MUTTS

SUNDAY AFTERNOONS

By Patrick McDonnell

Andrews McMeel
Publishing

Kansas City

Other Books by Patrick McDonnell

Mutts
Cats and Dogs: Mutts II
More Shtuff: Mutts III
Yesh!: Mutts IV
Our Mutts: Five
A Little Look-See: Mutts VI
What Now: Mutts VII
I Want to Be the Kitty: Mutts No. Eight

Mutts Sundays
Mutts Sunday Mornings

The Mutts Little Big Book

Mutts is distributed internationally by King Features Syndicate, Inc. For information, write King Features Syndicate, Inc., 888 Seventh Ave., New York, New York 10019.
Mutts Sunday Afternoons copyright © 2004 by Patrick McDonnell. All rights reserved. Printed in the United States of America. No part of this book may be used or reproduced in any manner whatsoever without written permission except in the case of reprints in the context of reviews.
For information, write Andrews McMeel Publishing, an Andrews McMeel Universal company, 4520 Main Street, Kansas City, Missouri 64111.

04 05 06 07 08 BAM 10 9 8 7 6 5 4 3 2 1
ISBN: 0-7407-4141-1

Library of Congress Control Number: 2003113025

Mutts Sunday Afternoons is printed on recycled paper.

Mutts can be found on the Internet at
www.muttscomics.com.

ATTENTION: SCHOOLS AND BUSINESSES
Andrews McMeel books are available at quantity discounts with bulk purchase for educational, business, or sales promotional use. For information, please write to:
Special Sales Department, Andrews McMeel Publishing, 4520 Main Street, Kansas City, Missouri 64111.

MUTTS

OOOOOH... MY NOSE IS ALL SHTUFFED UP...
AAACHOOEY.
OOOOOOH... I HAVE DA SHNIFFLES...
OOOOOO NUTHIN'S SADDER THAN A LI'L SHICK KITTY...
MOMMY.
OOOOOH... I COULD REALLY USE SHOME CHICKY SHNOODLE.
OOOOH... POOR PO MOOCHIE...
OOOOOH... POOR PO PUDDY...
OOOOOH, EARL, ARE YOU PRAYING FOR ME TO GET BETTER...?
YES...
THAT... OR LARYNGITIS.
MUTTS © 2001 PATRICK McDONNELL · DISTRIBUTED BY KING 1/14

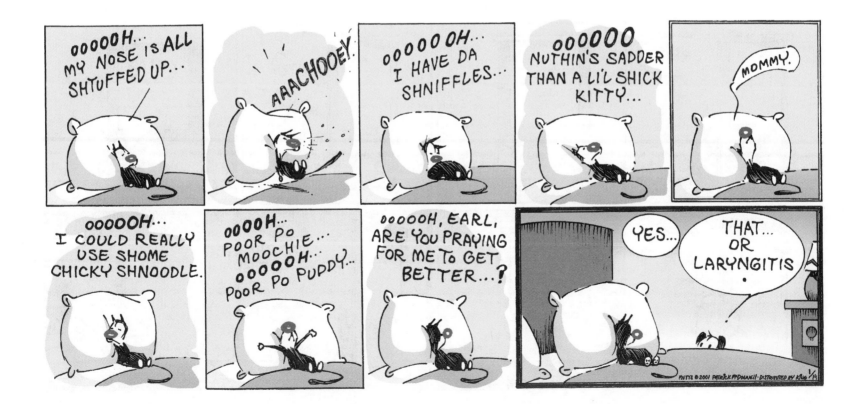

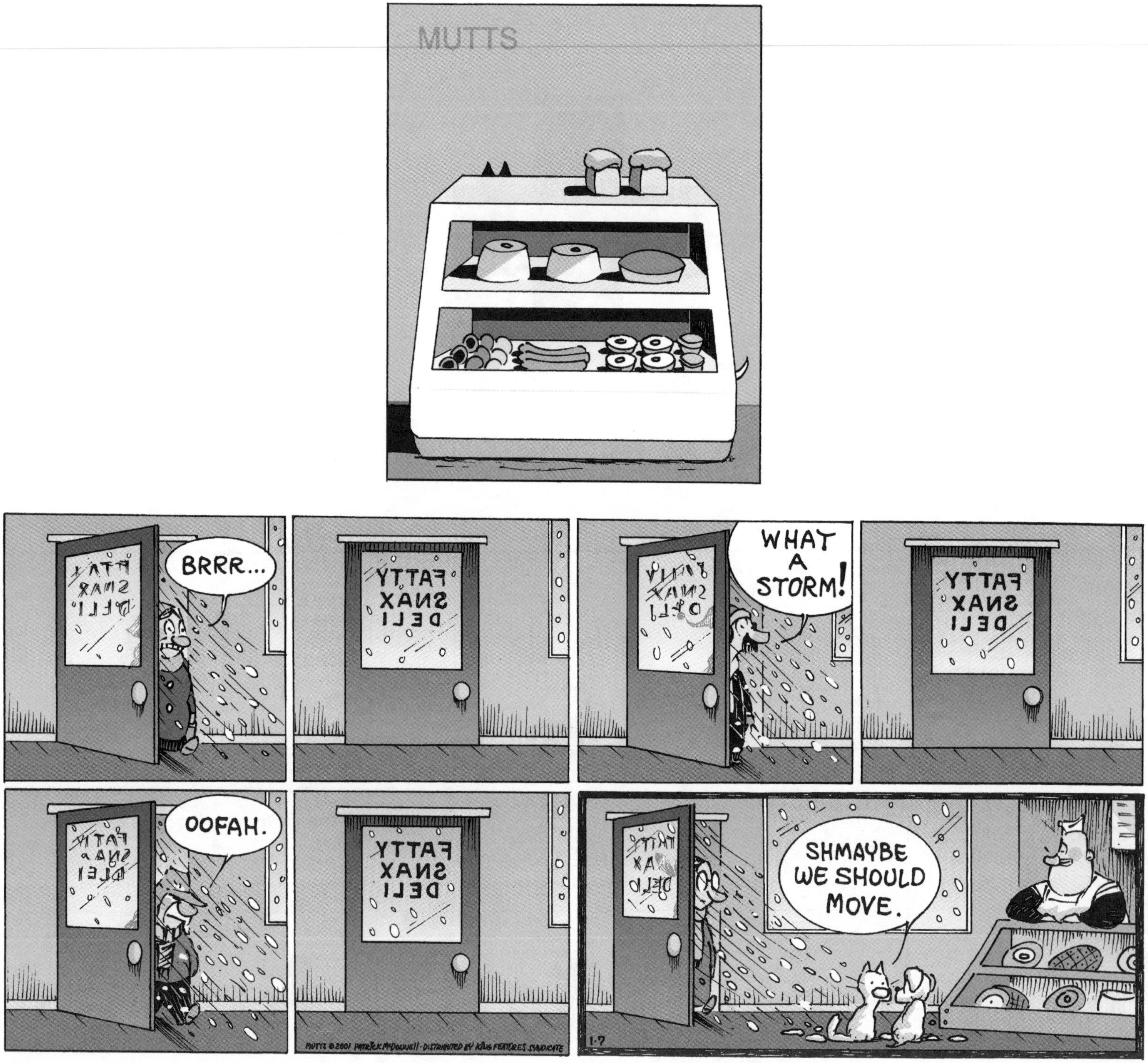
MUTTS
BRRR...
FATTY SNAX DELI
WHAT A STORM!
OOFAH.
SHMAYBE WE SHOULD MOVE.
MUTTS © 2001 PATRICK McDONNELL · DISTRIBUTED BY KING FEATURES SYNDICATE
1-7

MY SON, THE MUTT

SON, "EVERY MAN IS THE ARCHITECT OF HIS OWN FORTUNE."
" A NUT SAVED IS A NUT EARNED" .
"A NUT IN THE HAND IS WORTH TWO IN THE BUSH."
1·21
" HOLD ON TIGHTLY — LET GO LIGHTLY."
BONK
MUTTS © 2001 PATRICK McDONNELL · DISTRIBUTED BY KING FEATURES SYNDICATE

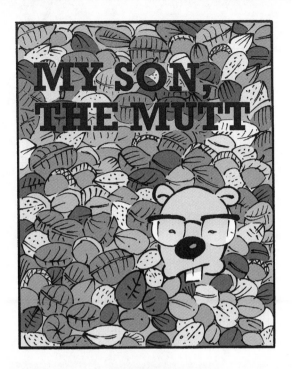

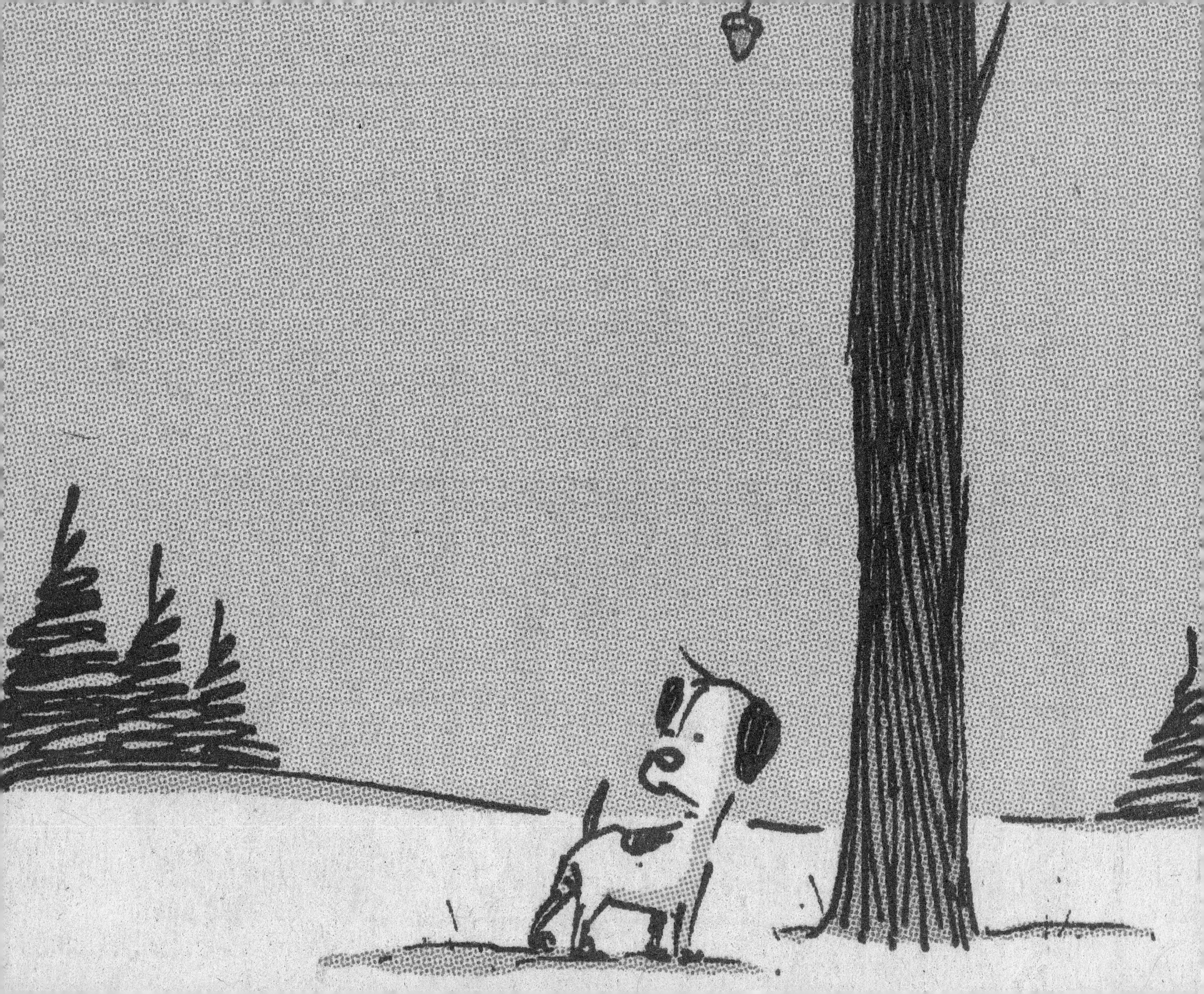

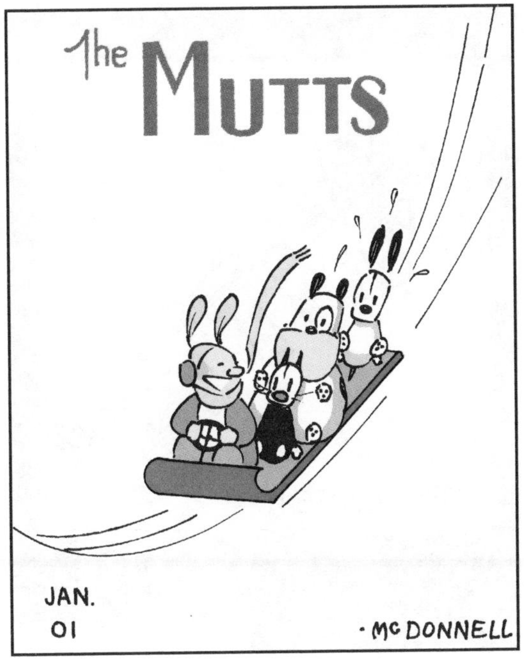

The MUTTS
JAN.
01
· McDONNELL

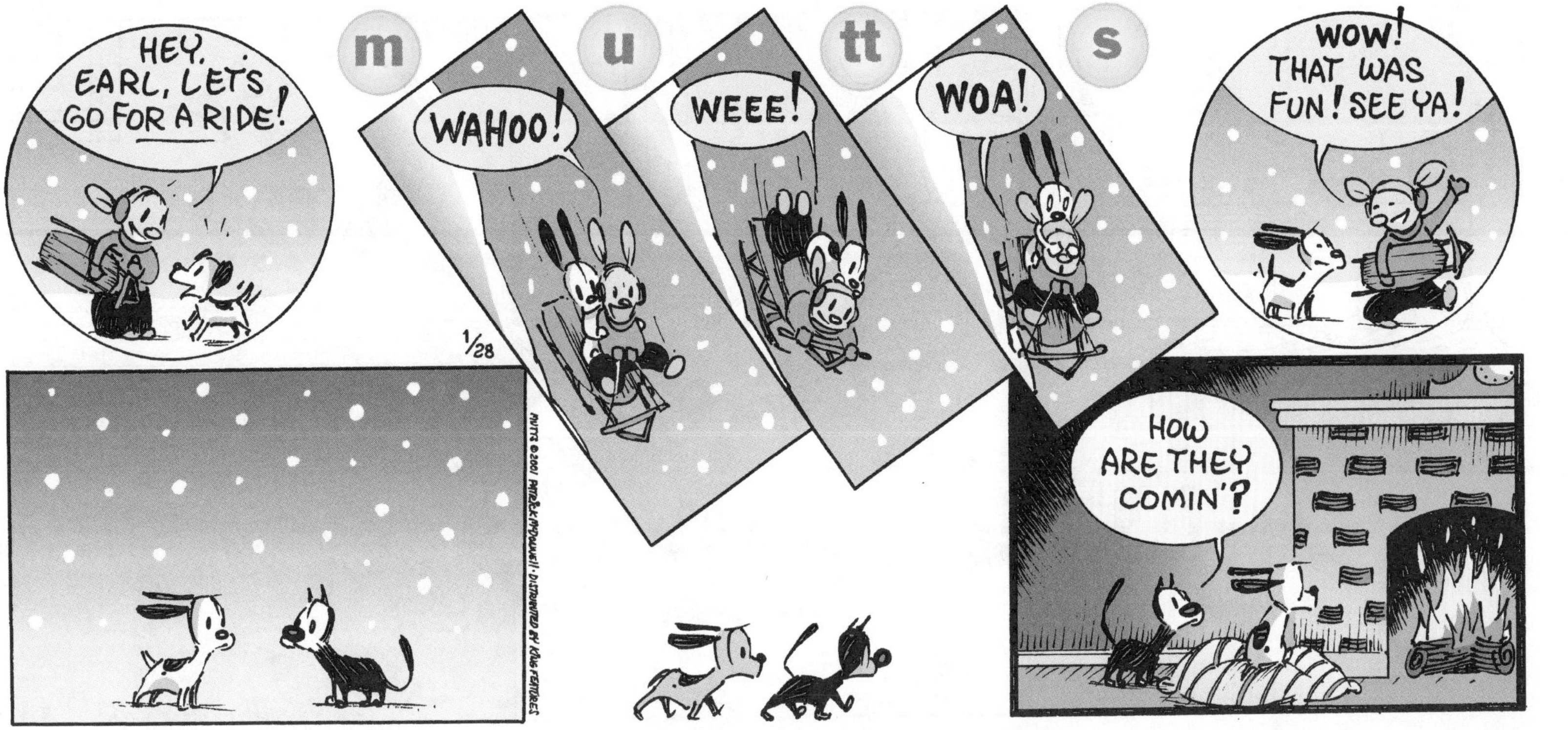

m u tt s
HEY, EARL, LET'S GO FOR A RIDE!
WAHOO!
WEEE!
WOA!
WOW! THAT WAS FUN! SEE YA!
1/28
MUTTS ©2001 PATRICK McDONNELL. DISTRIBUTED BY KING FEATURES
HOW ARE THEY COMIN'?

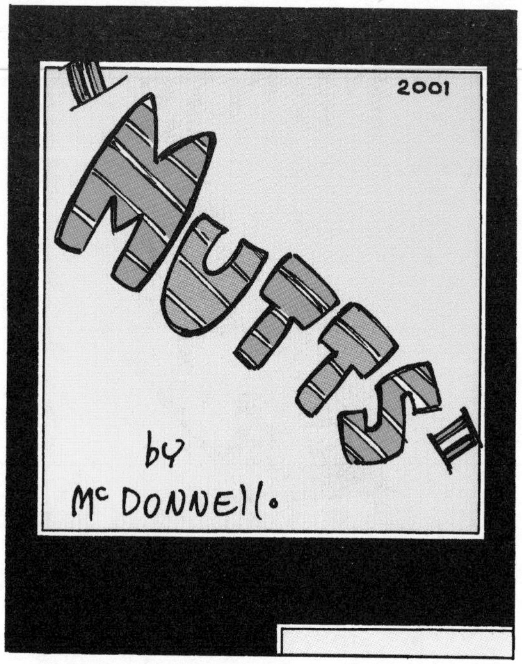
2001
MUTTS
by
Mc DONNELL

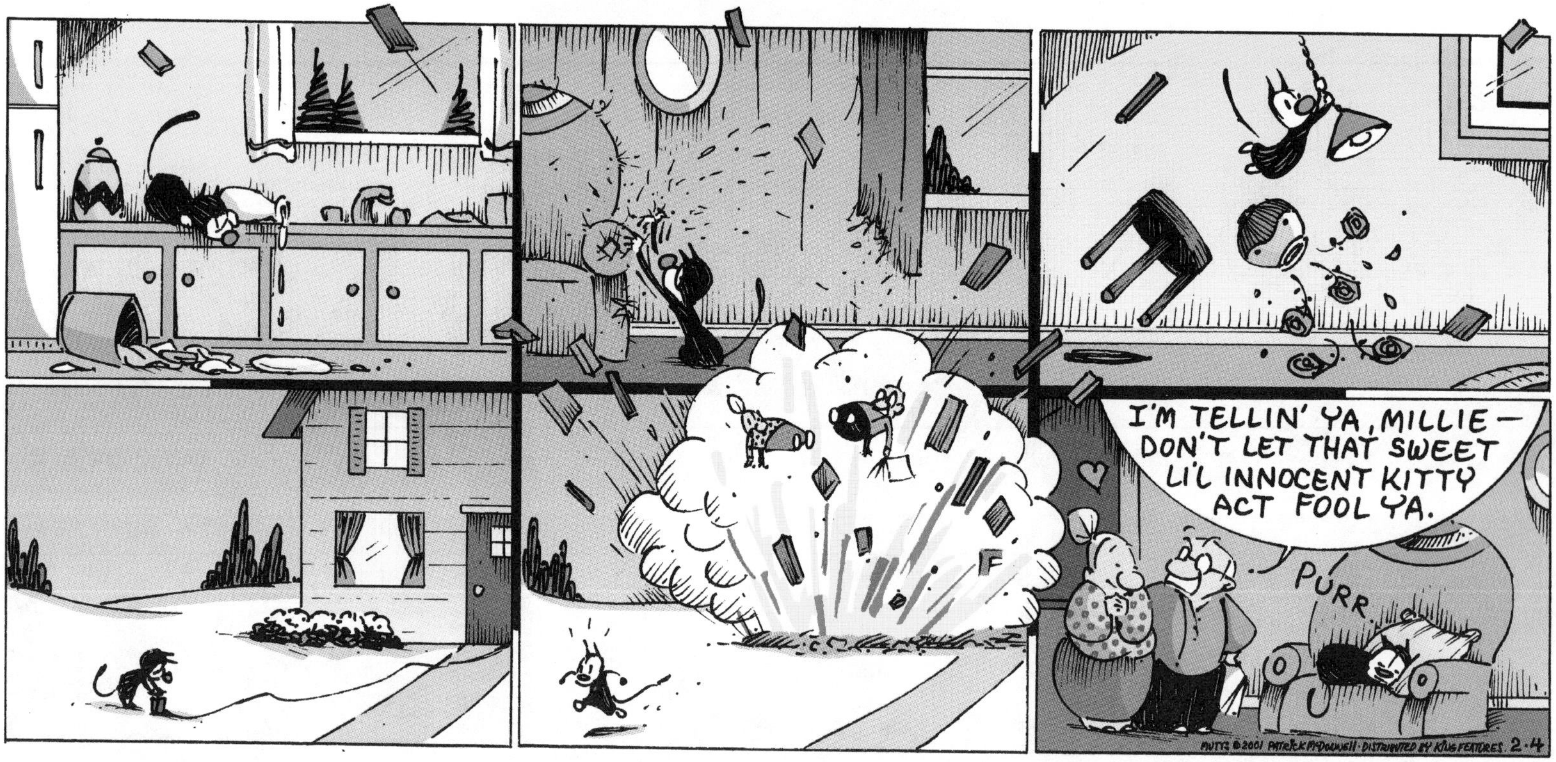
I'M TELLIN' YA, MILLIE— DON'T LET THAT SWEET LI'L INNOCENT KITTY ACT FOOL YA.
PURR
MUTTS © 2001 PATRICK McDONNELL · DISTRIBUTED BY KING FEATURES. 2·4

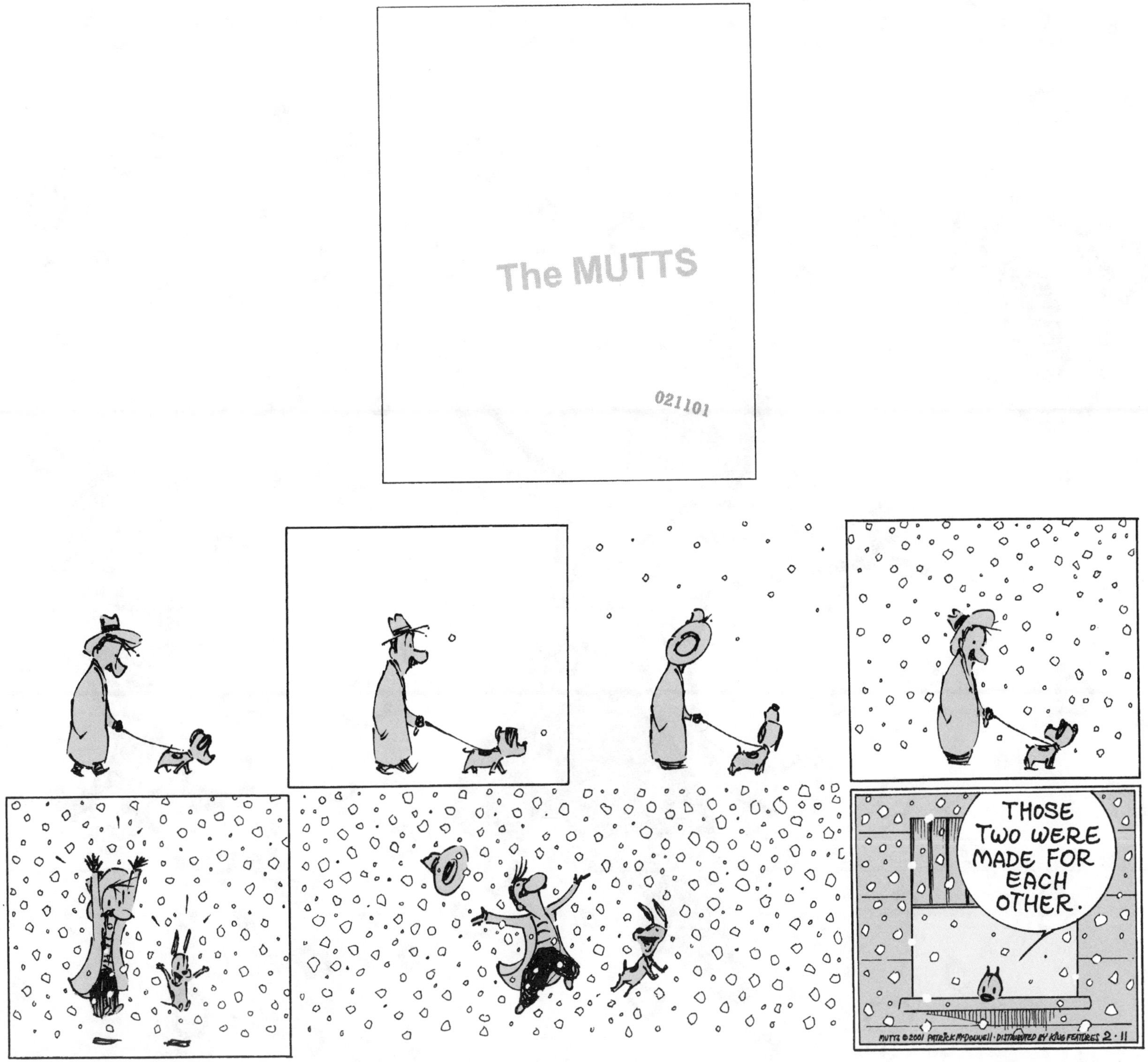
The MUTTS
021101
THOSE TWO WERE MADE FOR EACH OTHER.
MUTTS © 2001 PATRICK McDONNELL · DISTRIBUTED BY KING FEATURES 2·11

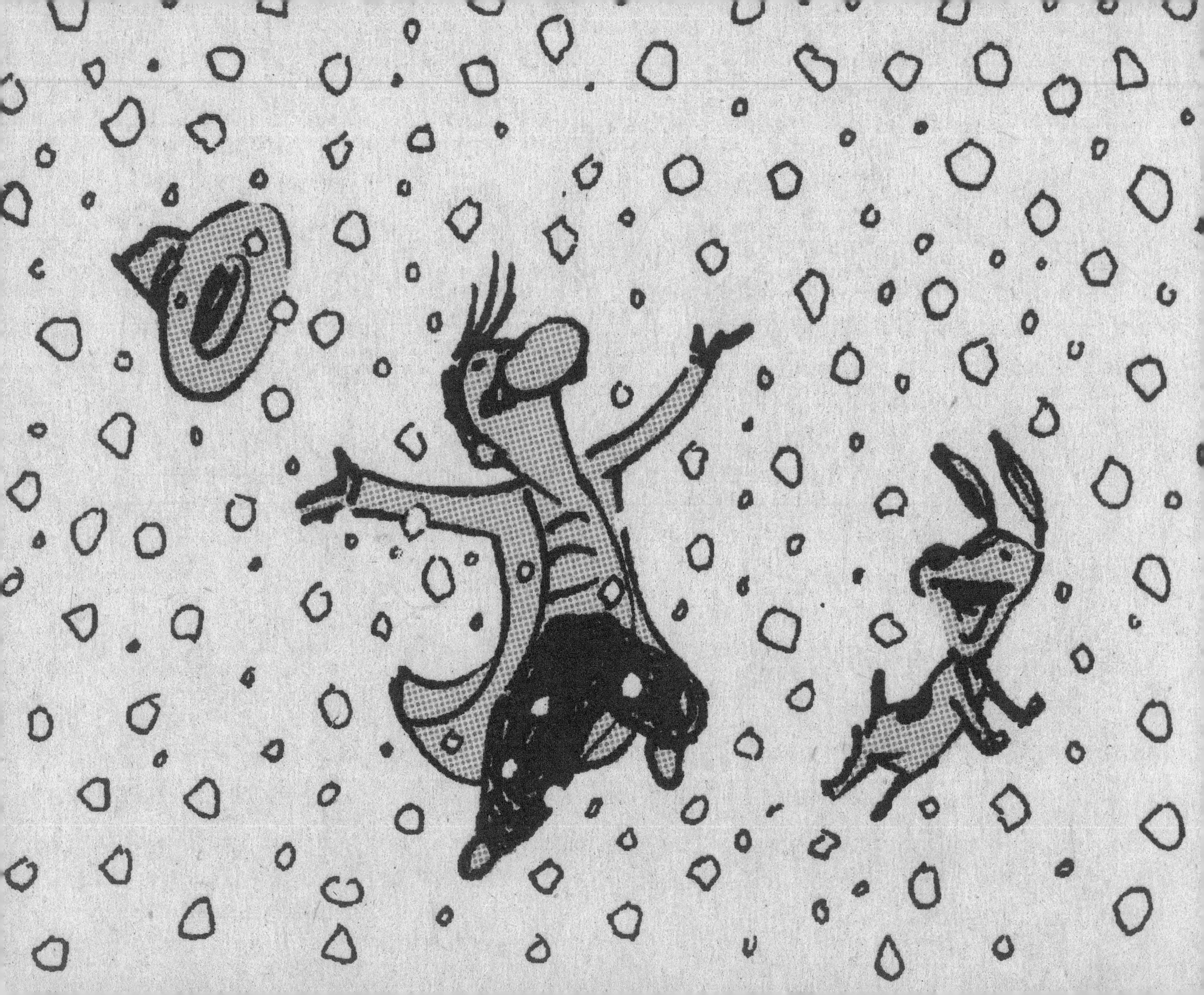

Earl & Mooch!
Mutts

McDONNELL

...AND WHAT DOES "ARF" MEAN?

"I WANT A TREAT."

WHAT ABOUT "BARK"?

"HEY, HOWZABOUT A TREAT?"

"WOOF"?

LOOSELY TRANSLATED THAT MEANS "GOOD TIME FOR A TREAT."

"RUFF."

NOW THAT COULD MEAN EITHER— "I SURE COULD GO FOR A LI'L SNACKY TREAT."

—OR "LET'S GO TO THE FRIDGE AND SEE IF THERE ARE ANY TREATS!"

WOW... LEARNING "DOG" IS VERY SHTIMULATING.

OH, YES...

MUTTS ©2001 PATRICK McDONNELL!

DISTRIBUTED BY KING FEATURES SYNDICATE

IT'S THE LANGUAGE OF LOVE.

2·25

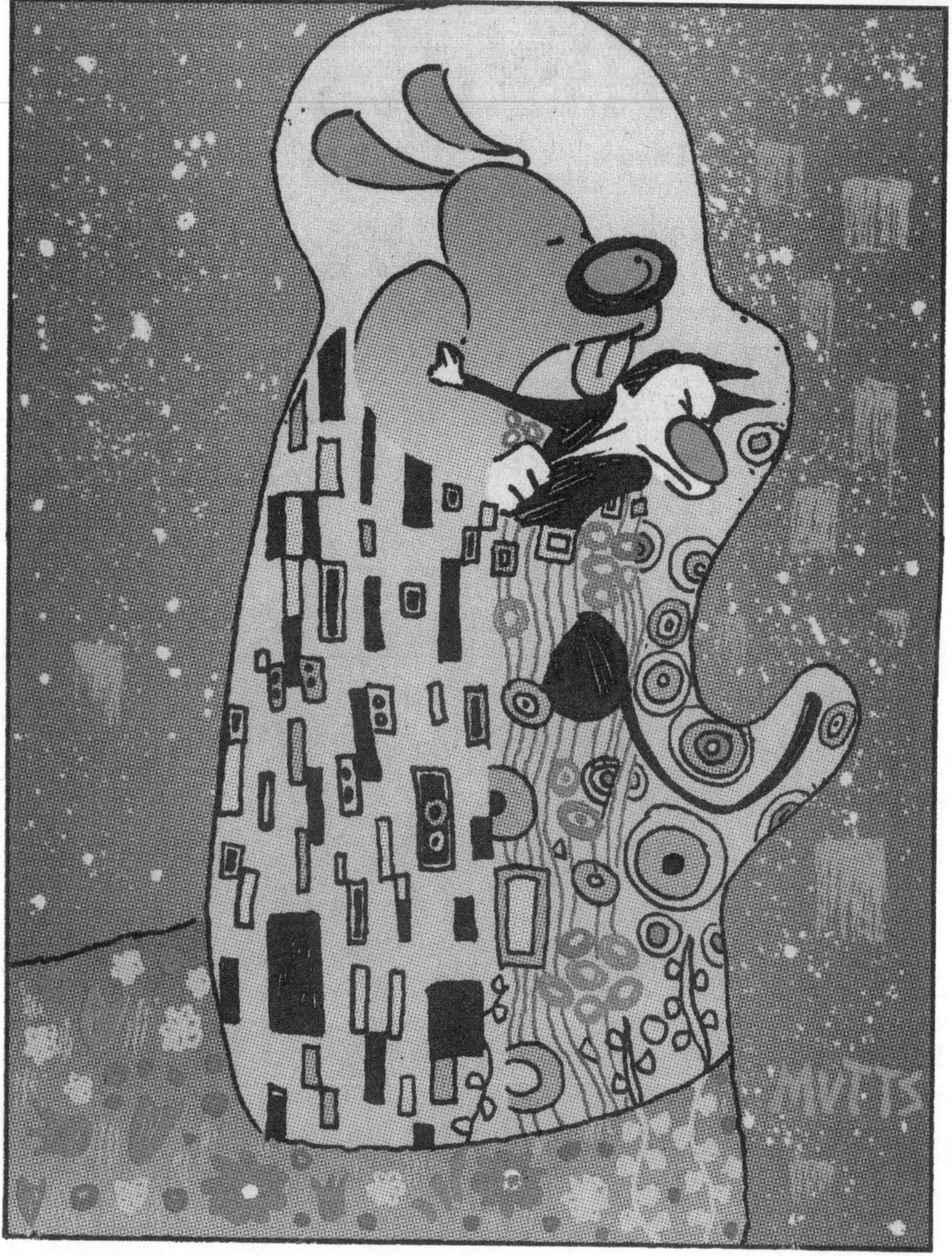
MUTTS

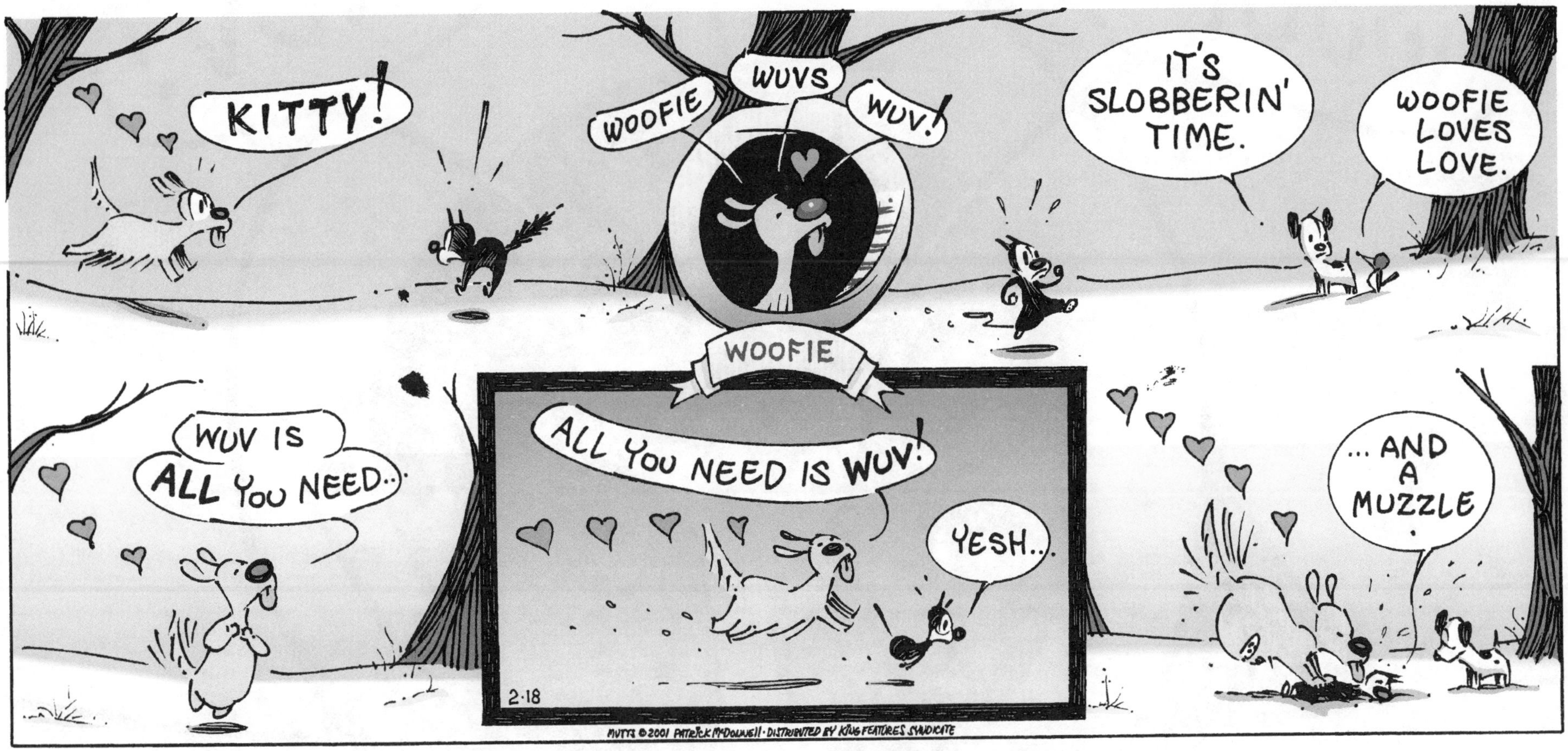
KITTY!
WOOFIE
WUVS
WUV!
WOOFIE
IT'S SLOBBERIN' TIME.
WOOFIE LOVES LOVE.
WUV IS ALL YOU NEED..
ALL YOU NEED IS WUV!
YESH..
... AND A MUZZLE.
2·18
MUTTS © 2001 PATRICK McDONNELL · DISTRIBUTED BY KING FEATURES SYNDICATE

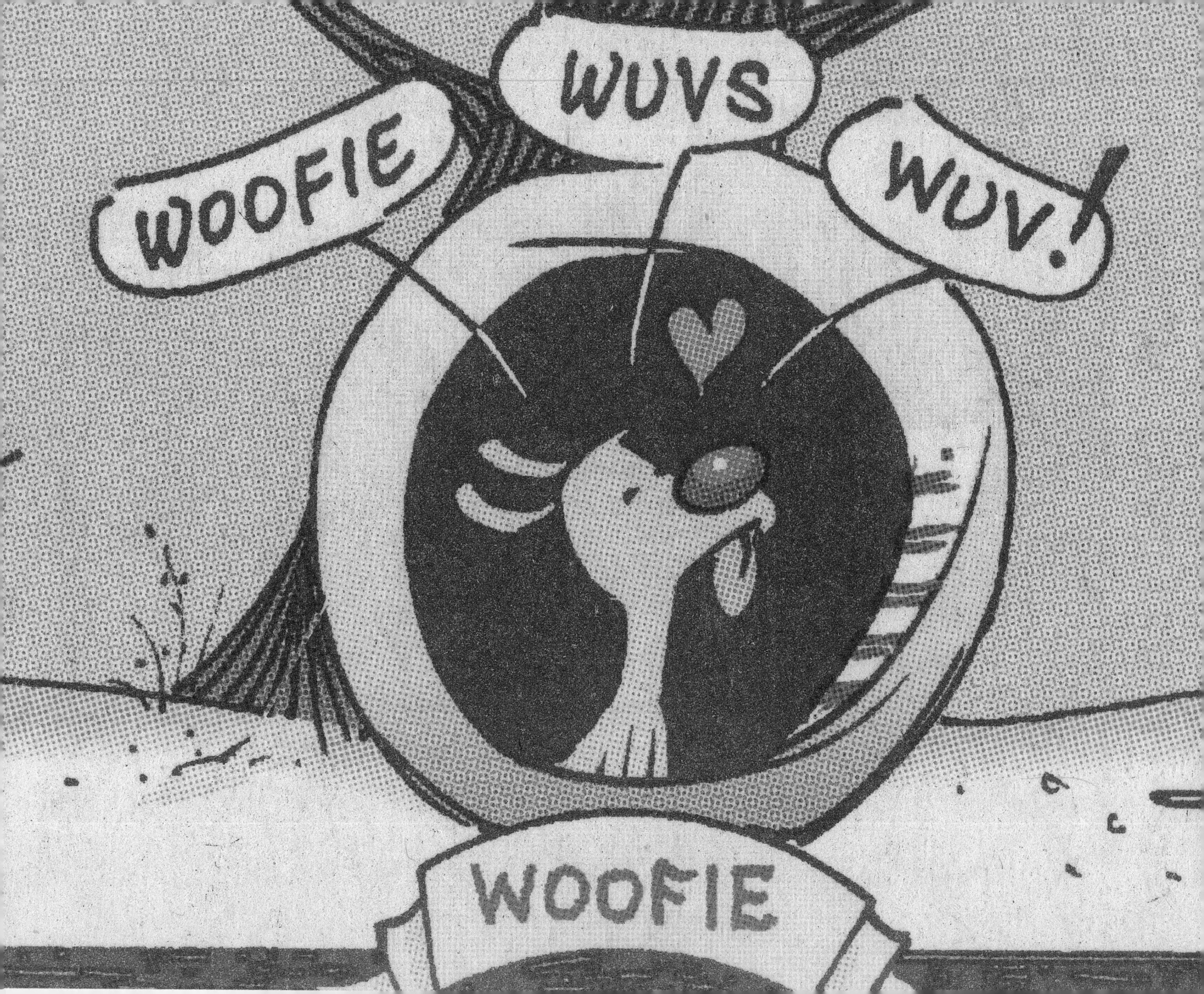
WOOFIE
WUVS
WUV!
WOOFIE

I'M THE MUTT
COMIC
BY PATRICK Mc DONNELL
©
·New Jersey·

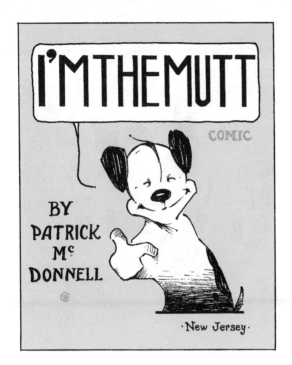

Earl's Automatic Belly-Rubber

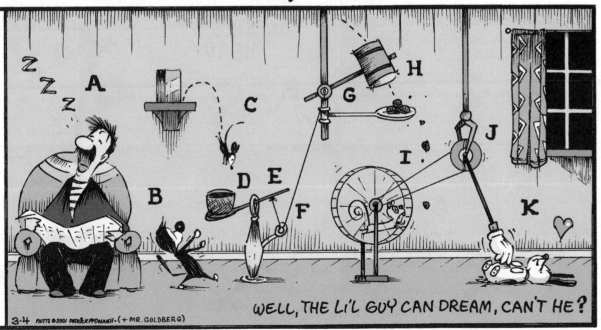

OZZIE'S SING-SONG SNORING (A) MAKES MOOCH (B) FEEL LIKE DANCING THUS SCARING MOUSE (C) WHO JUMPS IN BASKET (D) CAUSING LEVER (E) TO PULL STRING (F) MAKING MALLET (G) CRACK WALNUTS (H) ENTICING SQUIRREL TO REVOLVE WHEEL (I) SPINNING GEAR (J) THUS MOVING ARM (K) WHICH GENTLY RUBS EARL'S BELLY.
DISTRIBUTED BY KING FEATURES SYNDICATE
Z Z Z
A
B
C
D
E
F
G
H
I
J
K
WELL, THE LI'L GUY CAN DREAM, CAN'T HE?
3·4 MUTTS ©2001 PATRICK McDONNELL·(+ MR. GOLDBERG)

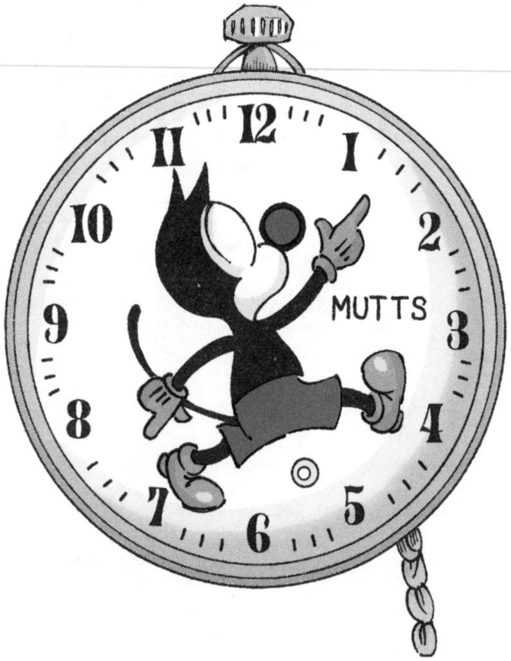
MUTTS

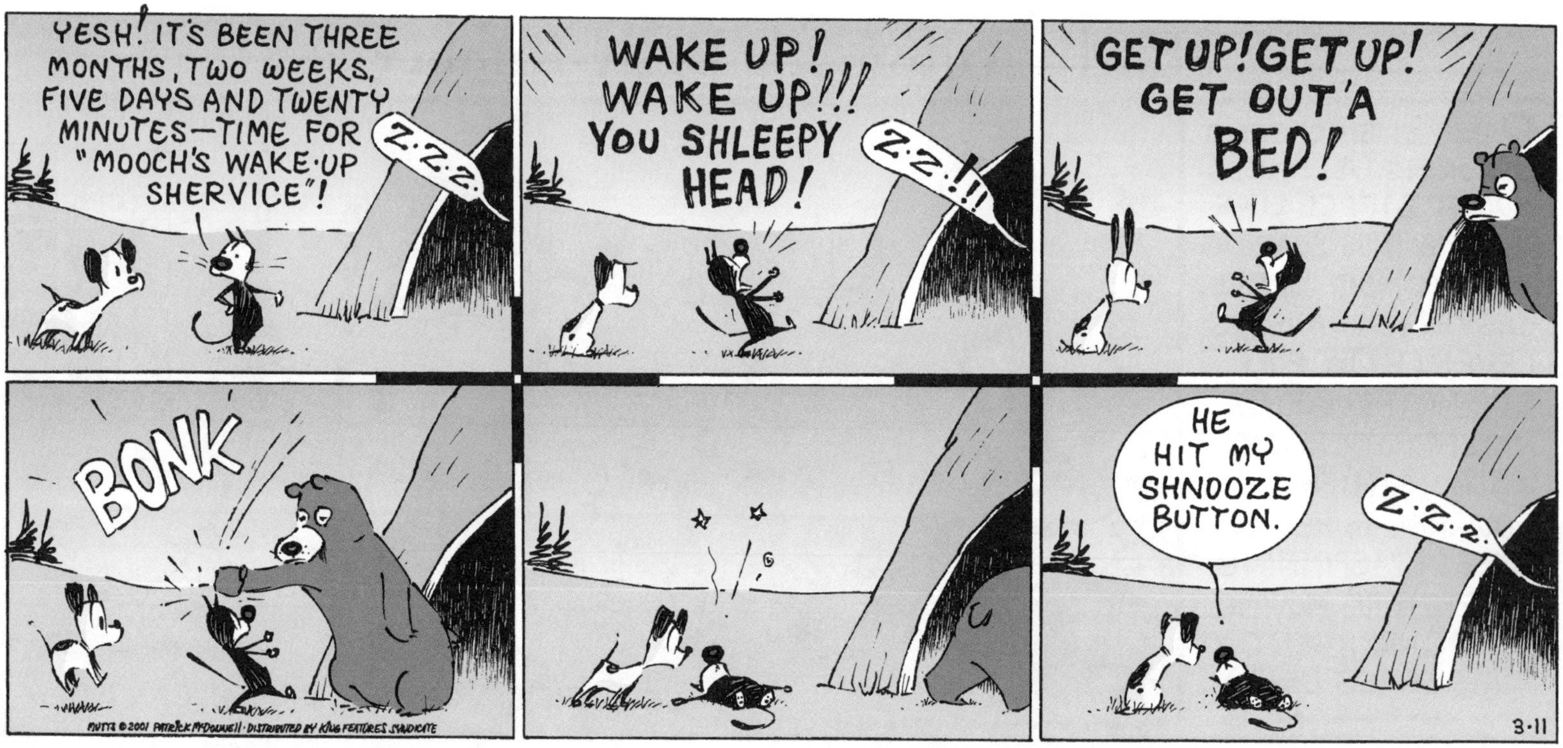
YESH! IT'S BEEN THREE MONTHS, TWO WEEKS, FIVE DAYS AND TWENTY MINUTES—TIME FOR "MOOCH'S WAKE-UP SHERVICE"!
Z·Z·Z
WAKE UP! WAKE UP!!! YOU SHLEEPY HEAD!
Z·Z·!!!
GET UP! GET UP! GET OUT'A BED!
BONK
HE HIT MY SHNOOZE BUTTON.
Z·Z·Z
MUTTS © 2001 PATRICK McDONNELL · DISTRIBUTED BY KING FEATURES SYNDICATE
3·11

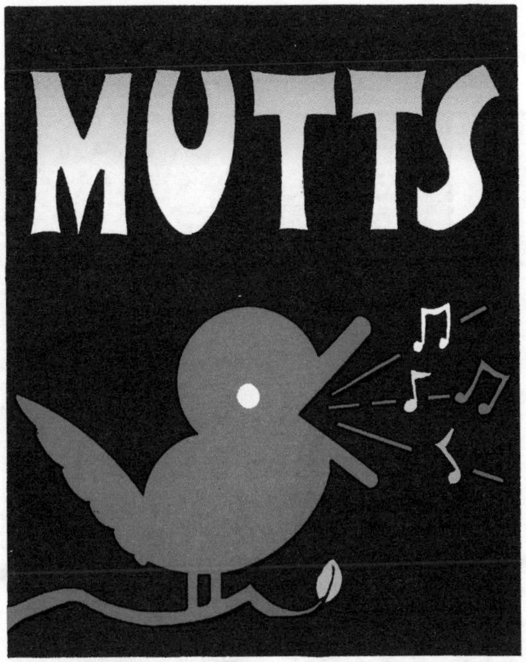
MUTTS

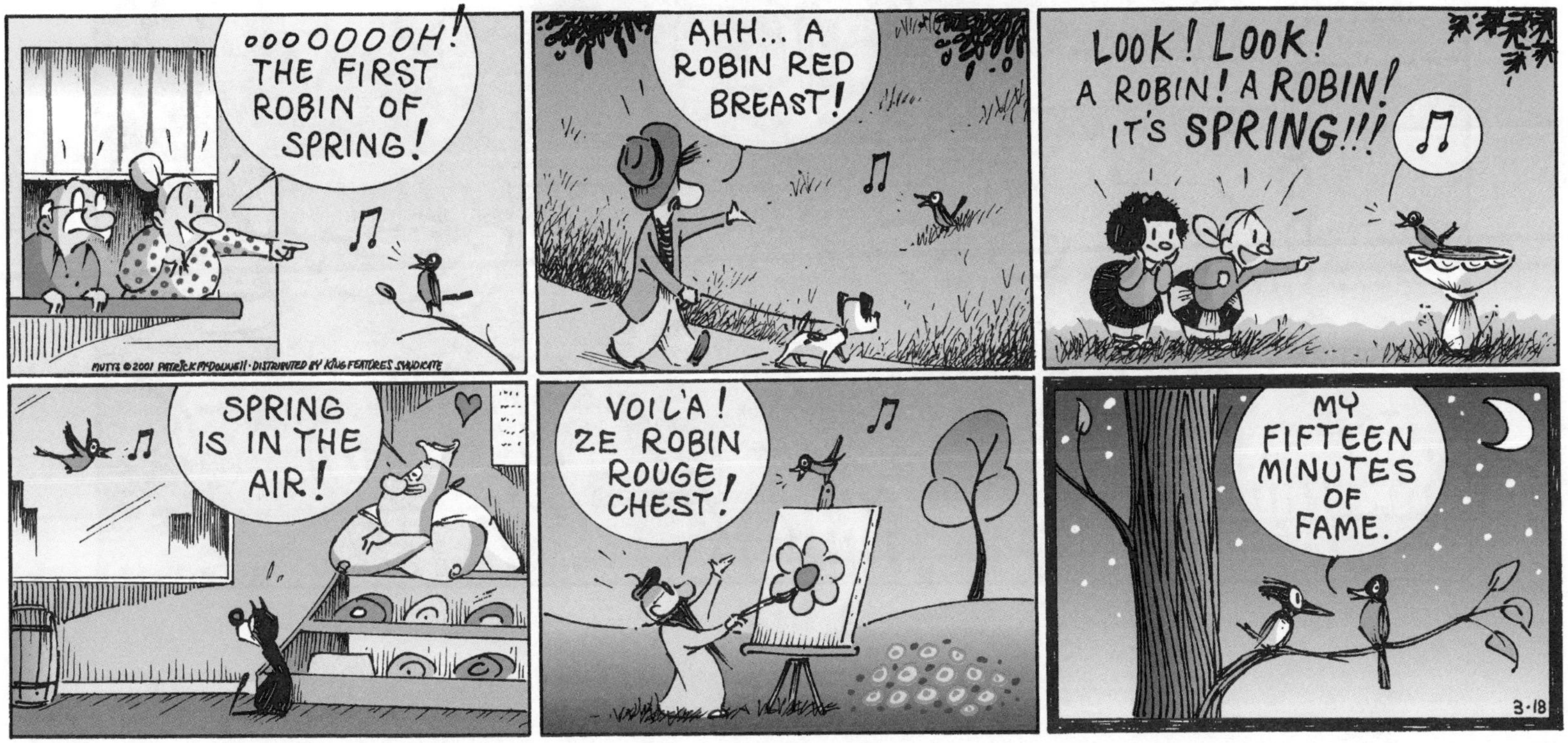
oooOOOOH! THE FIRST ROBIN OF SPRING!
MUTTS © 2001 PATRICK McDONNELL · DISTRIBUTED BY KING FEATURES SYNDICATE
AHH... A ROBIN RED BREAST!
LOOK! LOOK! A ROBIN! A ROBIN! IT'S SPRING!!!
SPRING IS IN THE AIR!
VOI'LA! ZE ROBIN ROUGE CHEST!
MY FIFTEEN MINUTES OF FAME.
3-18

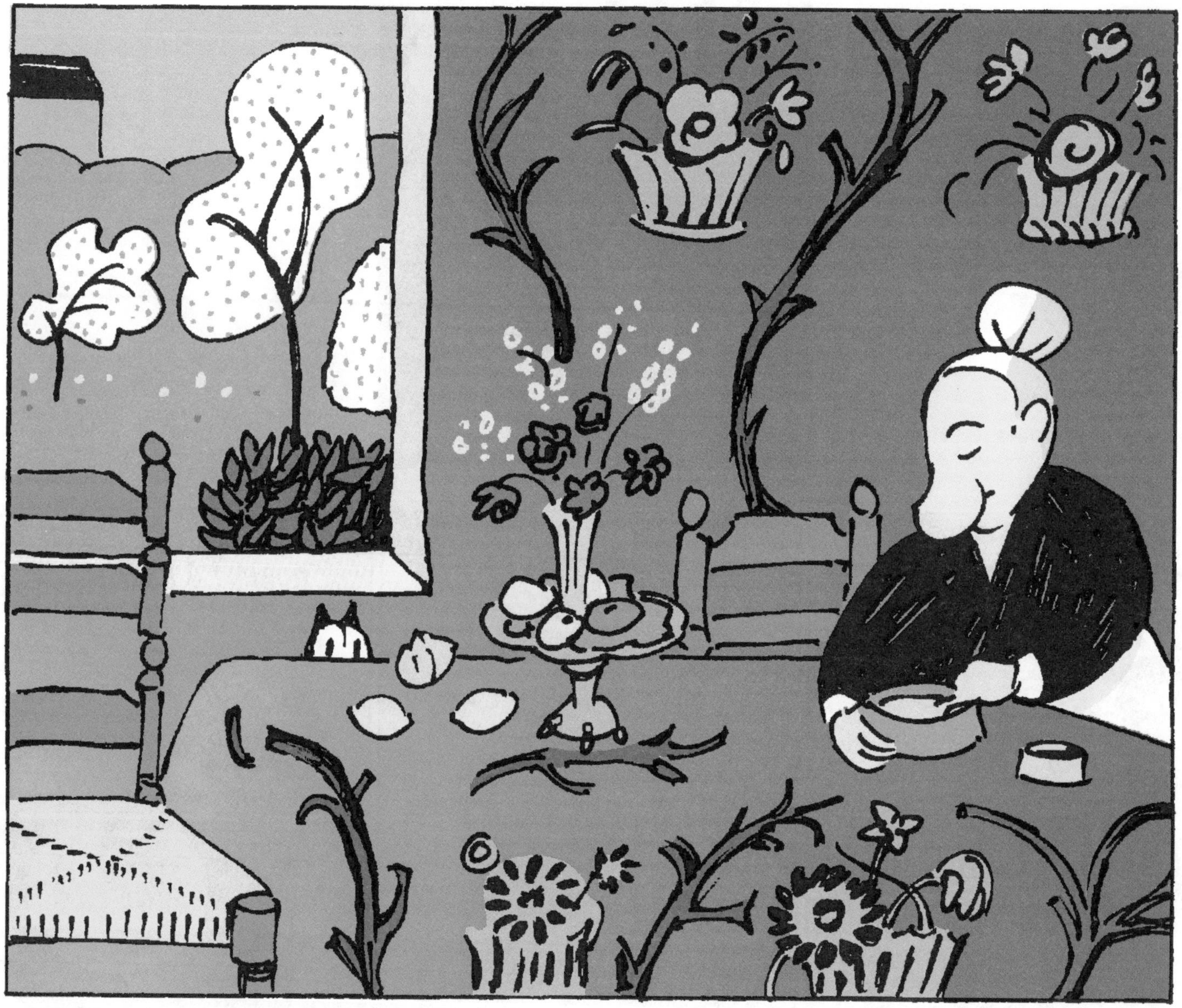

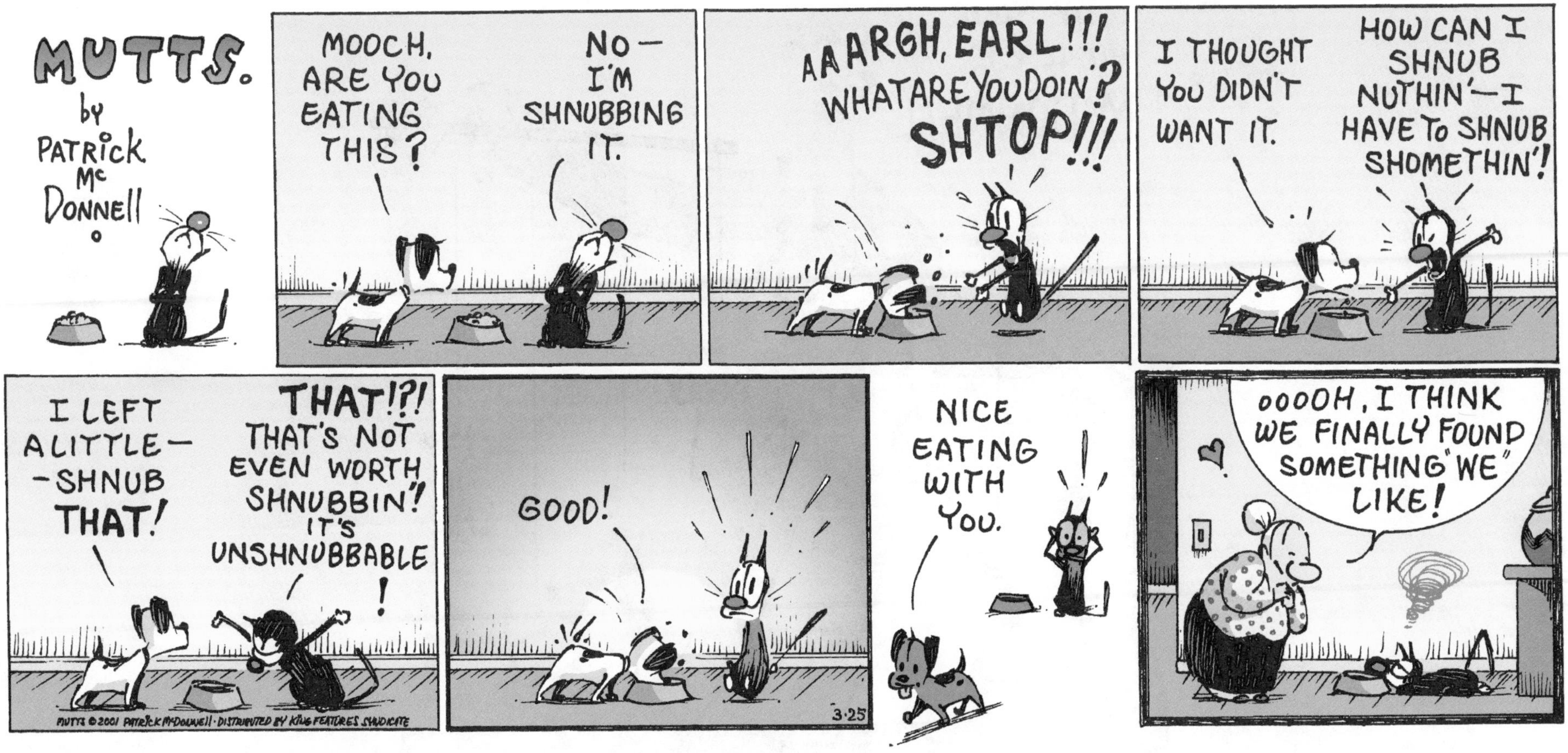
MUTTS.
by PATRICK McDONNELL
MOOCH, ARE YOU EATING THIS?
NO— I'M SHNUBBING IT.
AAARGH, EARL!!! WHATAREYOUDOIN'? SHTOP!!!
I THOUGHT YOU DIDN'T WANT IT.
HOW CAN I SHNUB NUTHIN'—I HAVE TO SHNUB SHOMETHIN'!
I LEFT A LITTLE— —SHNUB THAT!
THAT!?! THAT'S NOT EVEN WORTH SHNUBBIN'! IT'S UNSHNUBBABLE!
MUTTS ©2001 PATRICK McDONNELL · DISTRIBUTED BY KING FEATURES SYNDICATE
GOOD!
3·25
NICE EATING WITH YOU.
OOOOH, I THINK WE FINALLY FOUND SOMETHING "WE" LIKE!

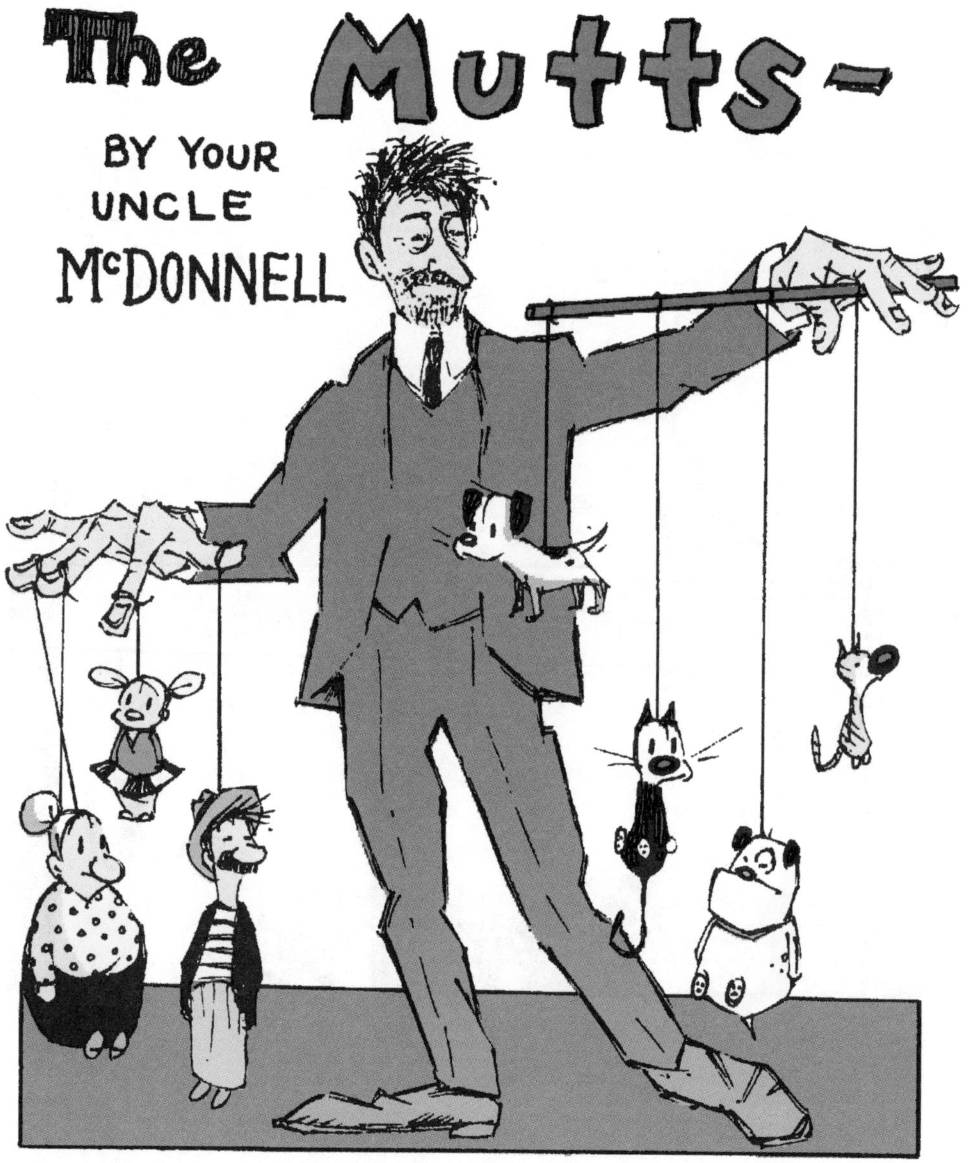
The Mutts-
BY YOUR UNCLE McDONNELL

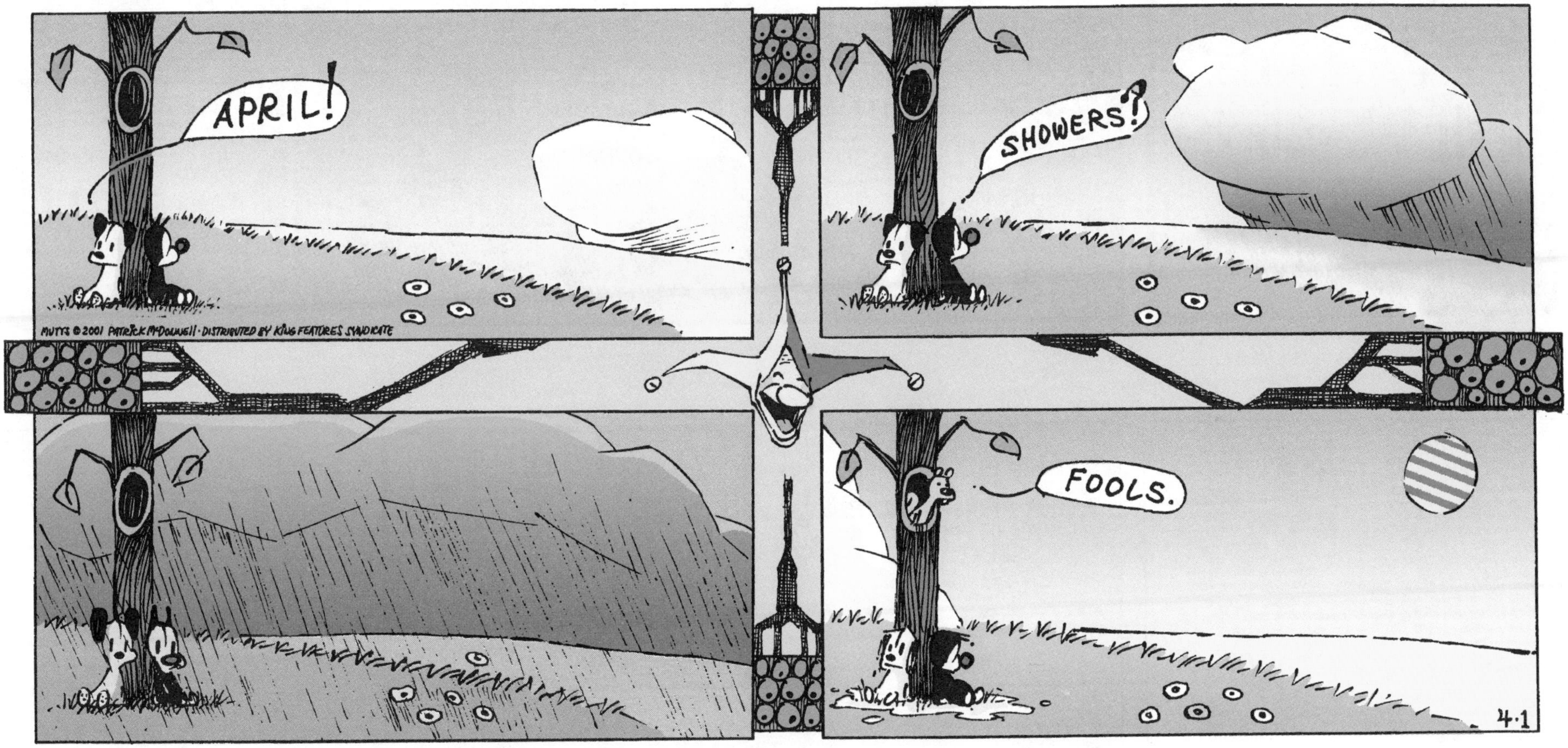
APRIL!
MUTTS © 2001 PATRICK McDONNELL · DISTRIBUTED BY KING FEATURES SYNDICATE
SHOWERS?
FOOLS.
4·1

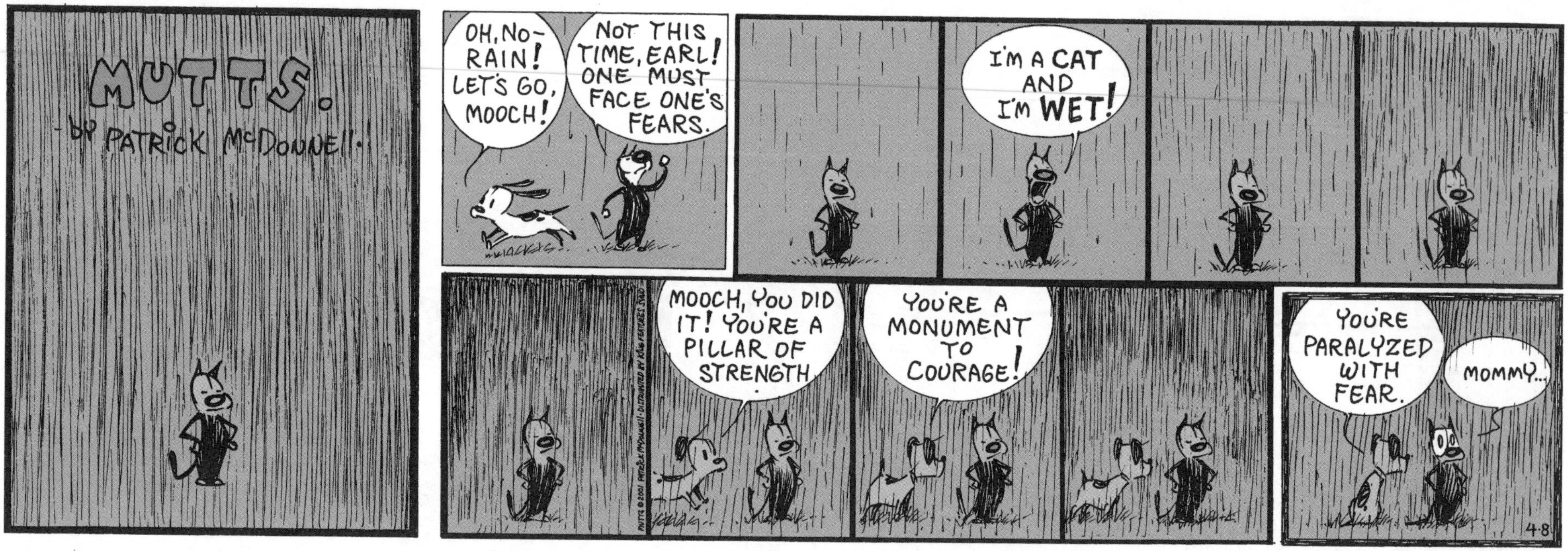
MUTTS.
by PATRICK McDONNELL
OH, NO- RAIN! LET'S GO, MOOCH!
NOT THIS TIME, EARL! ONE MUST FACE ONE'S FEARS.
I'M A CAT AND I'M WET!
MOOCH, YOU DID IT! YOU'RE A PILLAR OF STRENGTH.
YOU'RE A MONUMENT TO COURAGE!
YOU'RE PARALYZED WITH FEAR.
MOMMY...
4·8

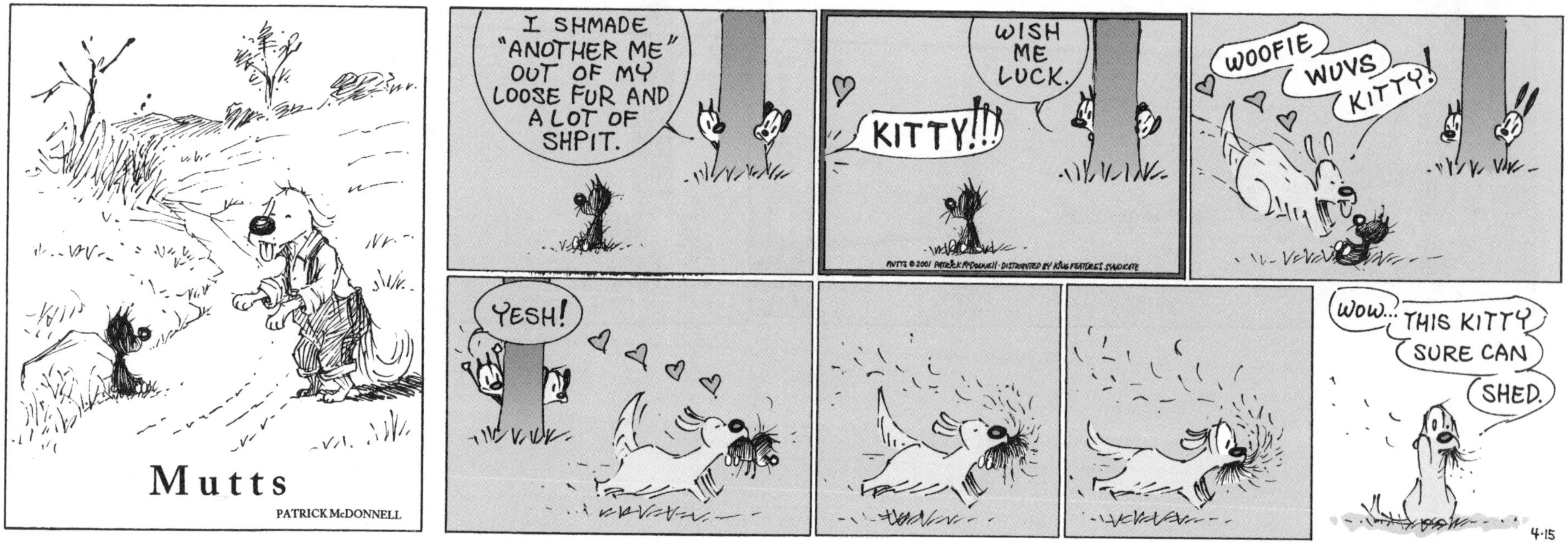
Mutts
PATRICK McDONNELL
I SHMADE "ANOTHER ME" OUT OF MY LOOSE FUR AND A LOT OF SHPIT.
WISH ME LUCK.
KITTY!!!
WOOFIE
WUVS
KITTY!
YESH!
WOW...
THIS KITTY
SURE CAN
SHED.
4·15

PLEASE.
PLEASE..
PLEASE...
PLEASE...

HAVE MERCY!!!

I'LL BE GOOD.

OH. POOR MOOCHIE. OH. POOR, PO ME!

HOW CAN I GO ON LIVING !?!

Mommy.

I MUST HANG ON! ..HANG ON!!!

OH. PUH-LEEZE PUH-LEEZE

MEOW MEOW-MEOW MEOW

THAT WAS THE LAST PIECE I'M GIVING HIM.

MUTTS © 2001 PATRICK McDONNELL · DISTRIBUTED BY KING FEATURES SYNDICATE

4-29

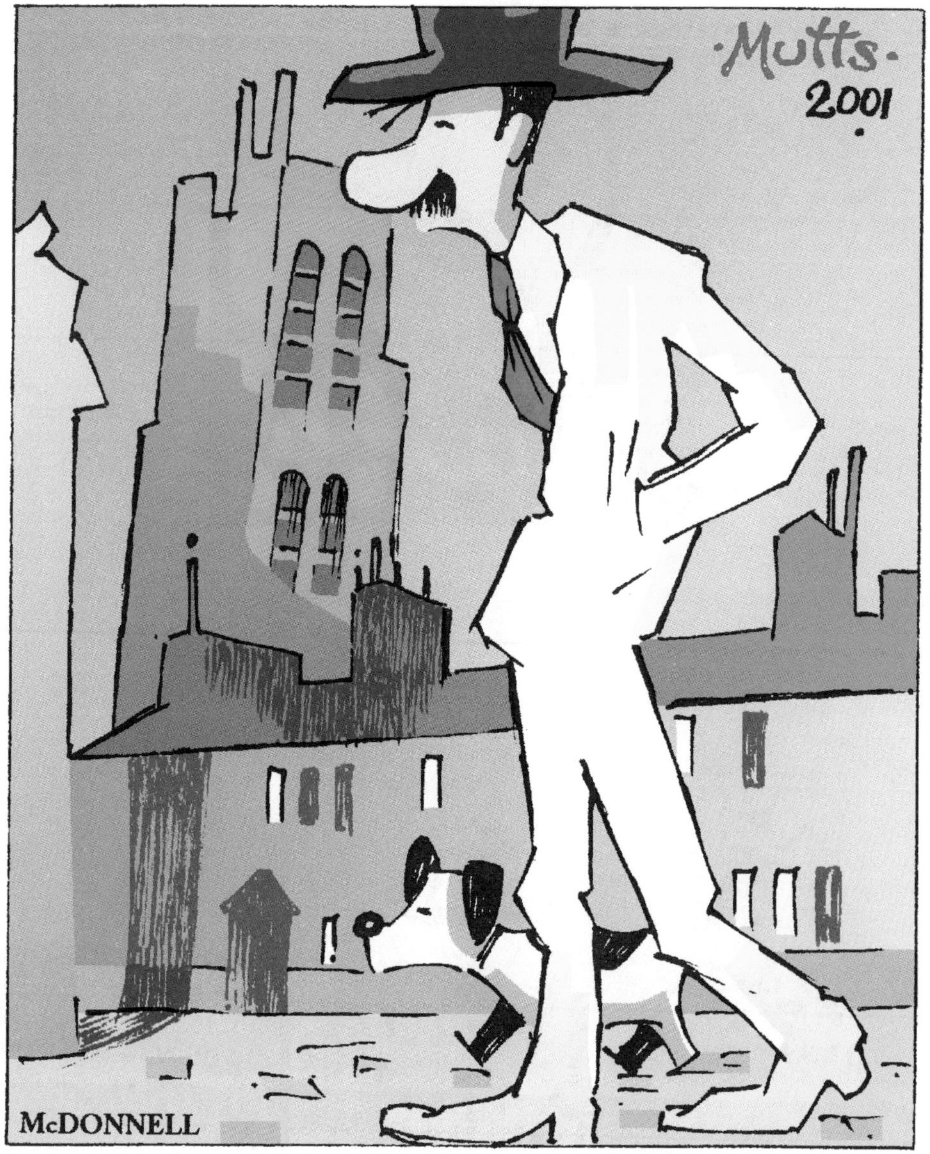
·Mutts·
2001
McDONNELL

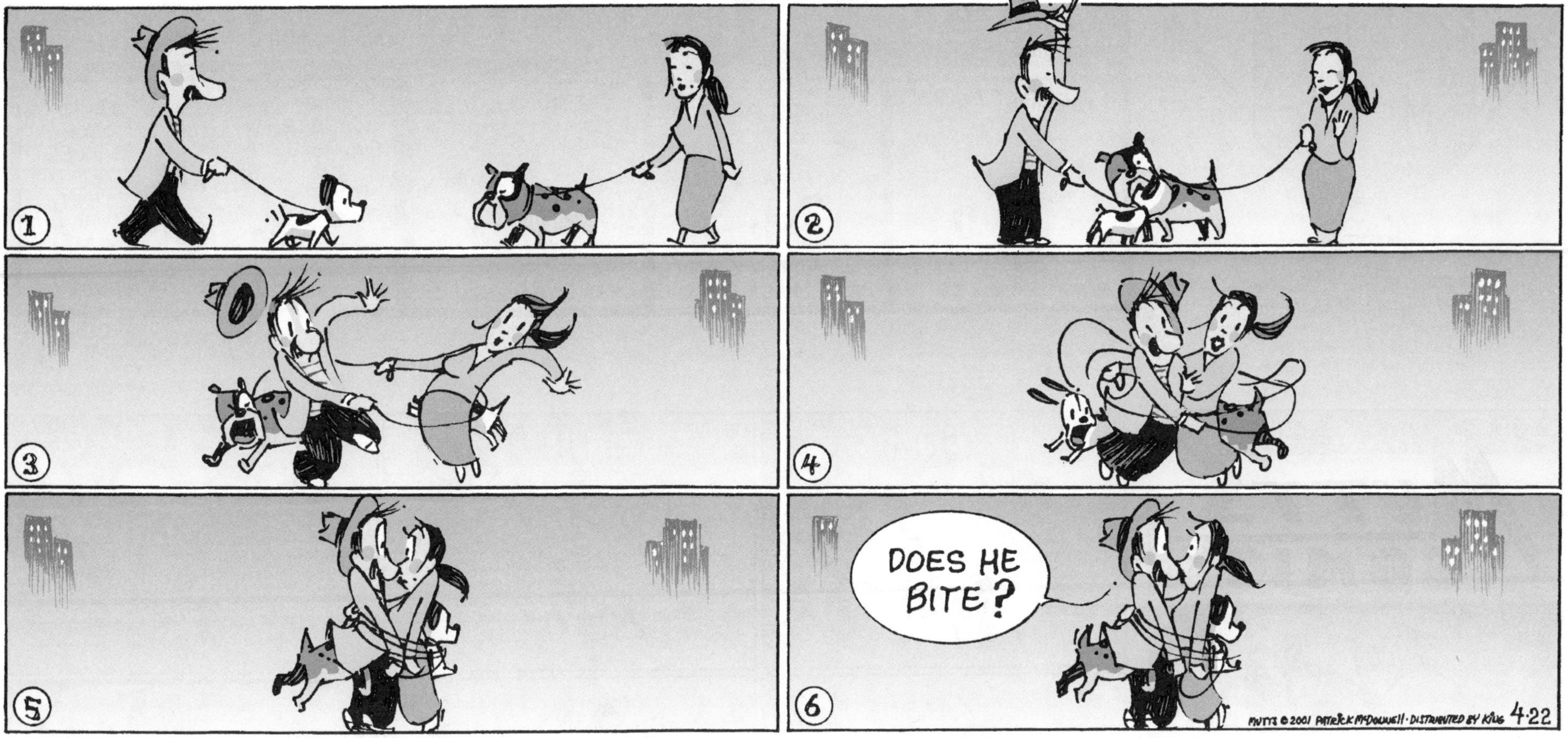
1
2
3
4
5
6
DOES HE BITE?
MUTTS © 2001 PATRICK McDONNELL · DISTRIBUTED BY KING 4·22

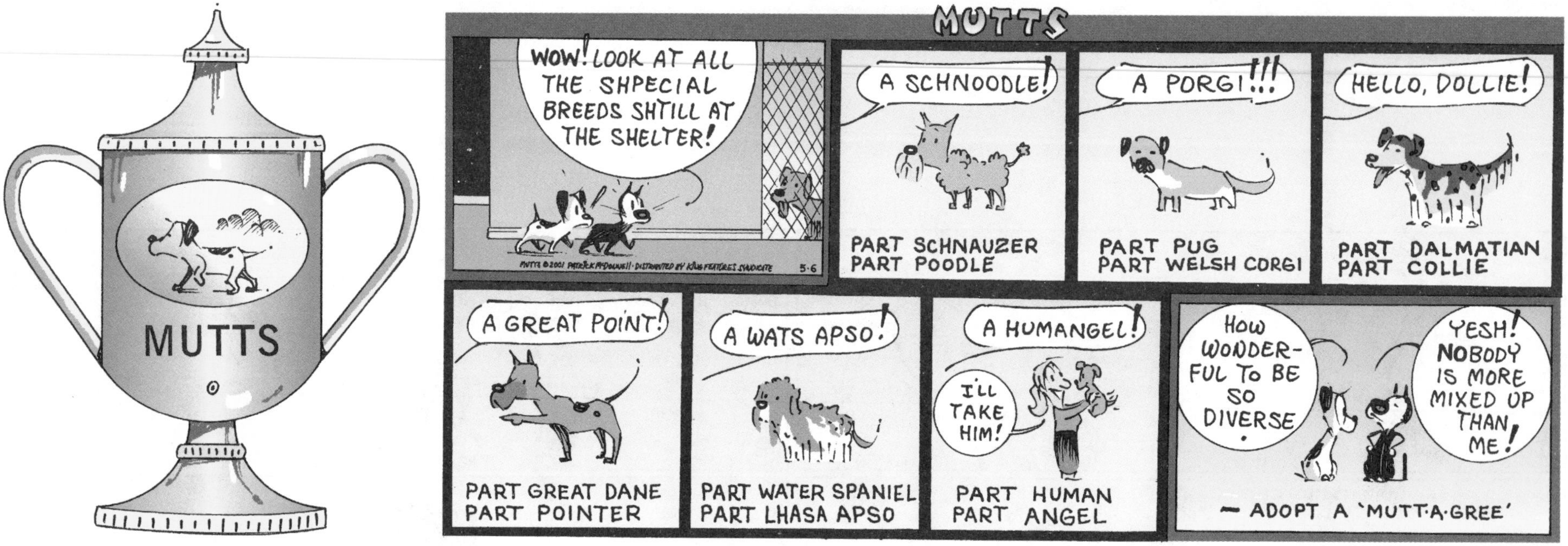
MUTTS
MUTTS
WOW! LOOK AT ALL THE SHPECIAL BREEDS SHTILL AT THE SHELTER!
MUTTS © 2001 PATRICK McDONNELL · DISTRIBUTED BY KING FEATURES SYNDICATE
5·6
A SCHNOODLE!
PART SCHNAUZER PART POODLE
A PORGI!!!
PART PUG PART WELSH CORGI
HELLO, DOLLIE!
PART DALMATIAN PART COLLIE
A GREAT POINT!
PART GREAT DANE PART POINTER
A WATS APSO!
PART WATER SPANIEL PART LHASA APSO
A HUMANGEL!
I'LL TAKE HIM!
PART HUMAN PART ANGEL
HOW WONDERFUL TO BE SO DIVERSE.
YESH! NOBODY IS MORE MIXED UP THAN ME!
— ADOPT A 'MUTT·A·GREE'

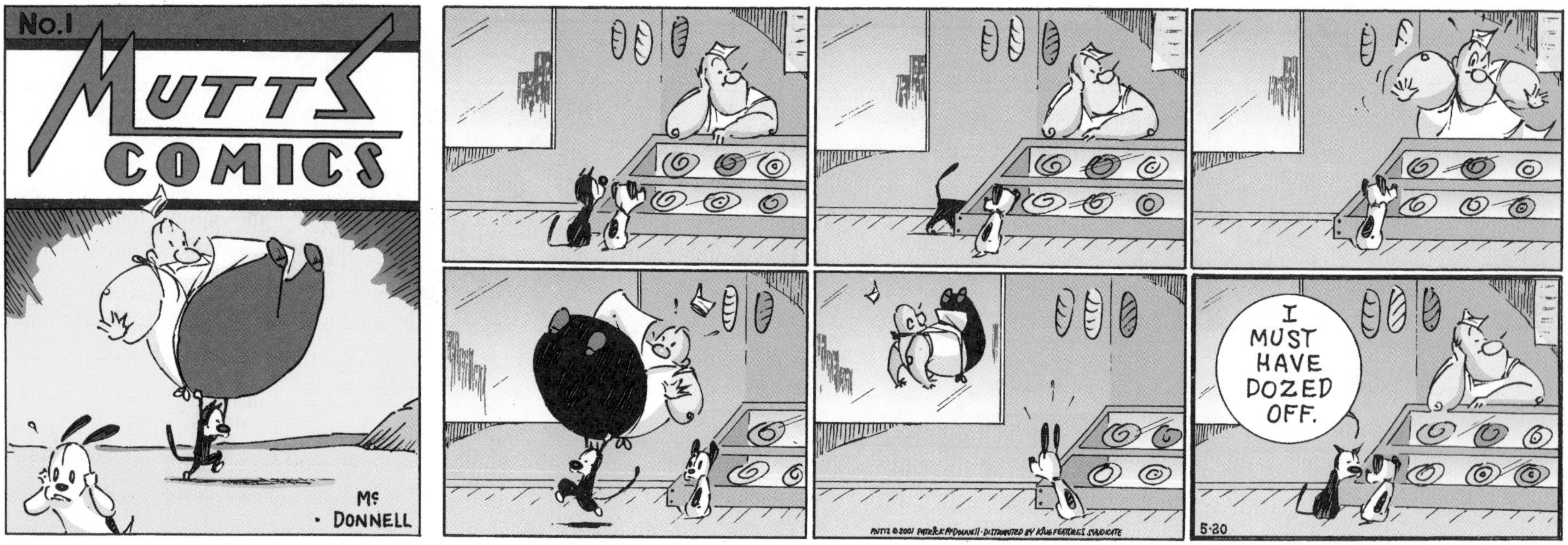
No. 1
MUTTS COMICS
McDONNELL
I MUST HAVE DOZED OFF.
MUTTS © 2001 PATRICK McDONNELL · DISTRIBUTED BY KING FEATURES SYNDICATE
5·20

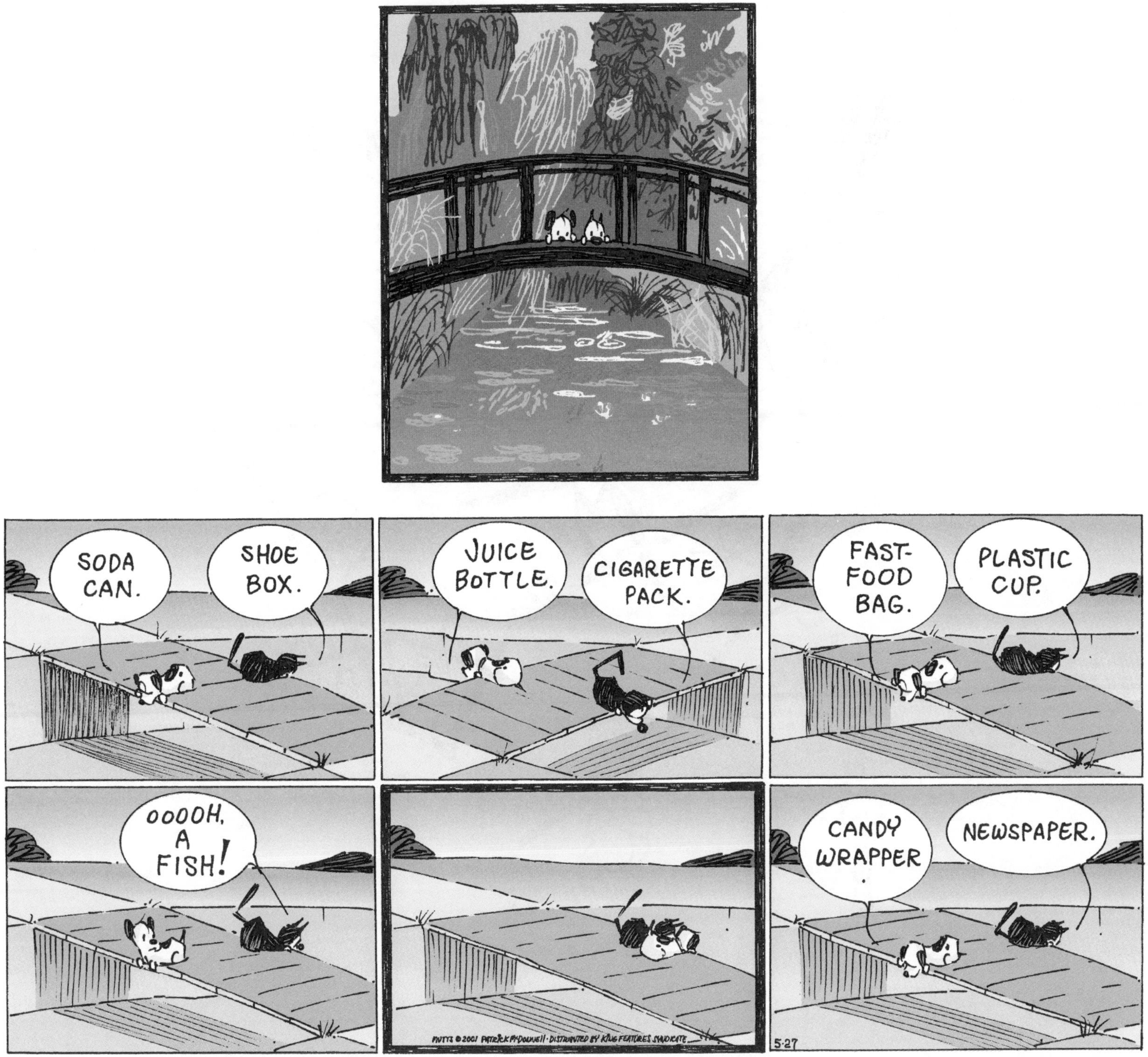
SODA CAN.
SHOE BOX.
JUICE BOTTLE.
CIGARETTE PACK.
FAST-FOOD BAG.
PLASTIC CUP.
OOOOH, A FISH!
CANDY WRAPPER.
NEWSPAPER.
MUTTS © 2001 PATRICK McDONNELL · DISTRIBUTED BY KING FEATURES SYNDICATE
5·27

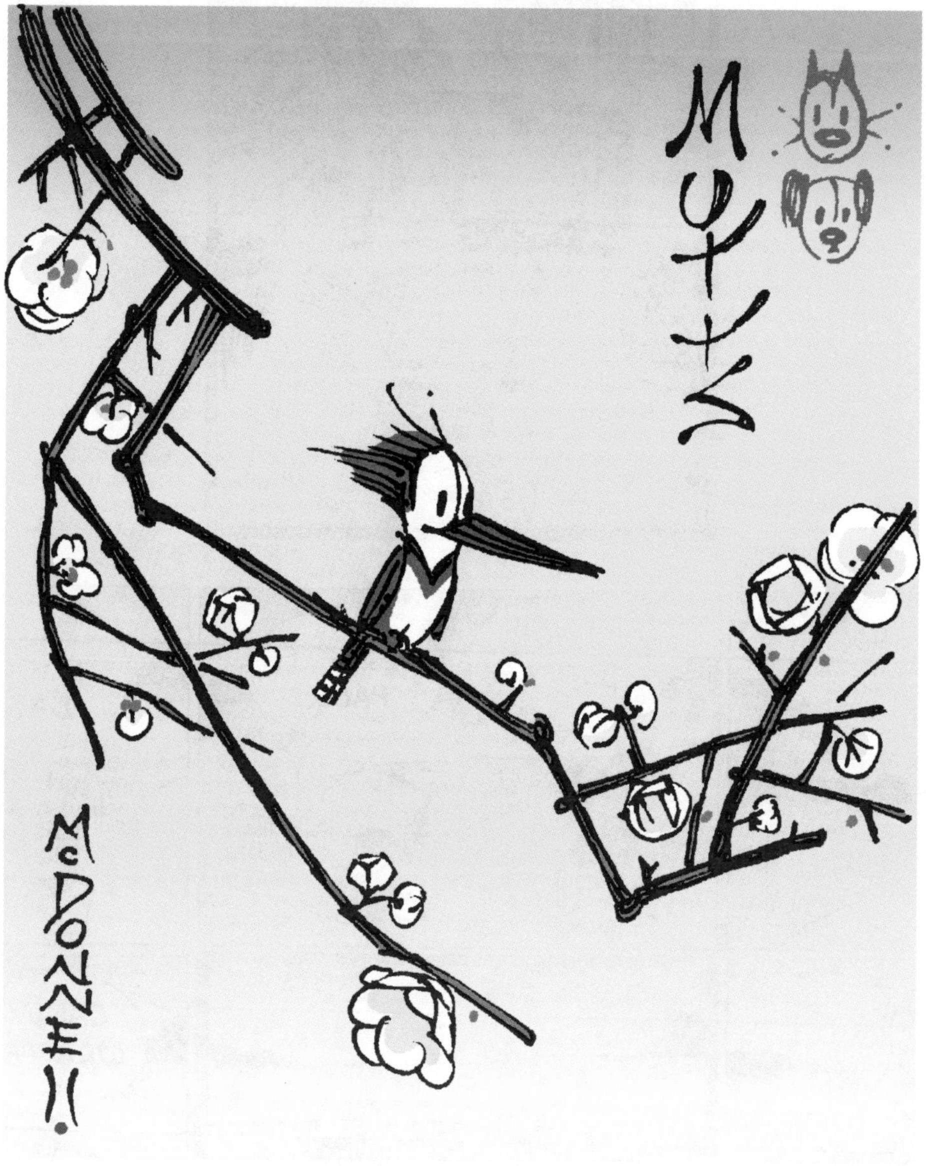
MUTTS
McDONNELL

I LOVE BIRD WATCHING!
LOOK! THERE'S A PEREGRINE FALCON!!! WOW! THAT'S A SCREECH OWL! LOOK! LOOK! A RUFOUS HUMMINGBIRD! A MAGPIE! A CHICKADEE!!! YOW! SO MANY WONDERFUL BIRDS! WHAT'S NEXT!?!
MUTTS © 2001 PATRICK McDONNELL · DISTRIBUTED BY KING FEATURES SYNDICATE
5·13
GEE, YOU'D THINK THEY NEVER SAW A BELTED KINGFISHER BEFORE!

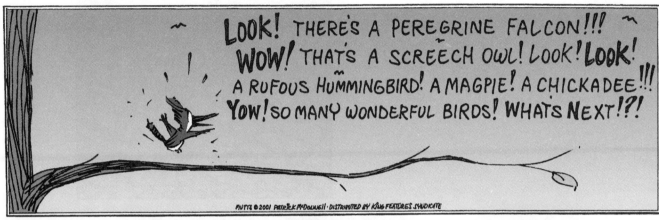

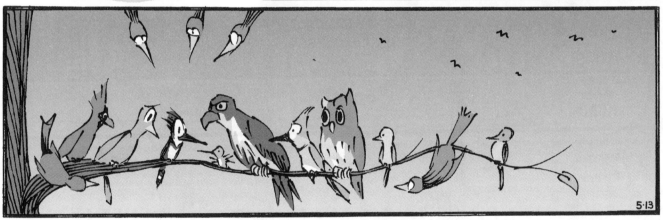

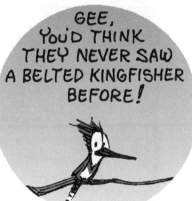

MUTTS

NIGHT FEVER, NIGHT FEVER
LOVE TO LOVE YA, SHBABY
SHAKE, SHAKE, SHAKE-SHAKE YOUR SHBOOTY!
WIGGLE IT—JUST A WITTLE BIT
MUTTS © 2001 PATRICK McDONNELL · DISTRIBUTED BY KING FEATURES SYNDICATE
GET DOWN, GET DOWN!
WOOPS...
BONK
SHTAYIN' ALIVE— SHTAYIN' ALIVE
6·3

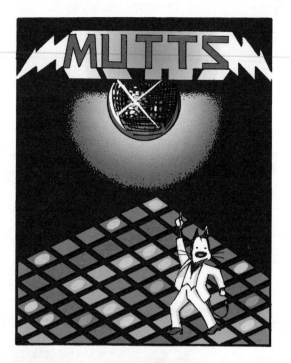

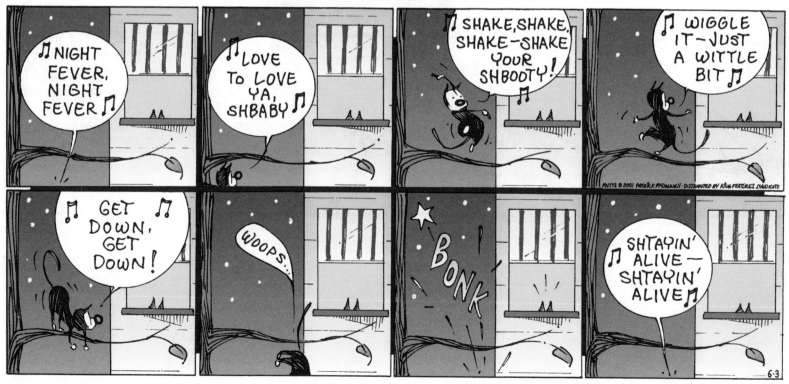

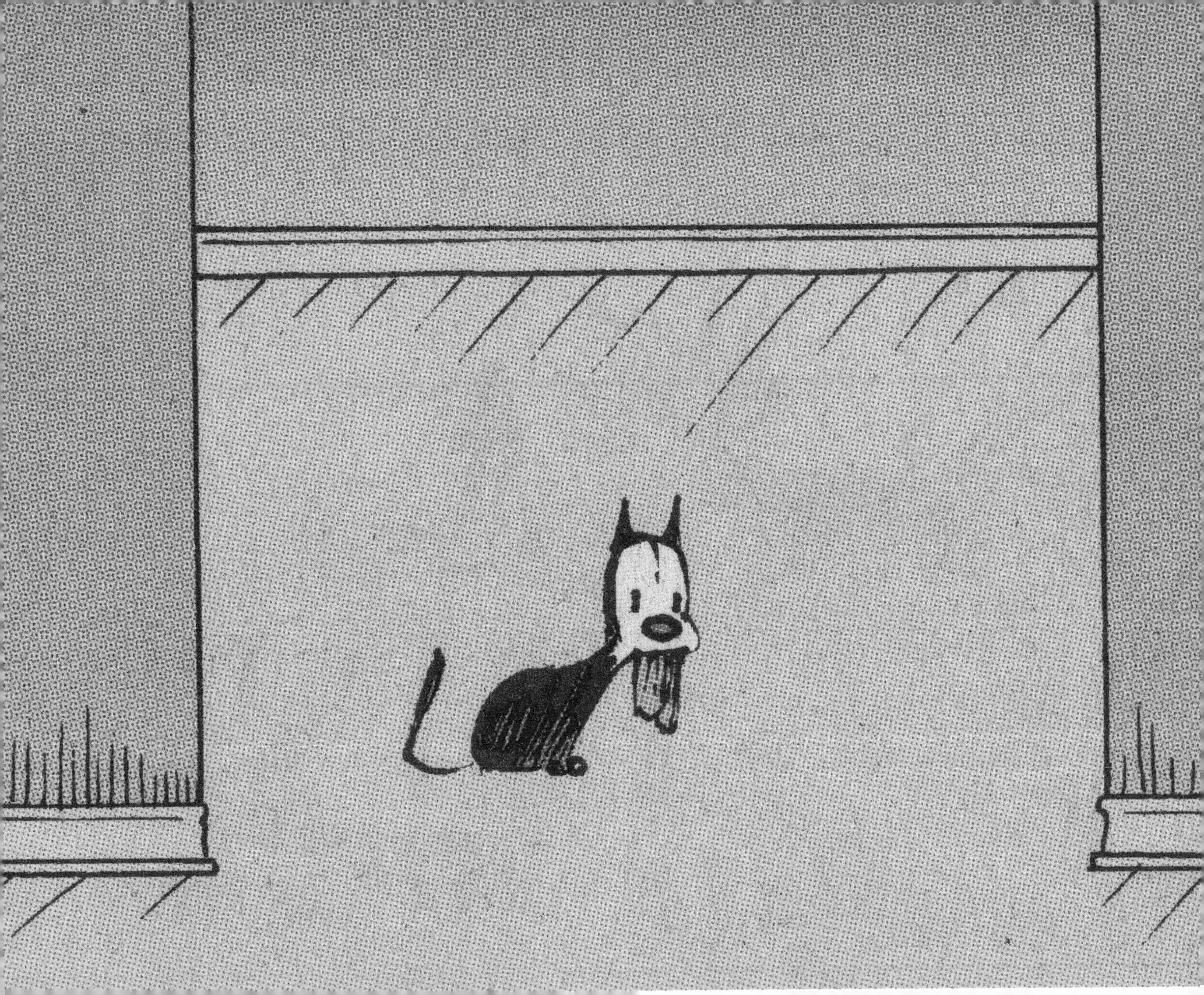

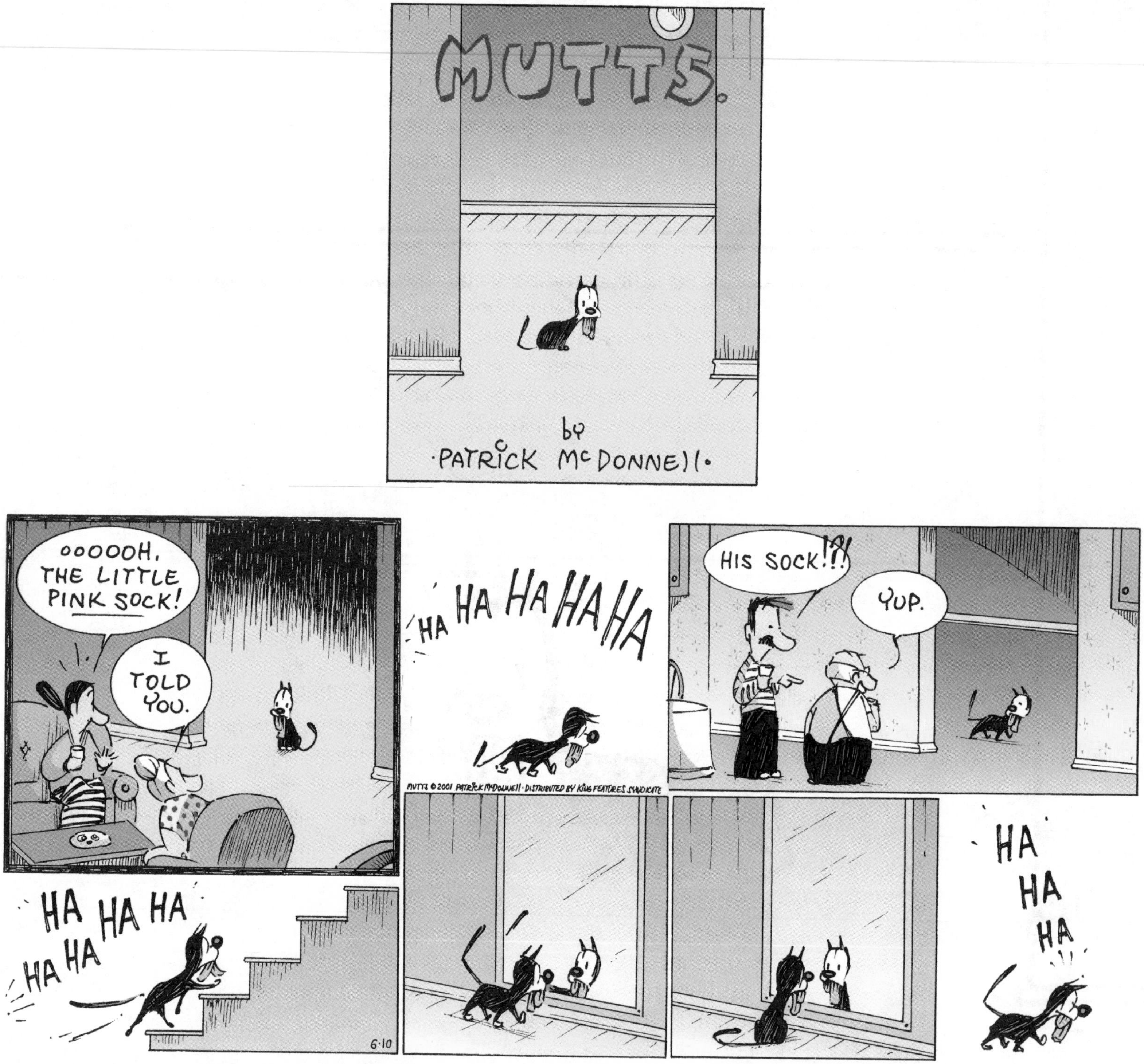

MUTTS.
by PATRICK McDONNELL
OOOOOH, THE LITTLE PINK SOCK!
I TOLD YOU.
HA HA HA HA HA
HIS SOCK!?!
YUP.
HA HA HA HA HA HA
6·10
MUTTS © 2001 PATRICK McDONNELL · DISTRIBUTED BY KING FEATURES SYNDICATE
HA HA HA

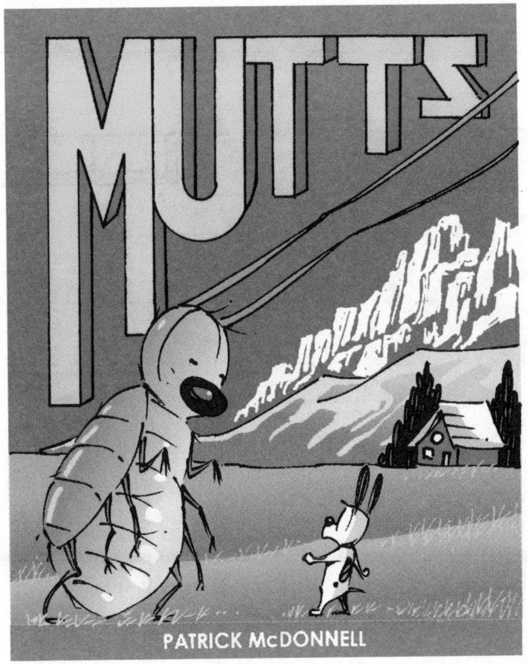
MUTTS
PATRICK McDONNELL

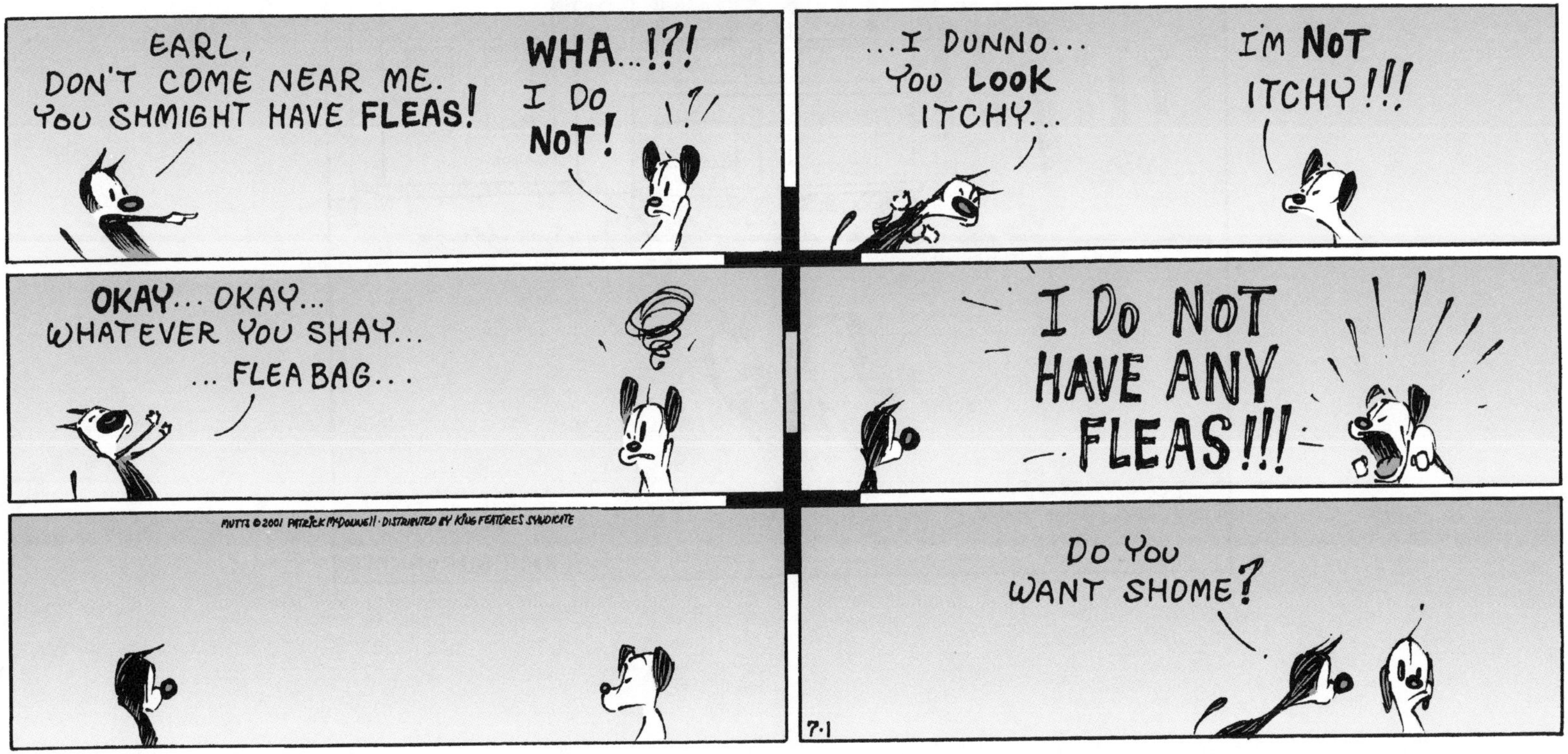
EARL, DON'T COME NEAR ME. YOU SHMIGHT HAVE FLEAS!
WHA...!?! I DO NOT!
...I DUNNO... YOU LOOK ITCHY...
I'M NOT ITCHY!!!
OKAY... OKAY... WHATEVER YOU SHAY...
... FLEABAG...
I DO NOT HAVE ANY FLEAS!!!
MUTTS © 2001 PATRICK McDONNELL · DISTRIBUTED BY KING FEATURES SYNDICATE
DO YOU WANT SHOME?
7·1

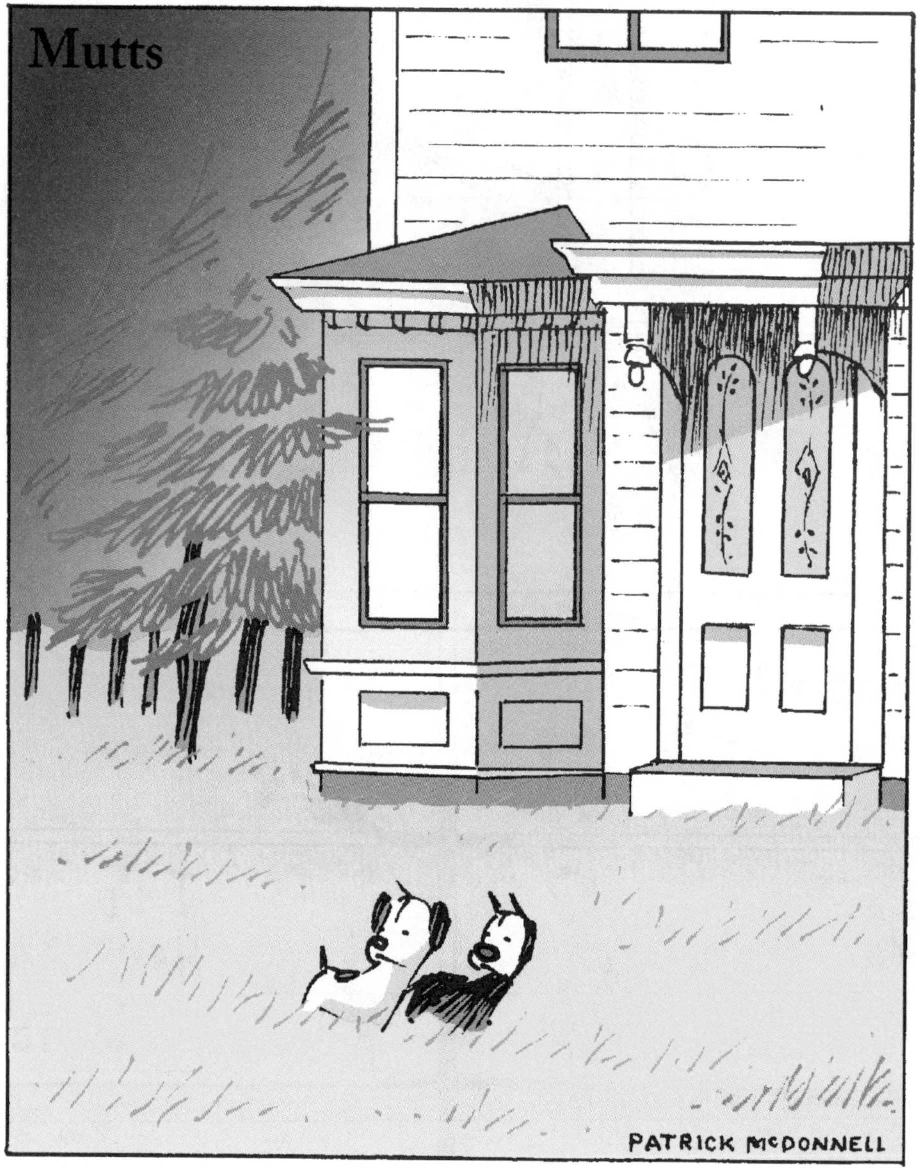
Mutts
PATRICK McDONNELL

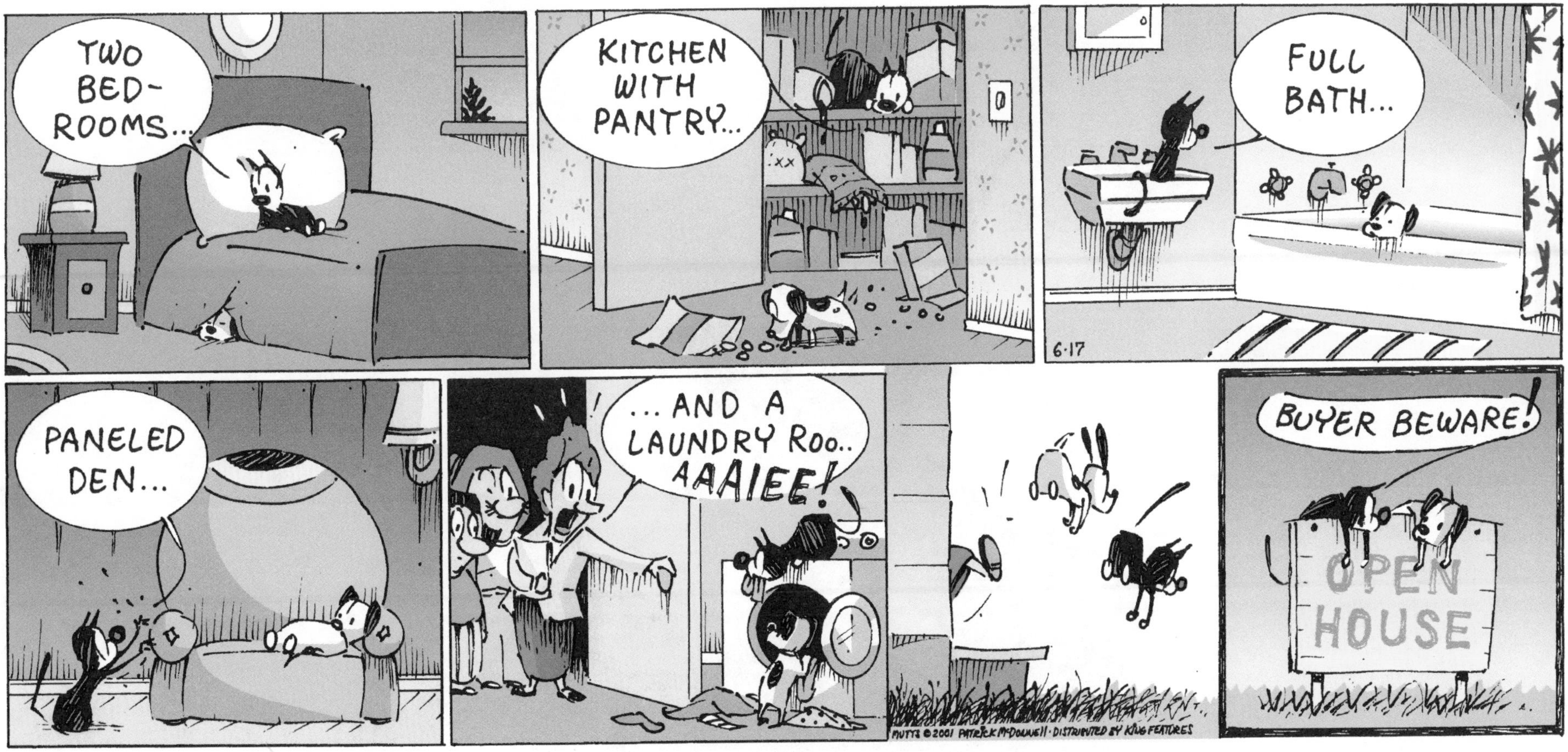
TWO BED-ROOMS...
KITCHEN WITH PANTRY...
FULL BATH...
6·17
PANELED DEN...
... AND A LAUNDRY ROO.. AAAIEE!
BUYER BEWARE!
OPEN HOUSE
MUTTS © 2001 PATRICK McDONNELL · DISTRIBUTED BY KING FEATURES

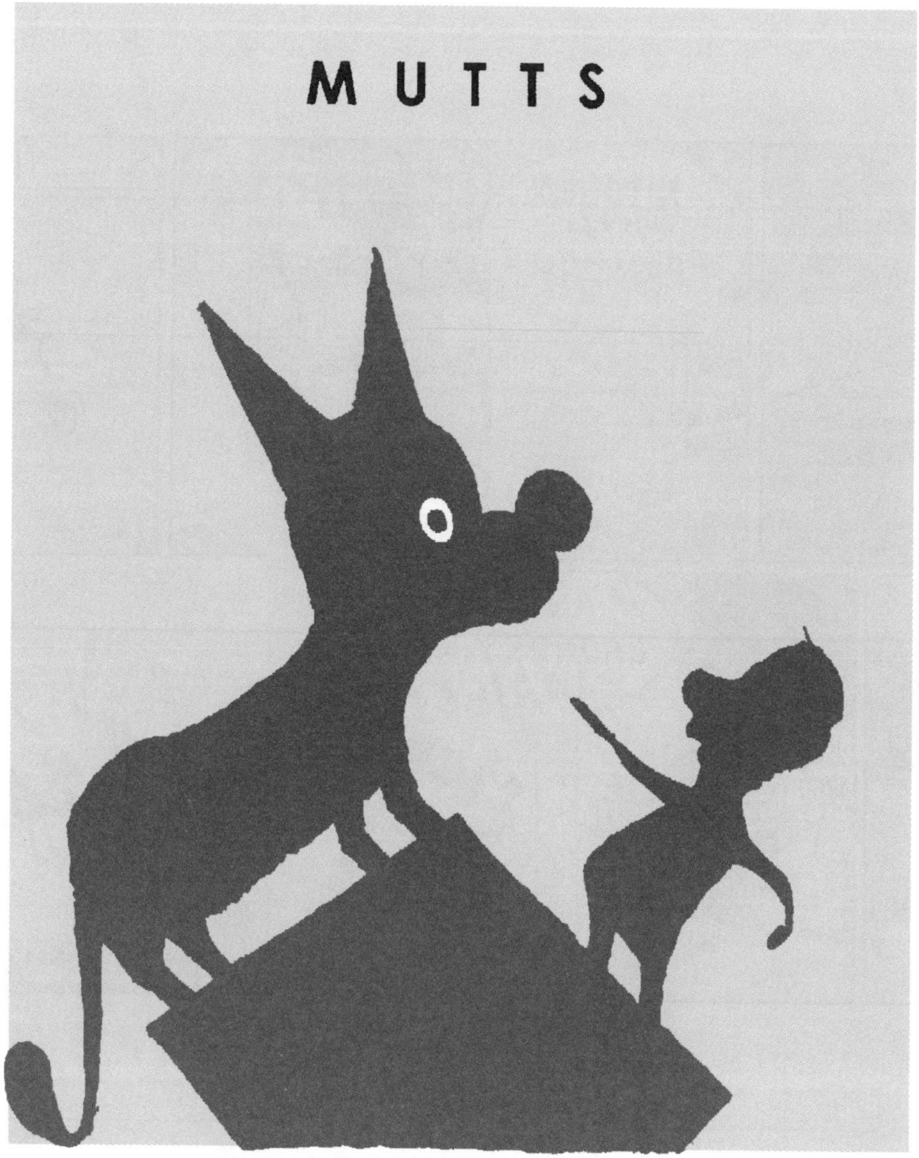
MUTTS

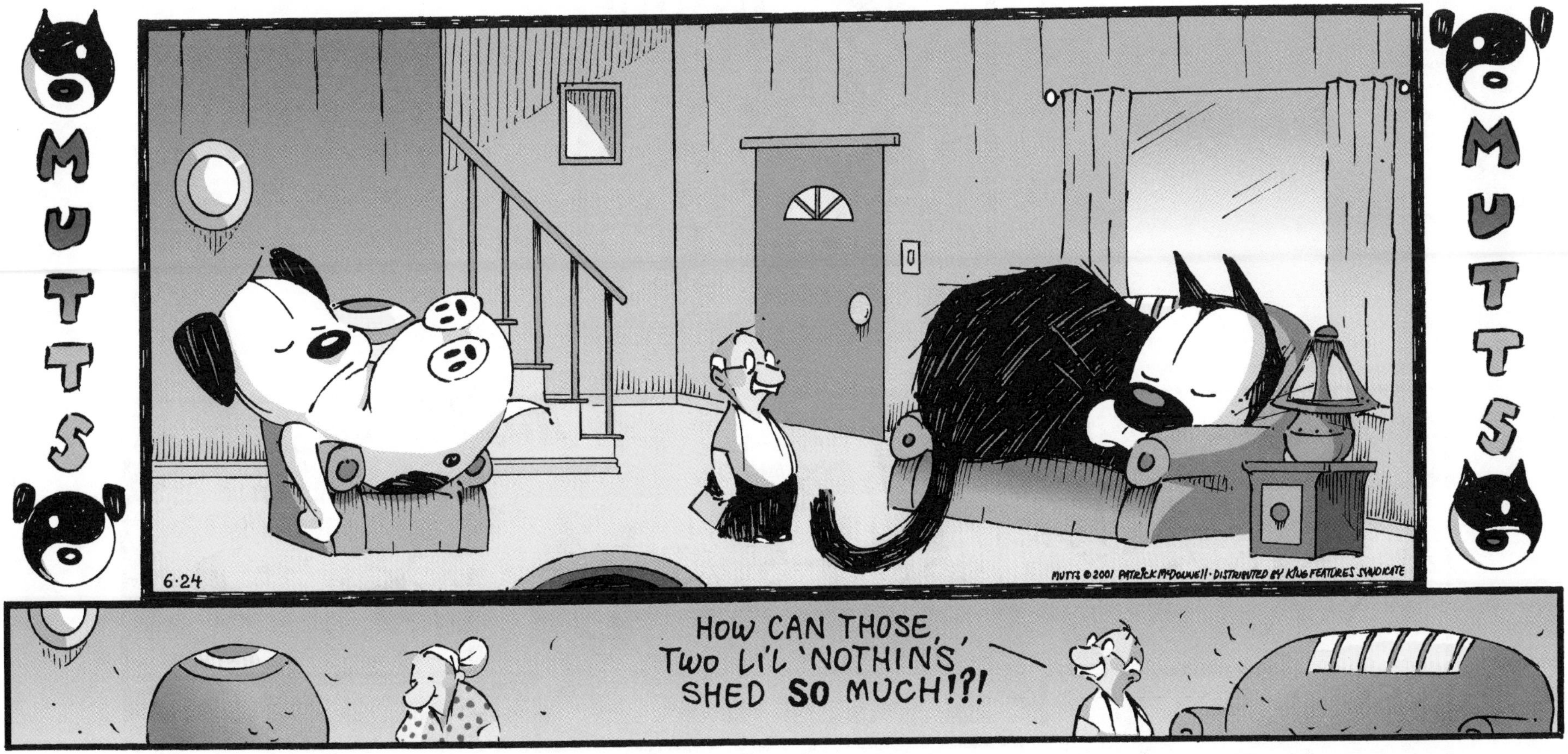
MUTTS
MUTTS
6·24
MUTTS © 2001 PATRICK McDONNELL · DISTRIBUTED BY KING FEATURES SYNDICATE
HOW CAN THOSE TWO LI'L 'NOTHIN'S' SHED **SO** MUCH!?!

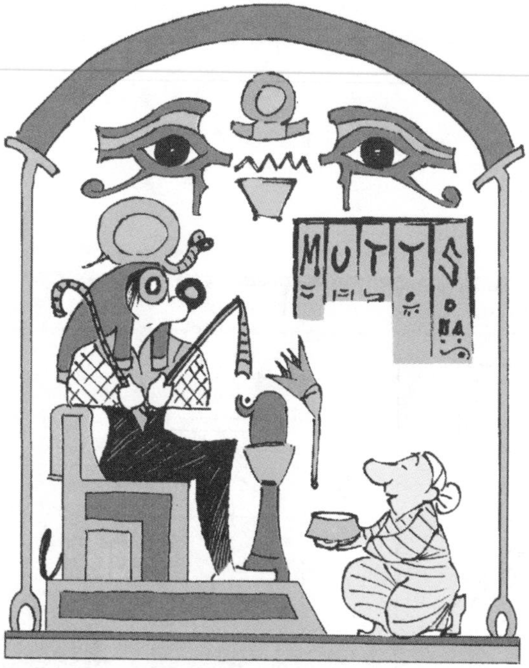
MUTTS

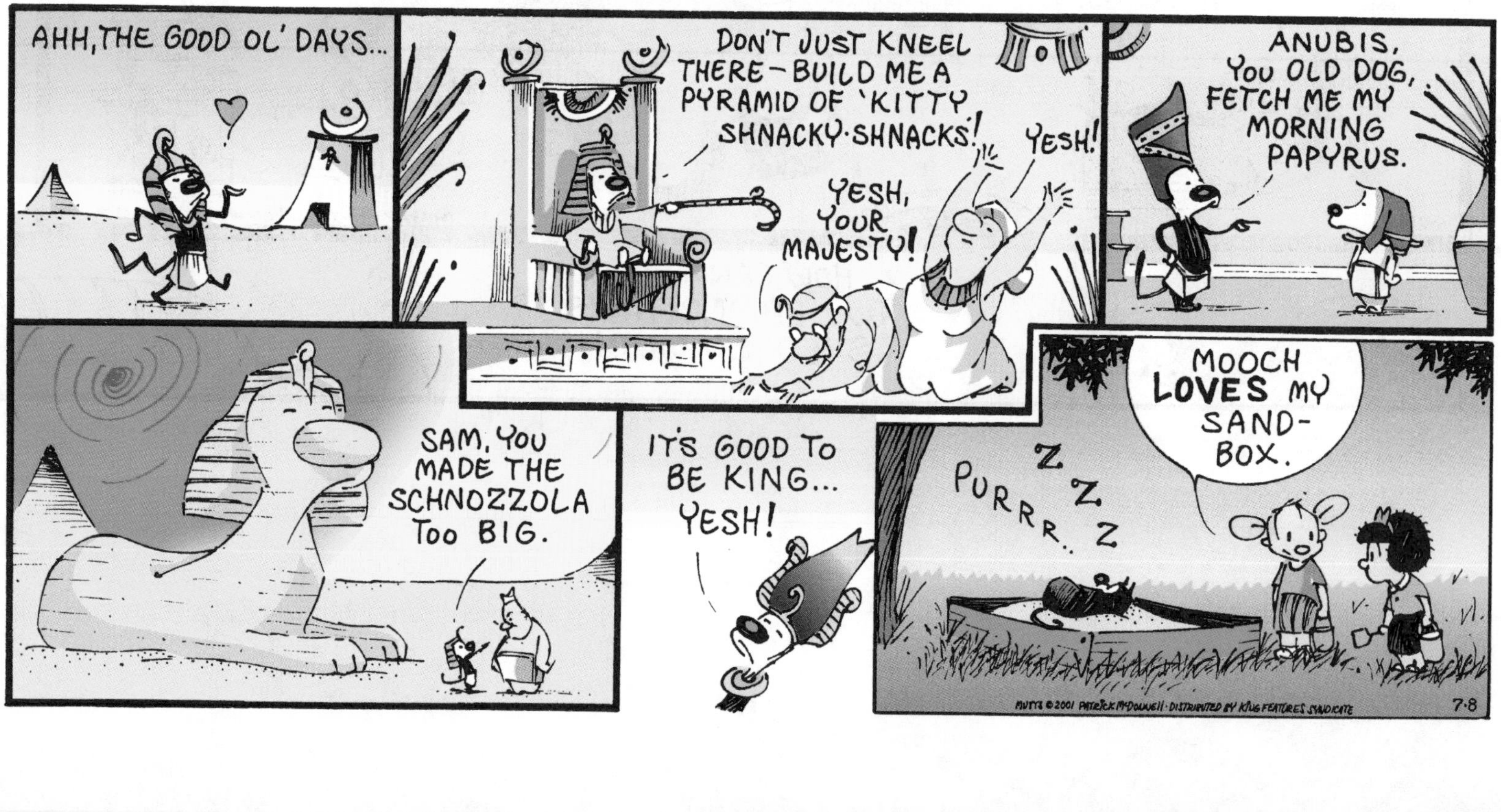
AHH, THE GOOD OL' DAYS...
DON'T JUST KNEEL THERE—BUILD ME A PYRAMID OF 'KITTY SHNACKY·SHNACKS'!
YESH!
YESH, YOUR MAJESTY!
ANUBIS, YOU OLD DOG, FETCH ME MY MORNING PAPYRUS.
SAM, YOU MADE THE SCHNOZZOLA TOO BIG.
IT'S GOOD TO BE KING... YESH!
PURRRR.. Z Z Z
MOOCH LOVES MY SAND-BOX.
MUTTS © 2001 PATRICK McDONNELL · DISTRIBUTED BY KING FEATURES SYNDICATE
7·8

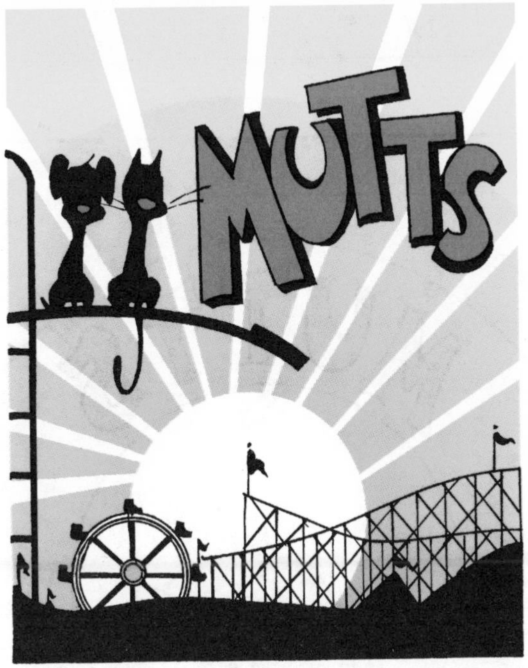
MUTTS

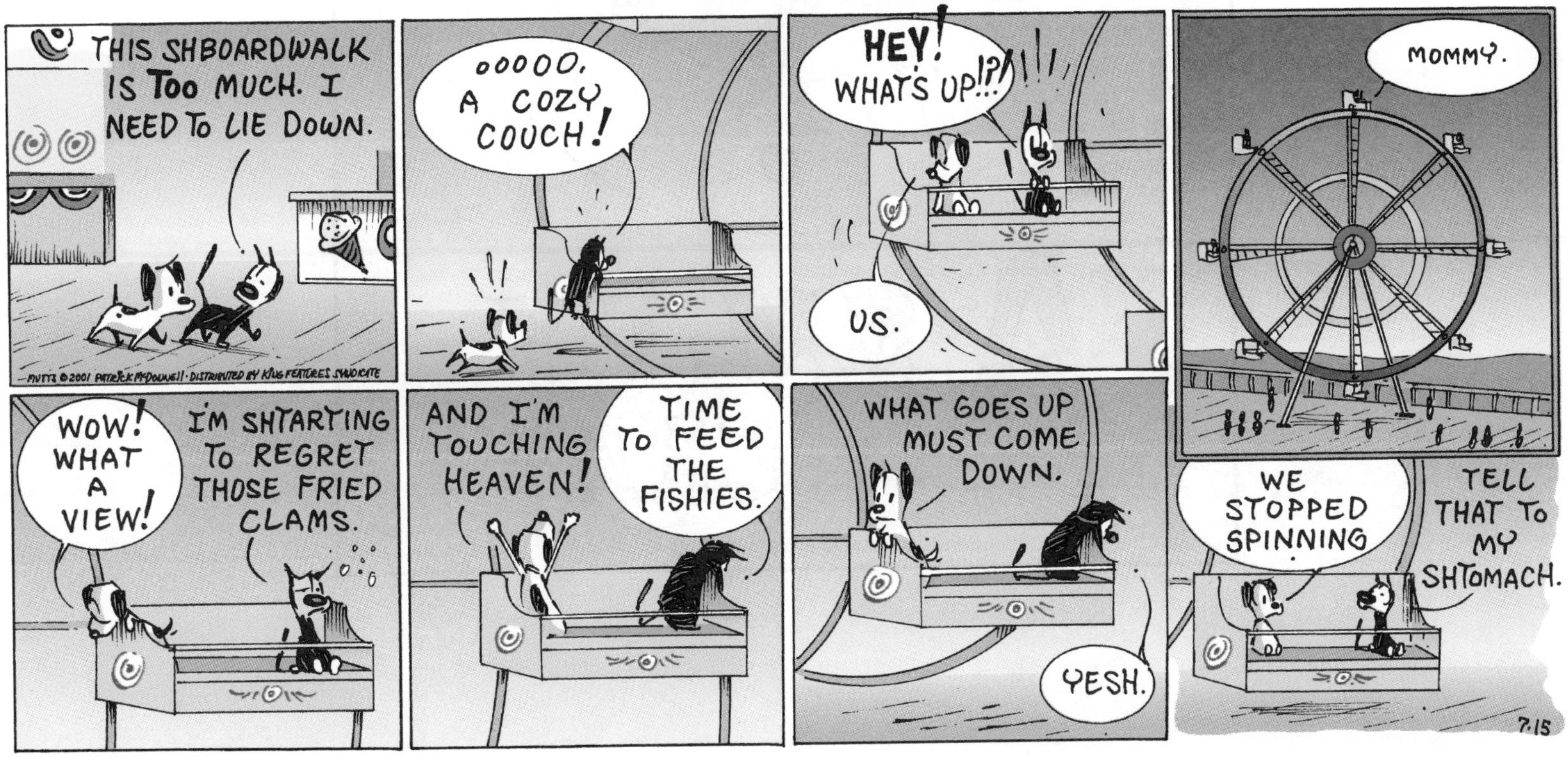
THIS SHBOARDWALK IS TOO MUCH. I NEED TO LIE DOWN.
MUTTS ©2001 PATRICK McDONNELL · DISTRIBUTED BY KING FEATURES SYNDICATE
OOOOO. A COZY COUCH!
HEY! WHAT'S UP!?!
US.
MOMMY.
WOW! WHAT A VIEW!
I'M SHTARTING TO REGRET THOSE FRIED CLAMS.
AND I'M TOUCHING HEAVEN!
TIME TO FEED THE FISHIES.
WHAT GOES UP MUST COME DOWN.
YESH.
WE STOPPED SPINNING.
TELL THAT TO MY SHTOMACH.
7·15

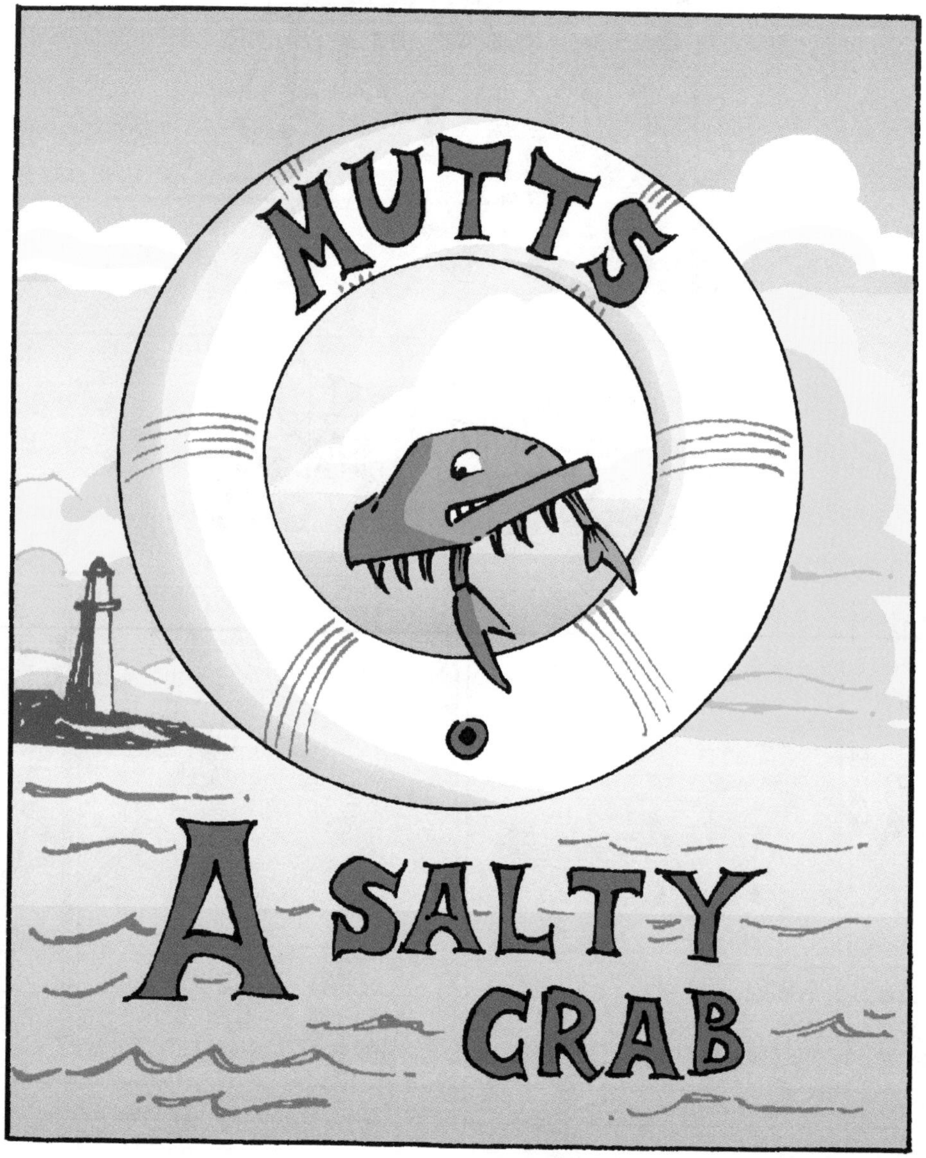
MUTTS
A SALTY CRAB

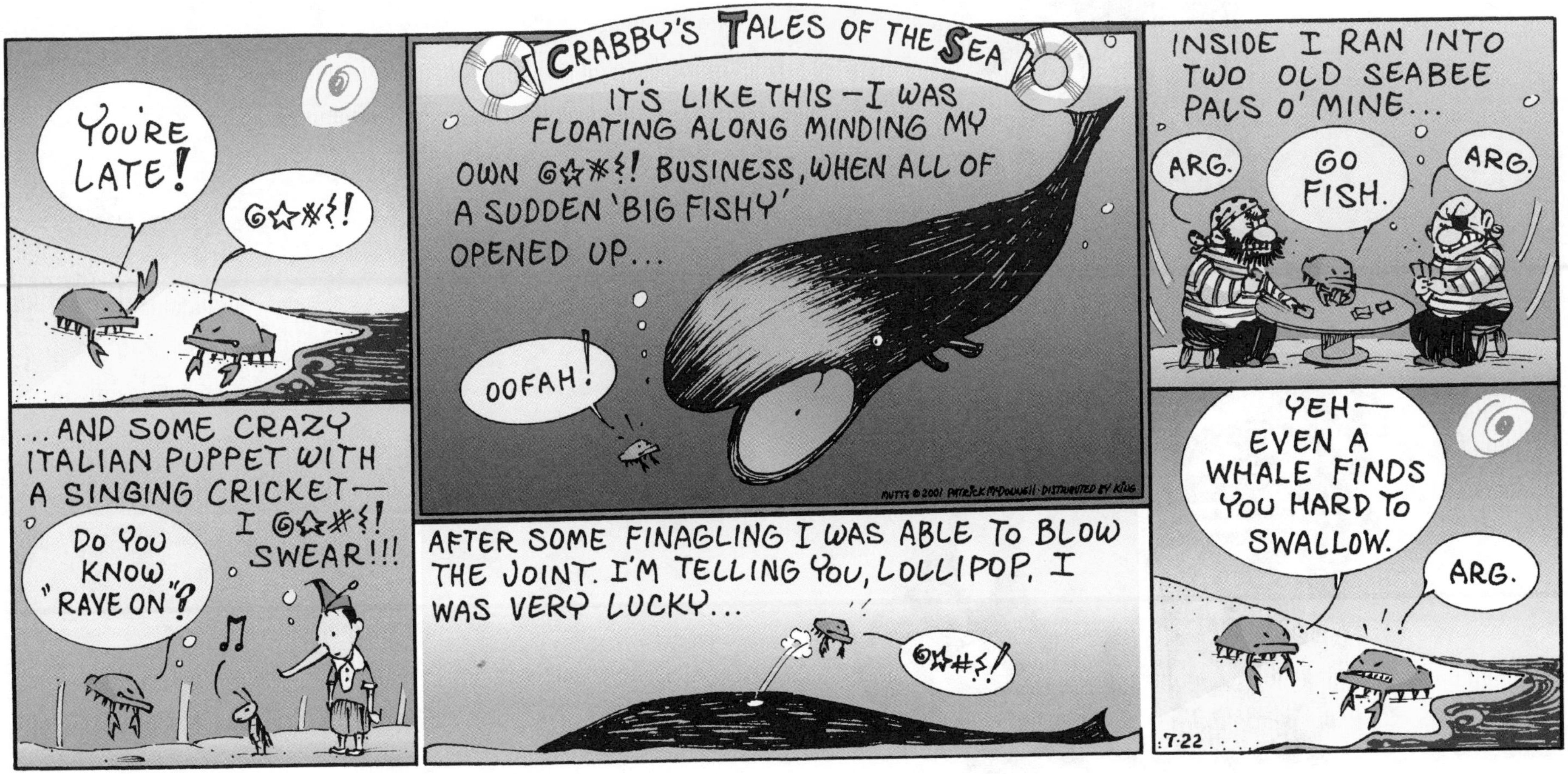
YOU'RE LATE!
G☆*$!
CRABBY'S TALES OF THE SEA
IT'S LIKE THIS—I WAS FLOATING ALONG MINDING MY OWN G☆*$! BUSINESS, WHEN ALL OF A SUDDEN 'BIG FISHY' OPENED UP...
OOFAH!
INSIDE I RAN INTO TWO OLD SEABEE PALS O' MINE...
ARG.
GO FISH.
ARG.
...AND SOME CRAZY ITALIAN PUPPET WITH A SINGING CRICKET—I G☆*$! SWEAR!!!
DO YOU KNOW "RAVE ON"?
AFTER SOME FINAGLING I WAS ABLE TO BLOW THE JOINT. I'M TELLING YOU, LOLLIPOP, I WAS VERY LUCKY...
G☆#$!
YEH—EVEN A WHALE FINDS YOU HARD TO SWALLOW.
ARG.
7·22

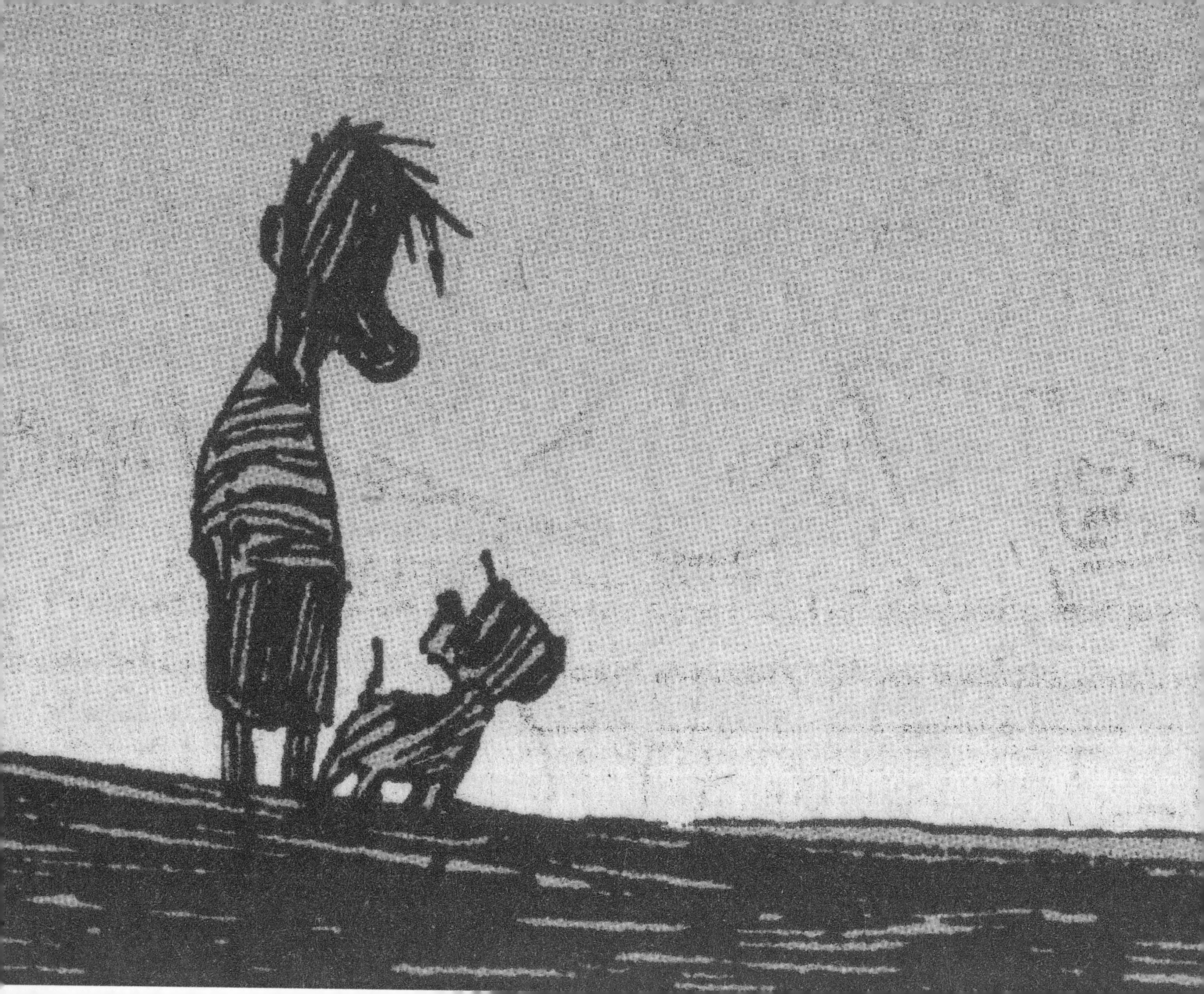

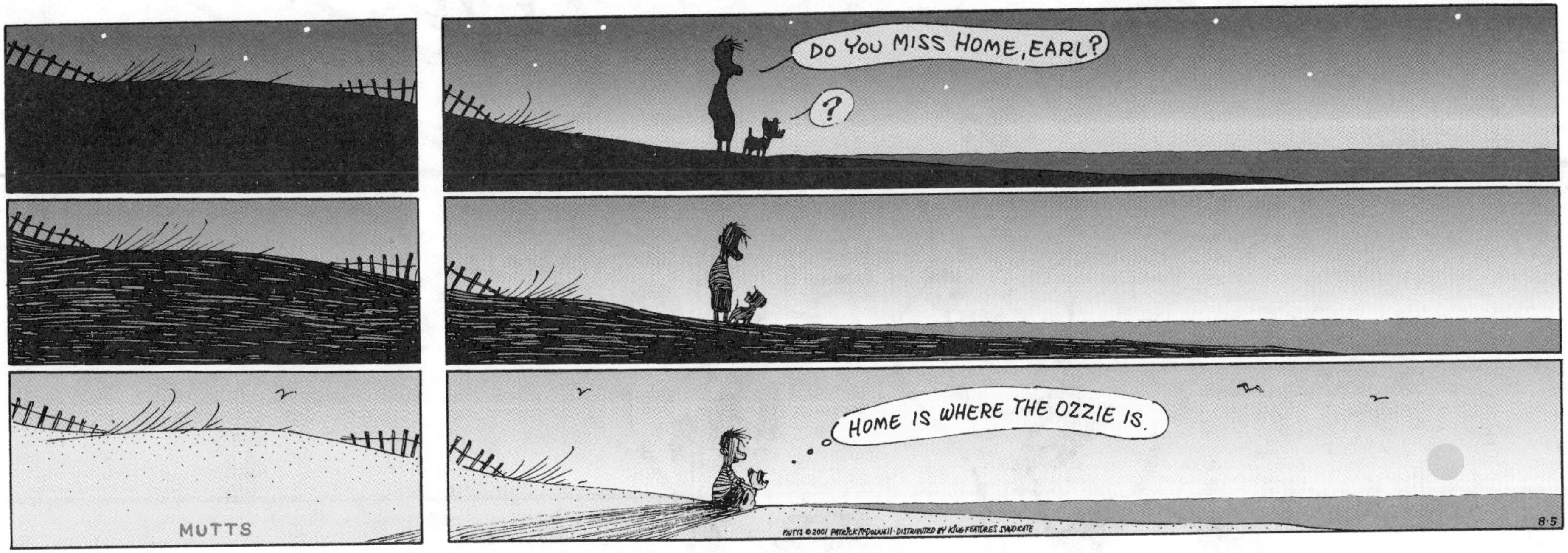
MUTTS
DO YOU MISS HOME, EARL?
?
HOME IS WHERE THE OZZIE IS.
8·5

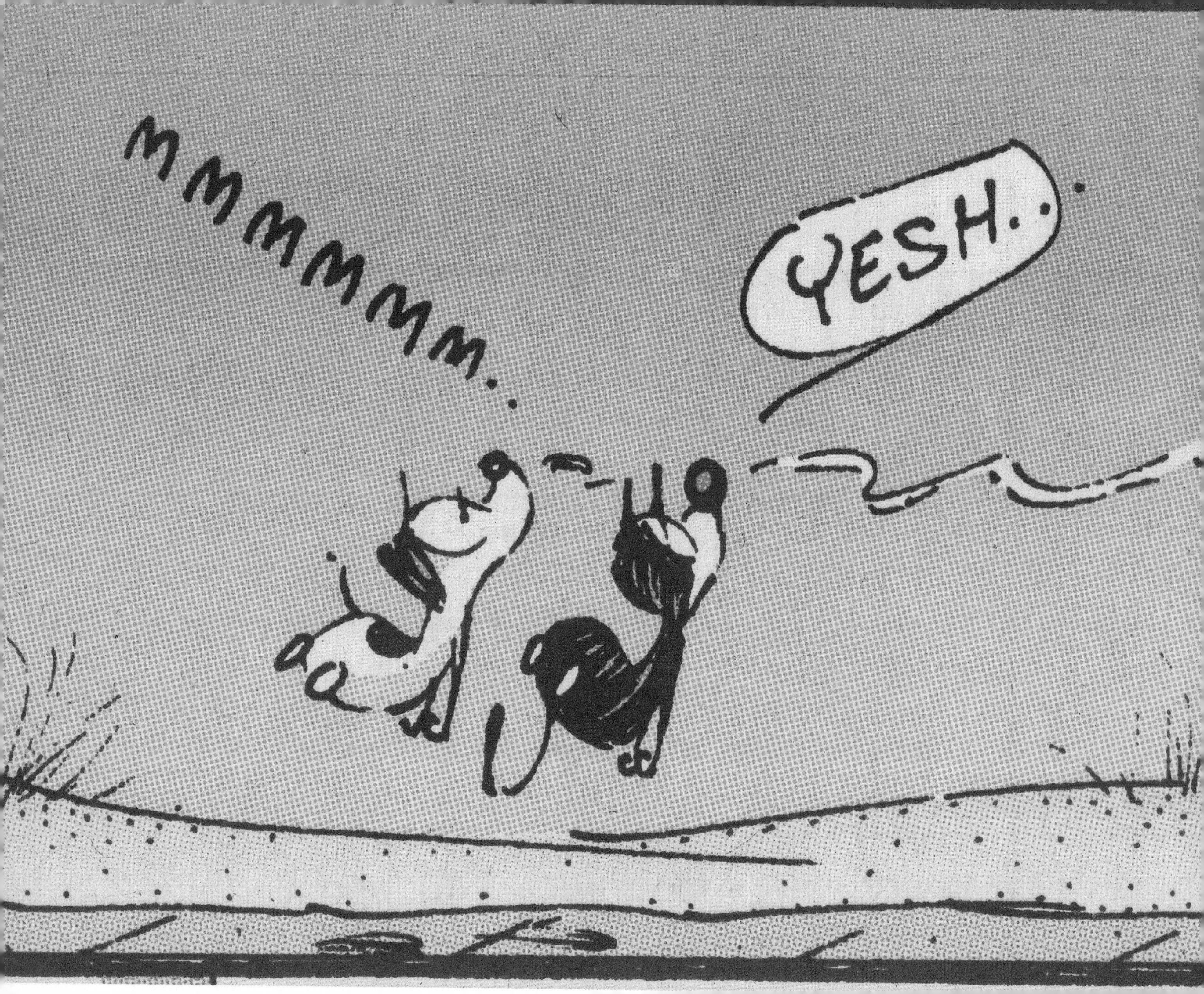
MMMMMMM..
YESH..

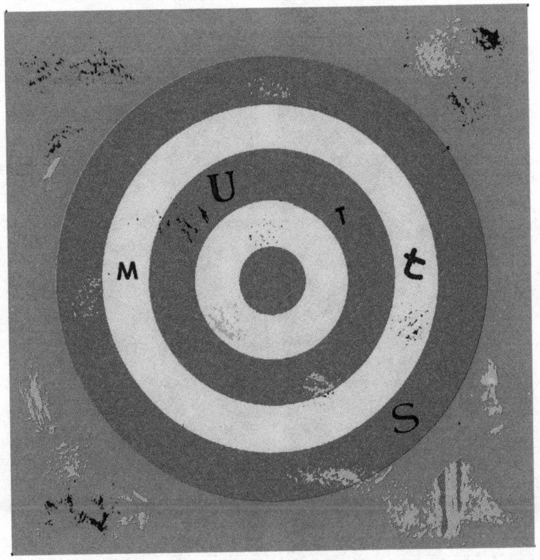

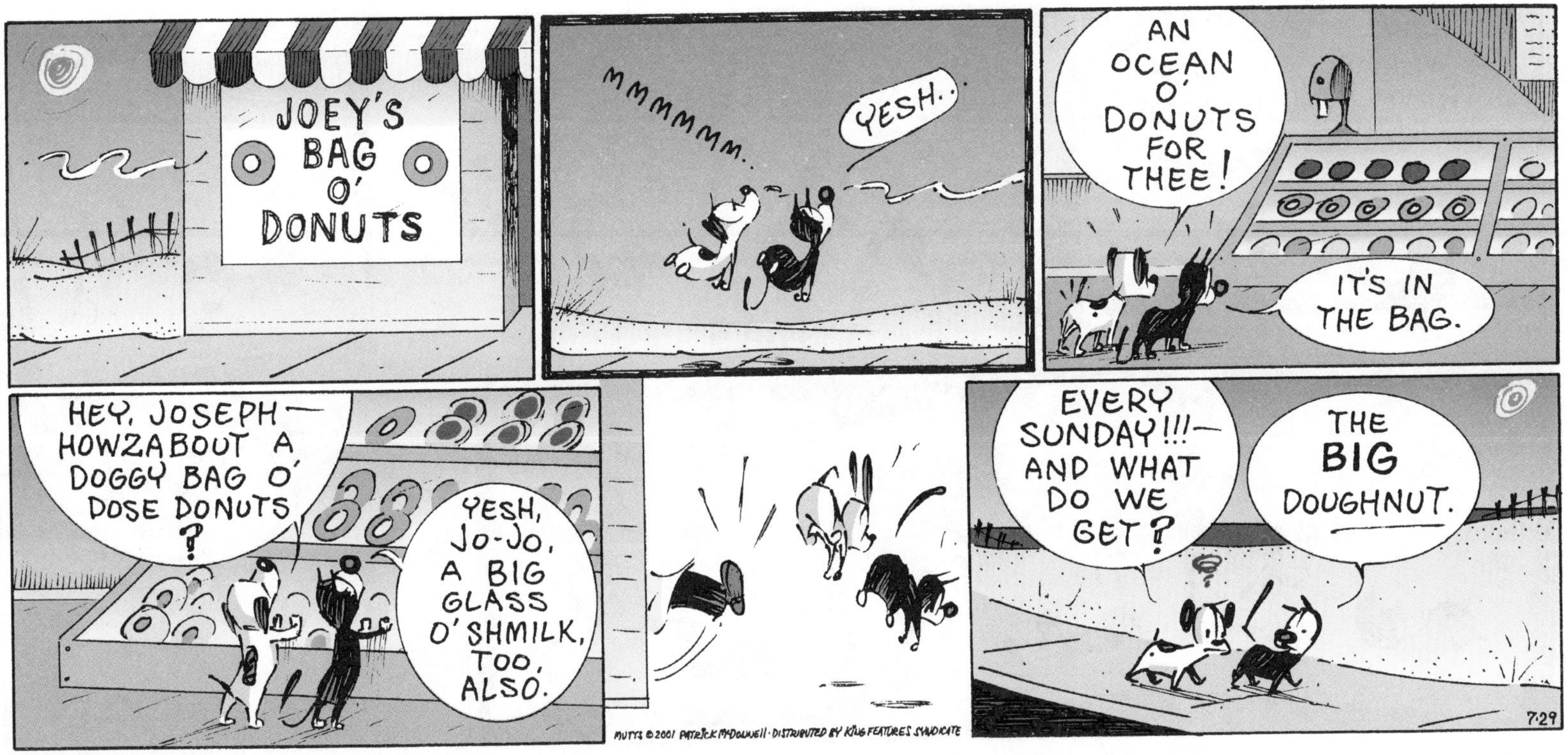
JOEY'S BAG O' DONUTS
MMMMMMM..
YESH..
AN OCEAN O' DONUTS FOR THEE!
IT'S IN THE BAG.
HEY, JOSEPH— HOWZABOUT A DOGGY BAG O' DOSE DONUTS?
YESH, JO-JO, A BIG GLASS O' SHMILK, TOO, ALSO.
EVERY SUNDAY!!!— AND WHAT DO WE GET?
THE BIG DOUGHNUT.
MUTTS © 2001 PATRICK McDONNELL · DISTRIBUTED BY KING FEATURES SYNDICATE
7·29

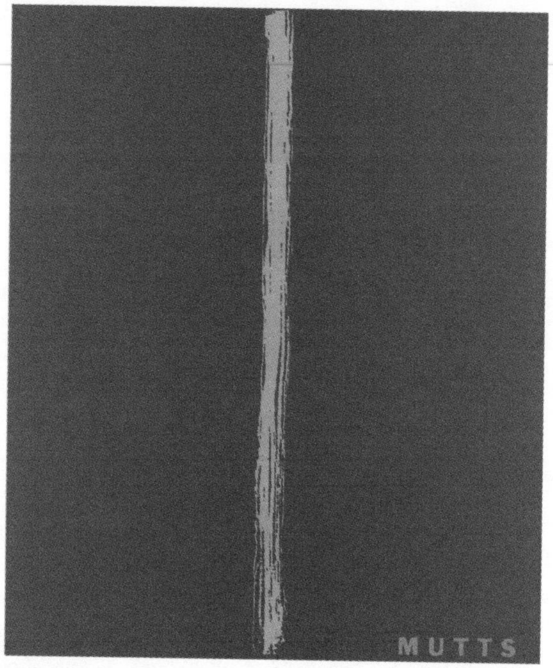
MUTTS

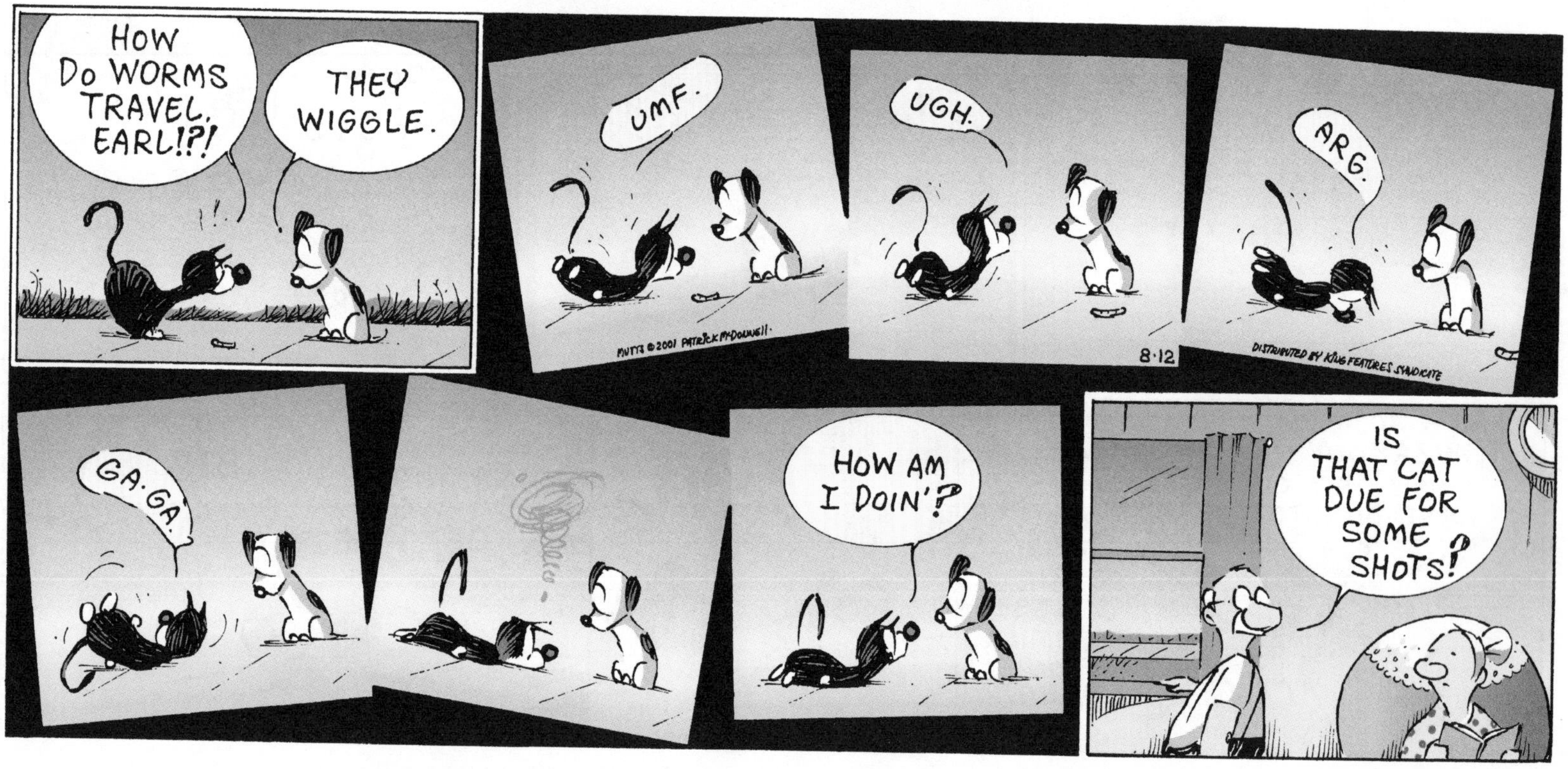
HOW DO WORMS TRAVEL, EARL!?!
THEY WIGGLE.
UMF.
UGH.
ARG.
MUTTS © 2001 PATRICK McDONNELL
8·12
DISTRIBUTED BY KING FEATURES SYNDICATE
GA·GA.
HOW AM I DOIN'?
IS THAT CAT DUE FOR SOME SHOTS?

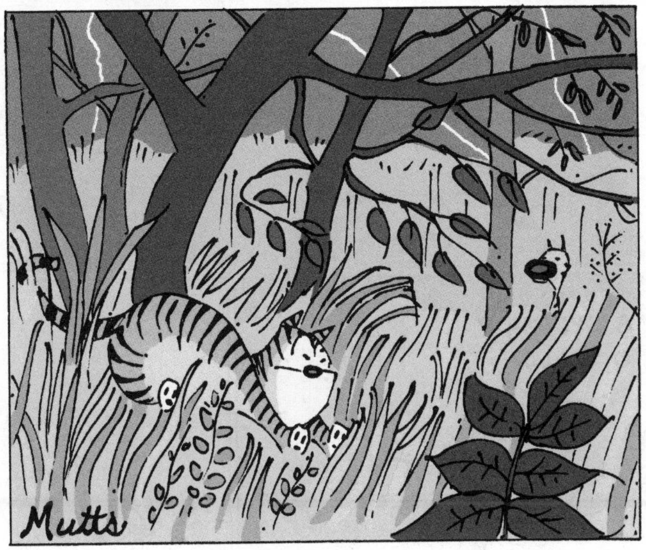
Mutts

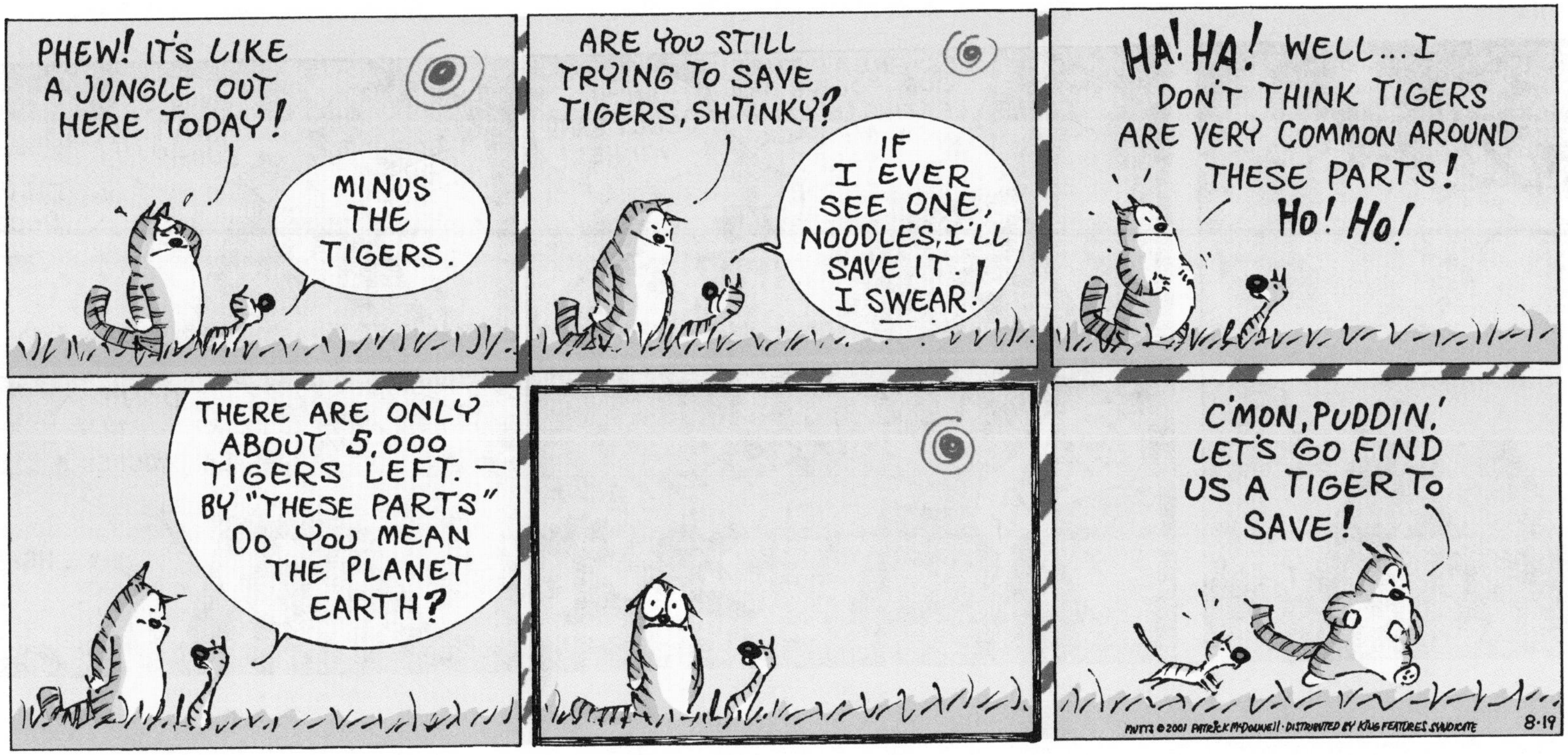
PHEW! IT'S LIKE A JUNGLE OUT HERE TODAY!
MINUS THE TIGERS.
ARE YOU STILL TRYING TO SAVE TIGERS, SHTINKY?
IF I EVER SEE ONE, NOODLES, I'LL SAVE IT. I SWEAR!
HA! HA! WELL... I DON'T THINK TIGERS ARE VERY COMMON AROUND THESE PARTS! HO! HO!
THERE ARE ONLY ABOUT 5,000 TIGERS LEFT. — BY "THESE PARTS" DO YOU MEAN THE PLANET EARTH?
C'MON, PUDDIN'! LET'S GO FIND US A TIGER TO SAVE!
MUTTS © 2001 PATRICK McDONNELL · DISTRIBUTED BY KING FEATURES SYNDICATE
8·19

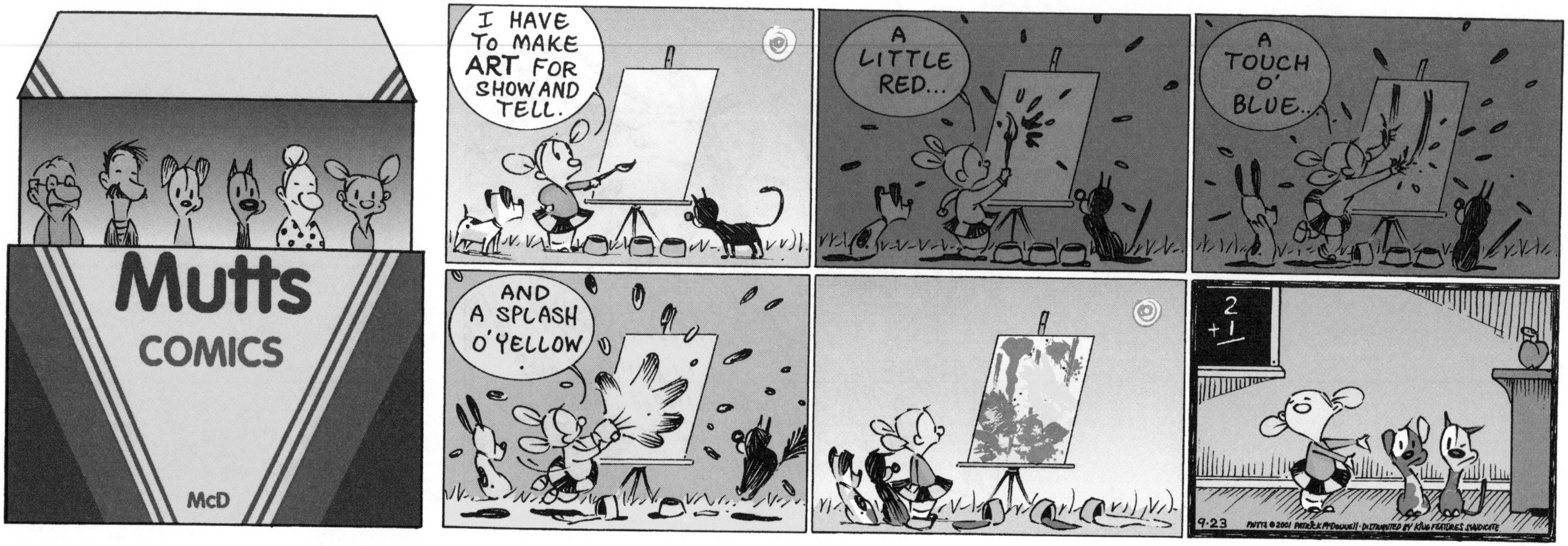
Mutts
COMICS
McD
I HAVE TO MAKE ART FOR SHOW AND TELL.
A LITTLE RED...
A TOUCH O' BLUE...
AND A SPLASH O' YELLOW.
2
+1
9·23
MUTTS © 2001 PATRICK McDONNELL · DISTRIBUTED BY KING FEATURES SYNDICATE

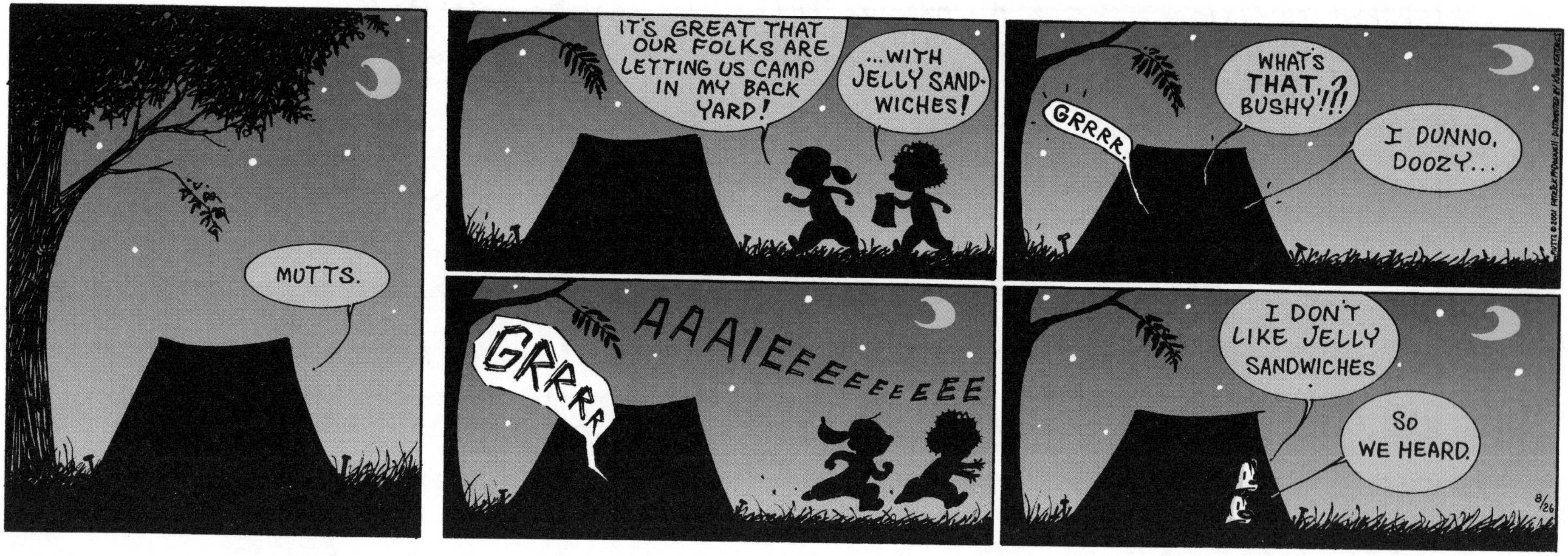
MUTTS.
IT'S GREAT THAT OUR FOLKS ARE LETTING US CAMP IN MY BACK YARD!
...WITH JELLY SANDWICHES!
GRRRR.
WHAT'S THAT, BUSHY ?!?!
I DUNNO, DOOZY...
GRRRR
AAAIEEEEEEEEEE
I DON'T LIKE JELLY SANDWICHES.
SO WE HEARD.
8/26

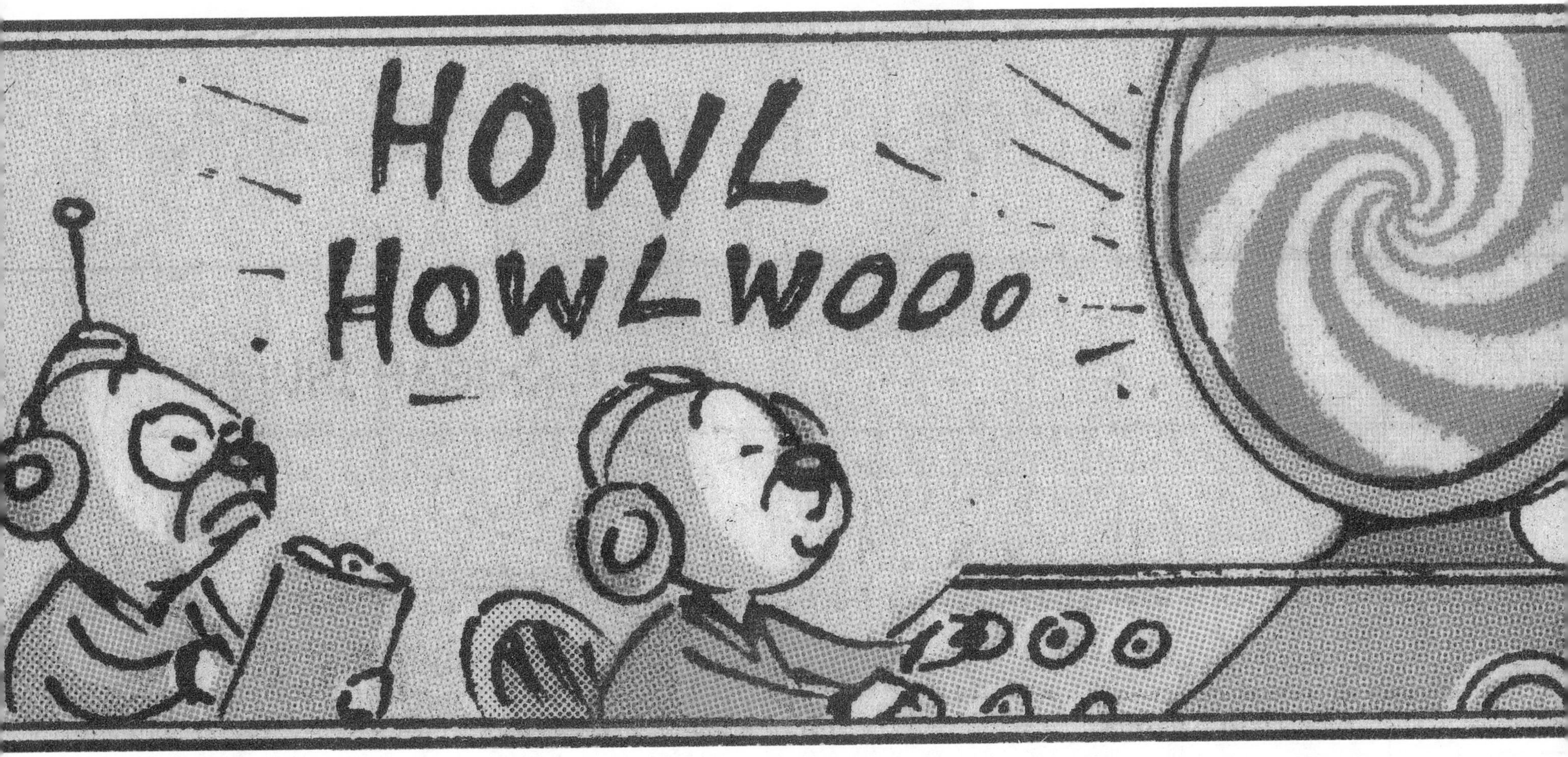
HOWL
HOWLWOOo

MUTTS

THE "MOONDOGS" ARE AT IT AGAIN–MONITORING ALL DOGGY TRANSMISSIONS FROM PLANET EARTH...
HOWL
HOWLWOOO
HOWL
EARL'S BEEN LEFT HOME ALONE, SIR.
WOOOOO
PETE IS STILL WAITING TO BE ADOPTED.
HOWL
AND GUARD DOG REMAINS CHAINED IN HIS YARD.
9·2
WHAT KIND OF UNCIVILIZED WORLD IS THIS!?!
HOWL
BUT NOT ALL THE NEWS IS BAD...
HOWLWOOO
WOOFIE LOVES A FULL MOON.
DON'T WE ALL, SIR.
MUTTS © 2001 PATRICK McDONNELL · DISTRIBUTED BY KING FEATURES

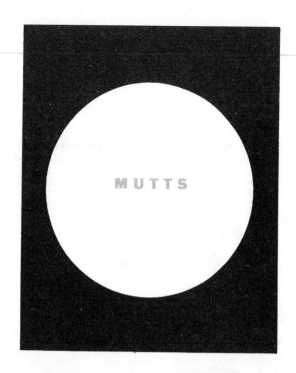

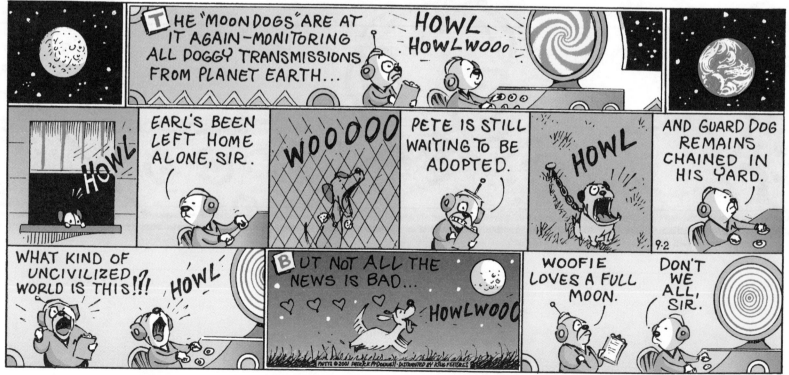

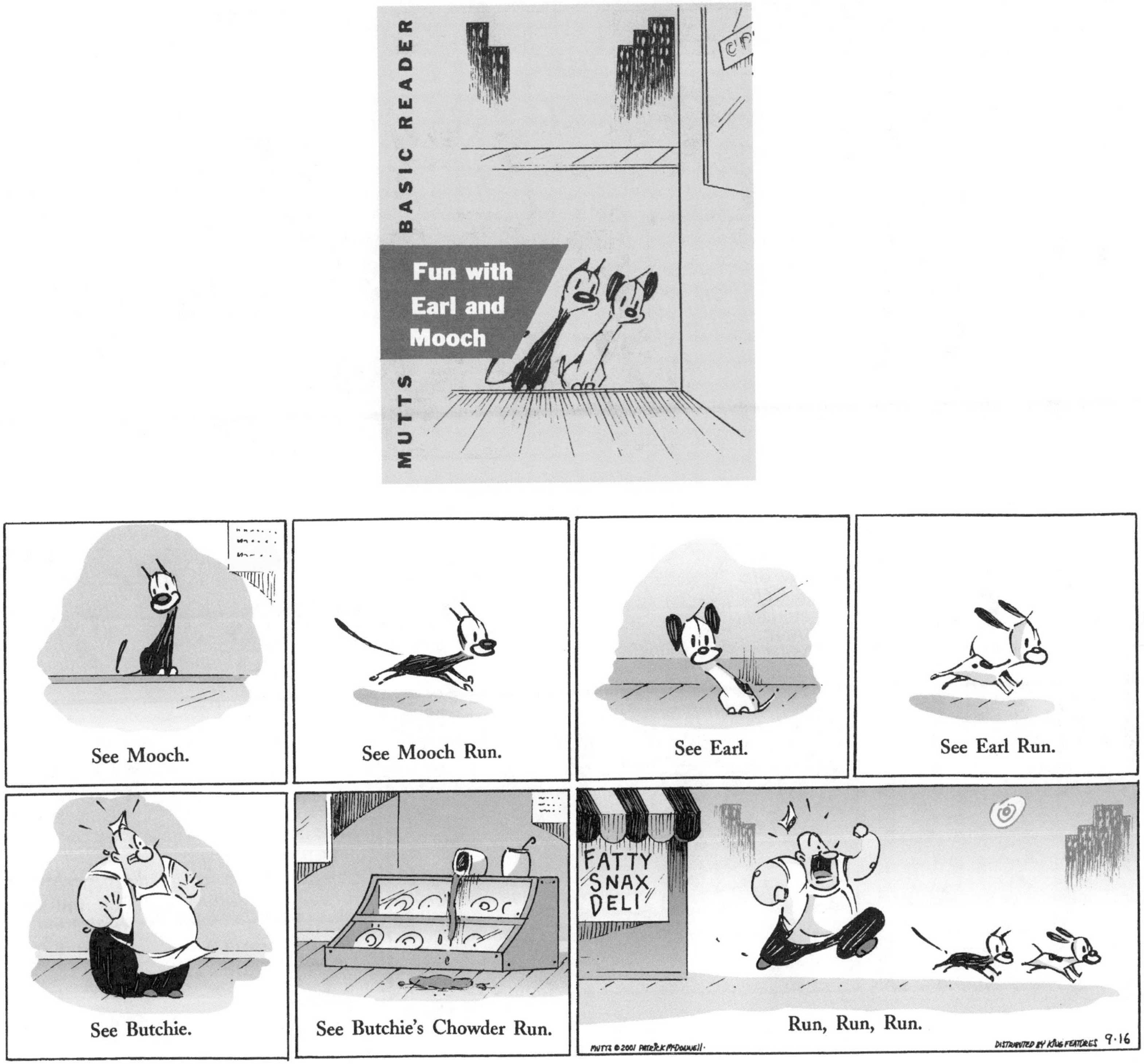
MUTTS BASIC READER
Fun with Earl and Mooch
See Mooch.
See Mooch Run.
See Earl.
See Earl Run.
See Butchie.
See Butchie's Chowder Run.
FATTY SNAX DELI
Run, Run, Run.
MUTTS © 2001 PATRICK McDONNELL
DISTRIBUTED BY KING FEATURES 9·16

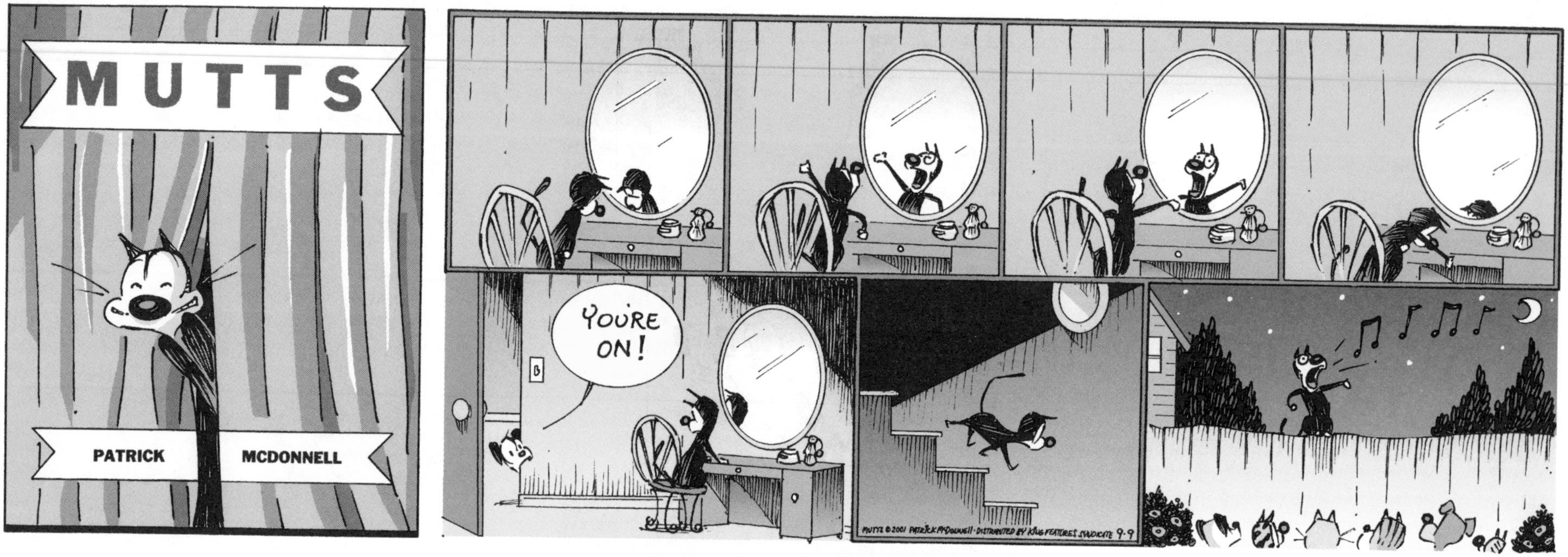
MUTTS
PATRICK
MCDONNELL
YOU'RE ON!
MUTTS © 2001 PATRICK McDONNELL · DISTRIBUTED BY KING FEATURES SYNDICATE 9-9

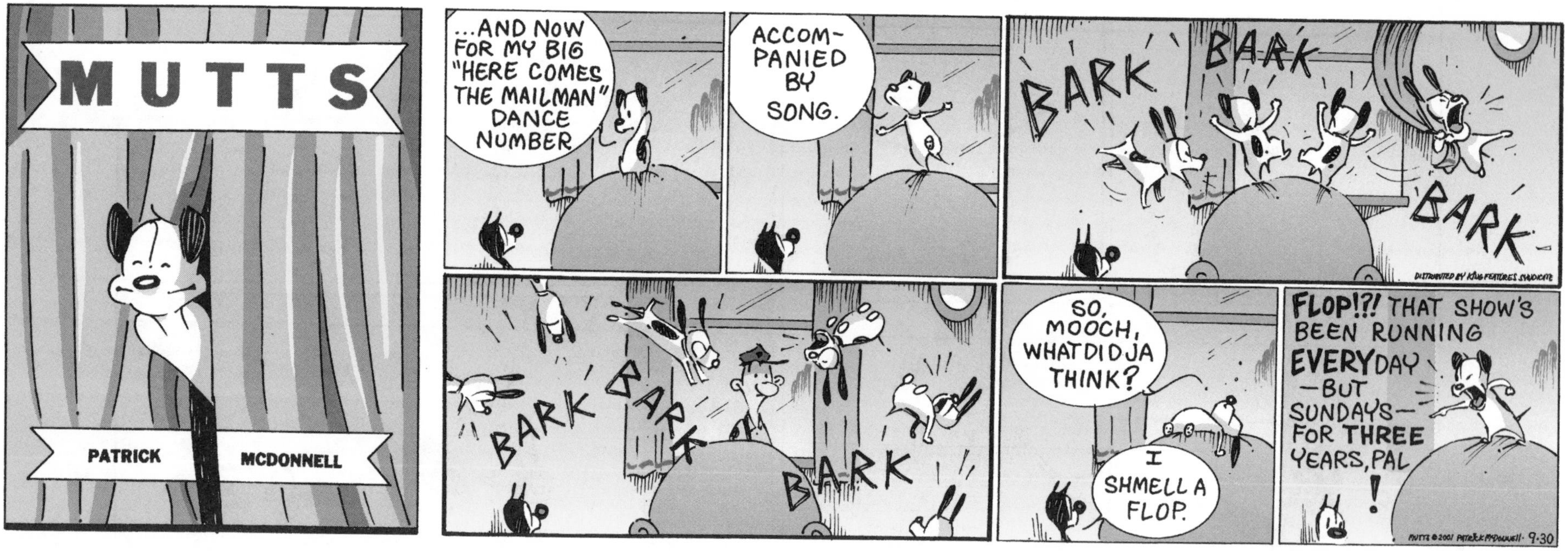
MUTTS
PATRICK
MCDONNELL
...AND NOW FOR MY BIG "HERE COMES THE MAILMAN" DANCE NUMBER
ACCOMPANIED BY SONG.
BARK
BARK
BARK
DISTRIBUTED BY KING FEATURES SYNDICATE
BARK
BARK
BARK
SO, MOOCH, WHATDIDJA THINK?
I SHMELL A FLOP.
FLOP!?! THAT SHOW'S BEEN RUNNING EVERYDAY —BUT SUNDAYS— FOR THREE YEARS, PAL!
MUTTS © 2001 PATRICK McDONNELL · 9-30

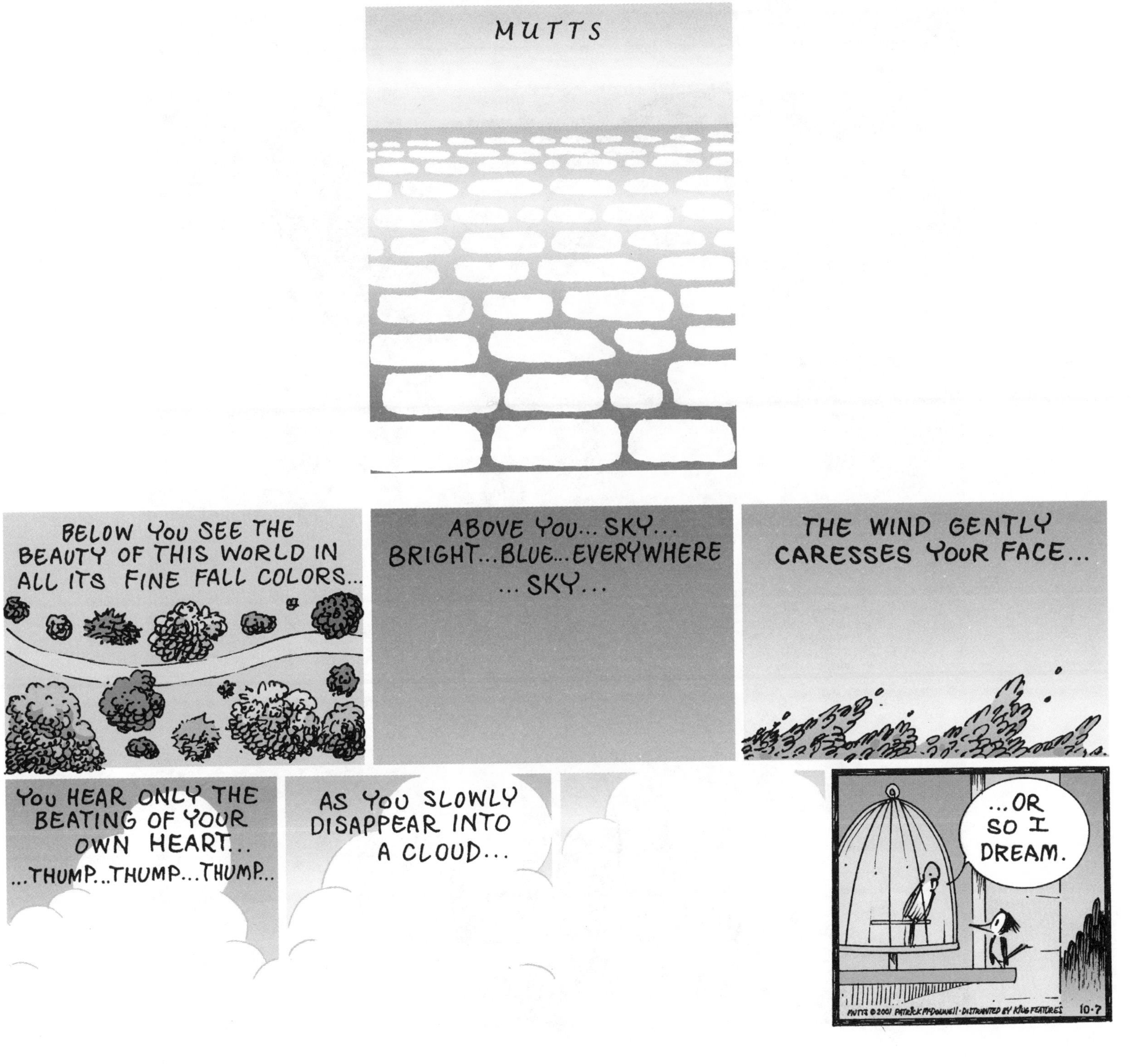
MUTTS
BELOW YOU SEE THE BEAUTY OF THIS WORLD IN ALL ITS FINE FALL COLORS...
ABOVE YOU... SKY... BRIGHT...BLUE...EVERYWHERE ... SKY...
THE WIND GENTLY CARESSES YOUR FACE...
YOU HEAR ONLY THE BEATING OF YOUR OWN HEART...
...THUMP...THUMP...THUMP...
AS YOU SLOWLY DISAPPEAR INTO A CLOUD...
...OR SO I DREAM.
MUTTS © 2001 PATRICK McDONNELL · DISTRIBUTED BY KING FEATURES
10·7

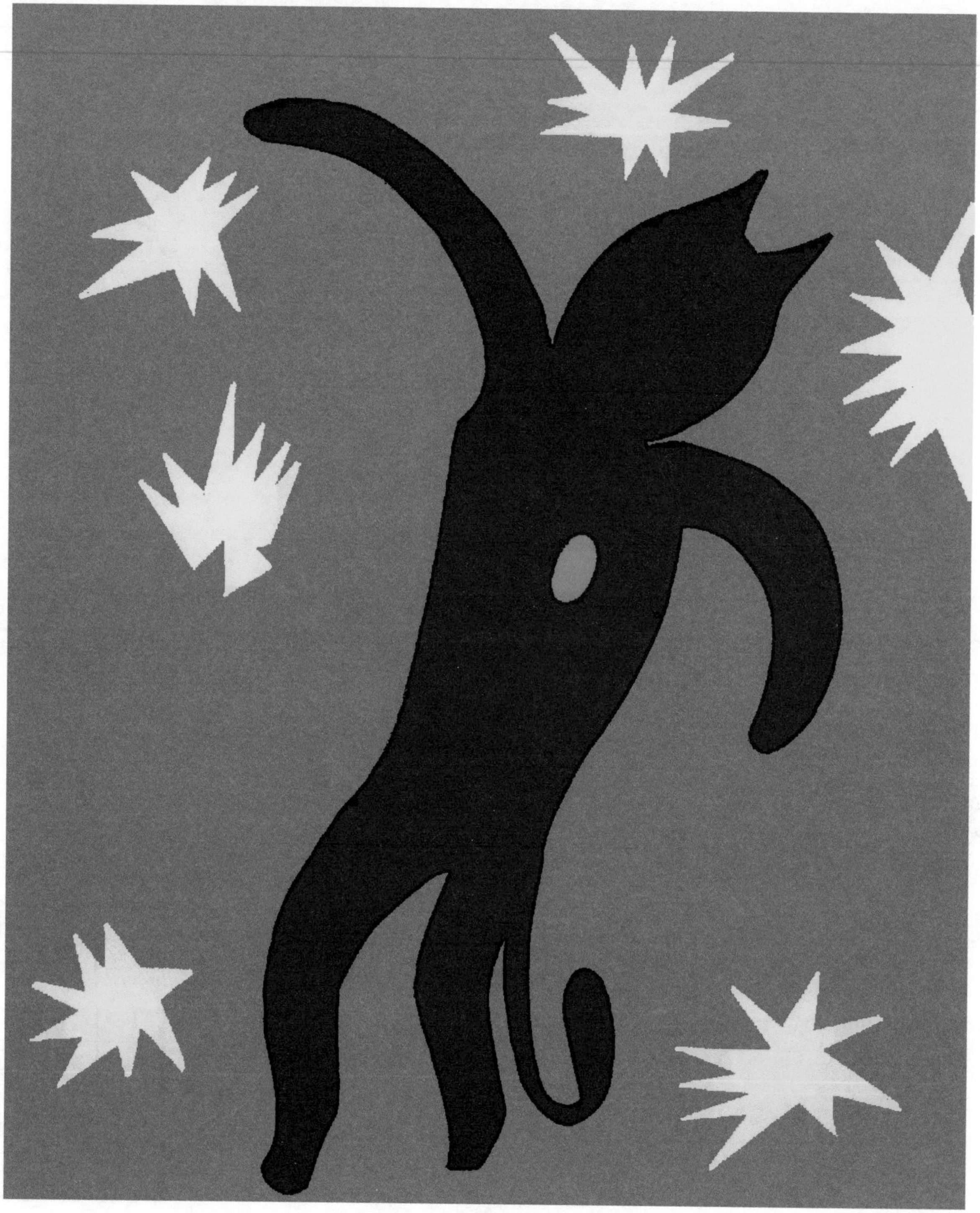

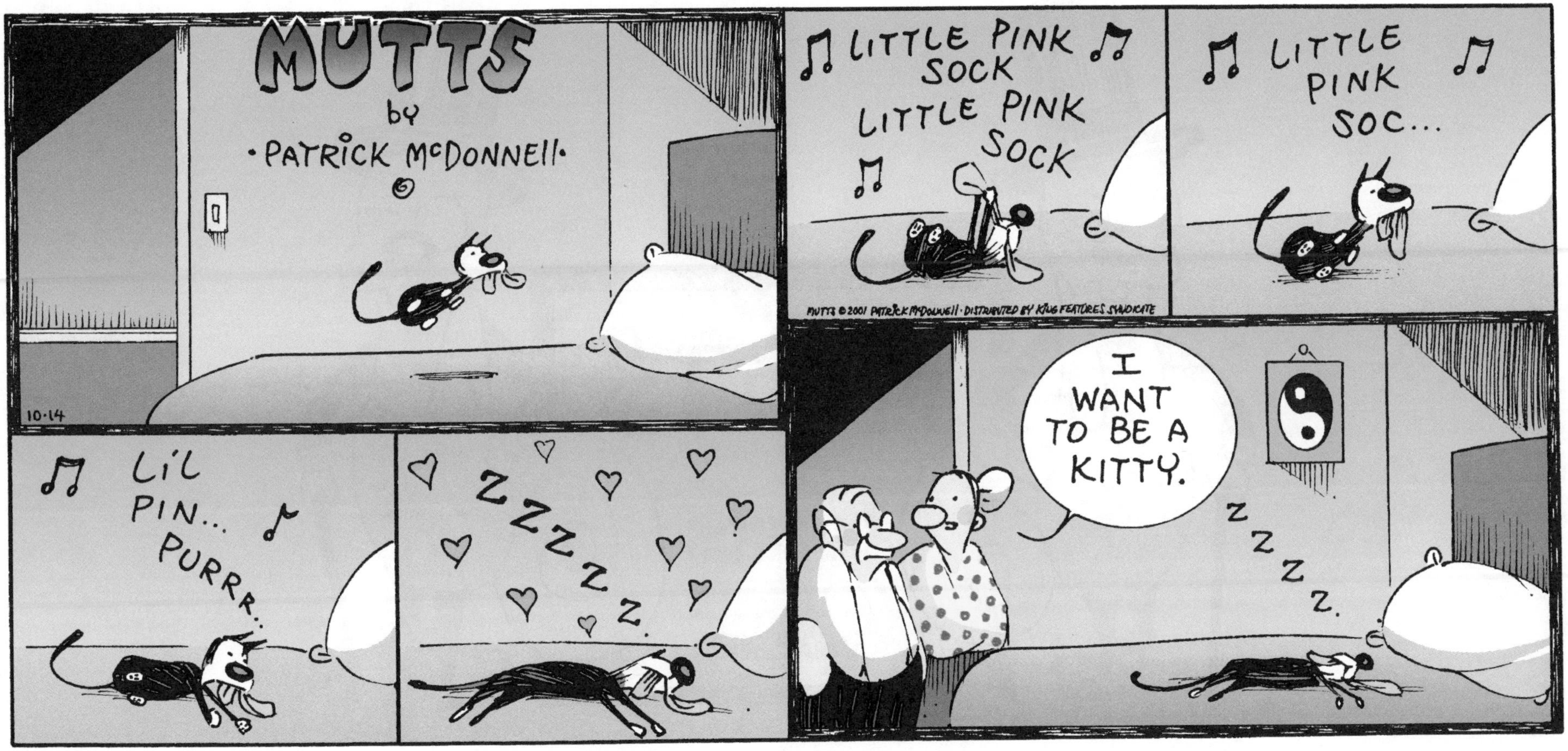
MUTTS
by
• PATRICK McDONNELL •
©
10·14
LITTLE PINK SOCK
LITTLE PINK SOCK
MUTTS © 2001 PATRICK McDONNELL · DISTRIBUTED BY KING FEATURES SYNDICATE
LITTLE PINK SOC...
LI'L PIN... PURRR...
Z Z Z Z Z Z.
I WANT TO BE A KITTY.
Z Z Z Z.

MUTTS
COMICS
McDONNELL

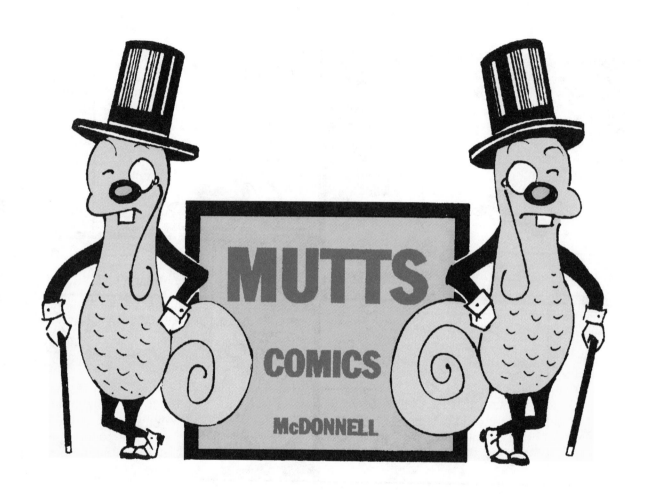

LO! A PISTACHIO! ALL THE WAY FROM THE DESERTS OF IRAN!
MUST BE A MIRAGE.
SAY "ALOHA" TO THE MACADAMIA NUT. A LULU FROM HONOLULU.
ALOHA!
ONE CAN ALMOST FEEL THE PALM TREES SWAYING...
HULA-HULA
BOW TO OUR HONORABLE GUEST FROM THE ORIENT ...THE LITCHI NUT!
MR. LITCHI.
"GOOD GRIEF"! THE COMMON PEANUT— THE GOOBER!
HEE-HAW!
... AND FINALLY— TALL AND TAN, THE BRAZIL. ONE TOUGH NUT!!!
AHH...
BONK
BONK
BONK
I LIKE TO MIX IT UP.
MUTTS © 2001 PATRICK McDONNELL · DISTRIBUTED BY KING FEATURES SYNDICATE
10-21

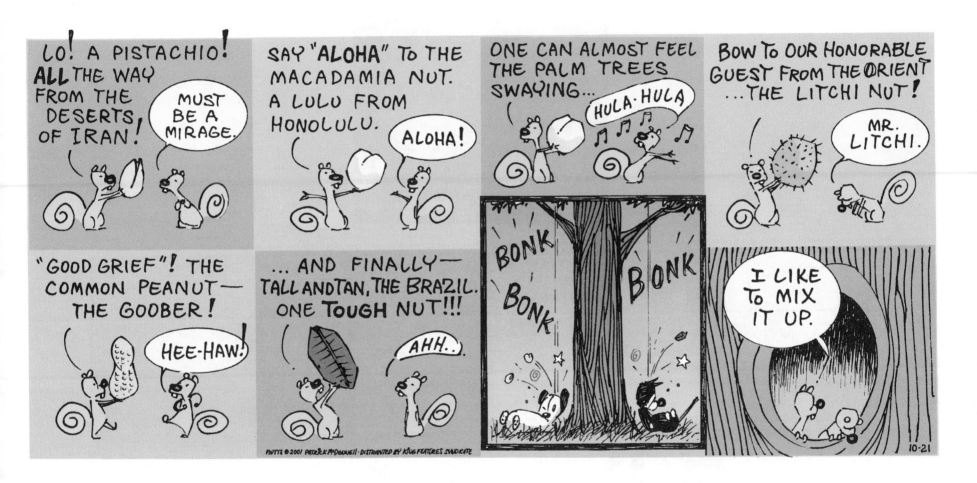

McDONNELL
MUTTS.

HOMEMADE, ...HUH?...
HOME-MADE PIES
...THEY MUST BE 'ANTIQUES.'
HA! HA! HA!
PIES
I'LL TAKE TWO.
HOME-MADE PIES
FATTY SNAX DELI
OPEN
MUTTS © 2001 PATRICK McDONNELL
DISTRIBUTED BY KING FEATURES SYNDICATE
HOME-MADE PIES
JUST LIKE HOME.
MMMM...
PIES
11-11

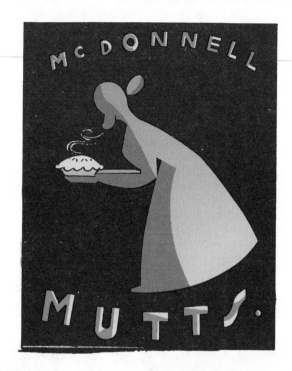

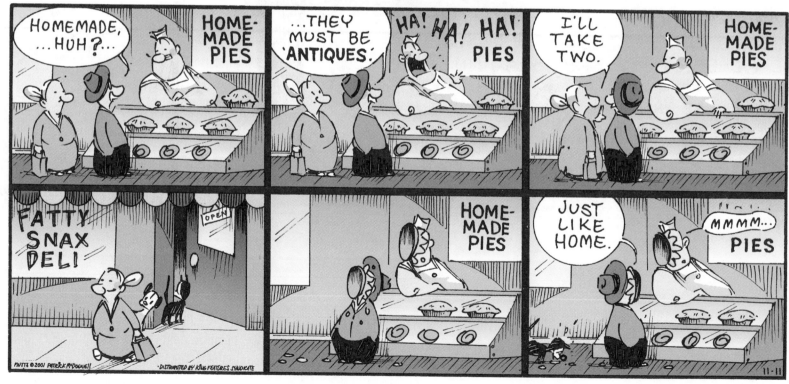

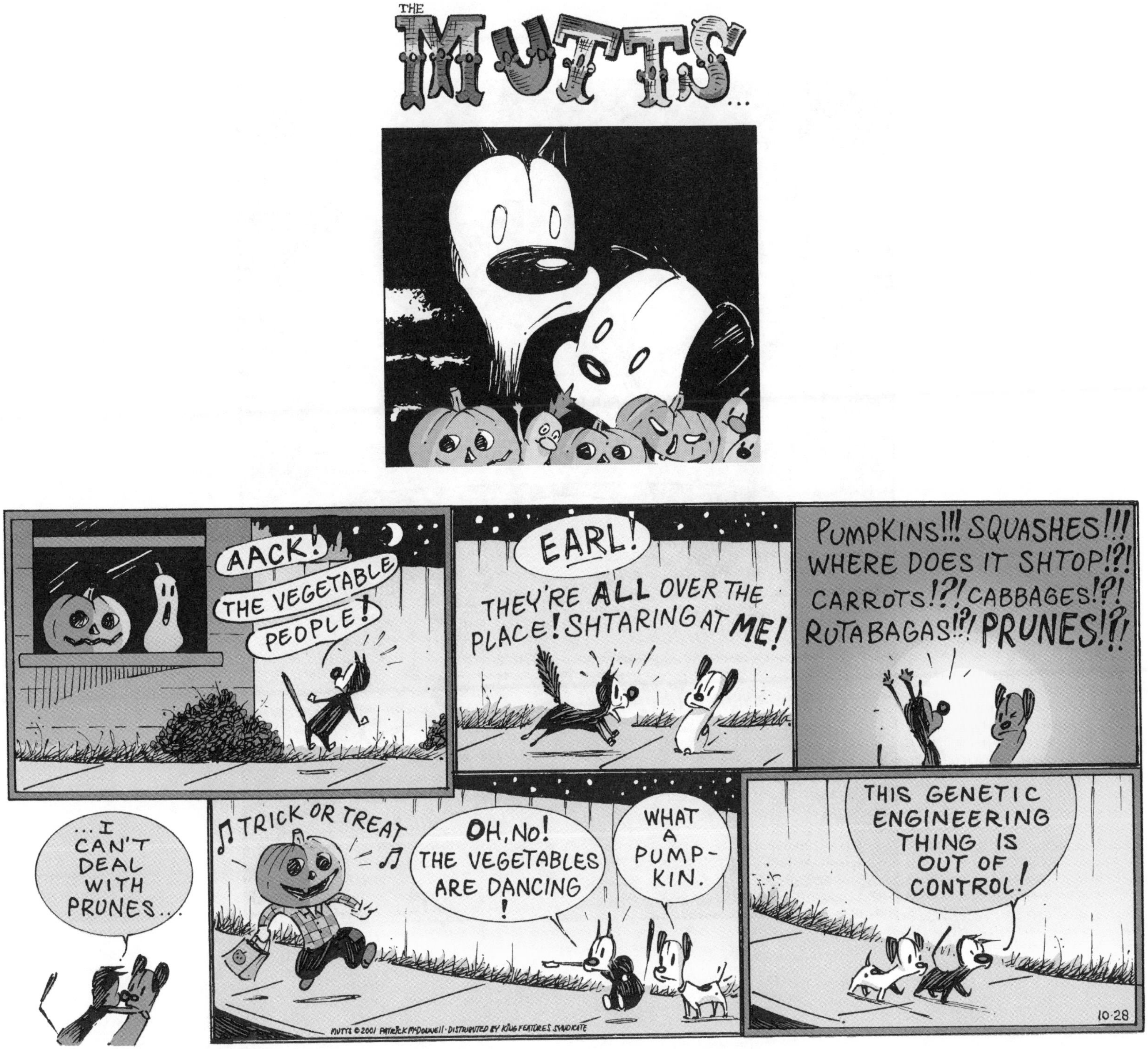
THE MUTTS...
AACK!
THE VEGETABLE PEOPLE!
EARL!
THEY'RE ALL OVER THE PLACE! SHTARING AT ME!
PUMPKINS!!! SQUASHES!!! WHERE DOES IT SHTOP!?! CARROTS!?! CABBAGES!?! RUTABAGAS!?! PRUNES!?!
TRICK OR TREAT
OH, NO! THE VEGETABLES ARE DANCING!
WHAT A PUMPKIN.
THIS GENETIC ENGINEERING THING IS OUT OF CONTROL!
...I CAN'T DEAL WITH PRUNES...
MUTTS © 2001 PATRICK McDONNELL · DISTRIBUTED BY KING FEATURES SYNDICATE
10·28

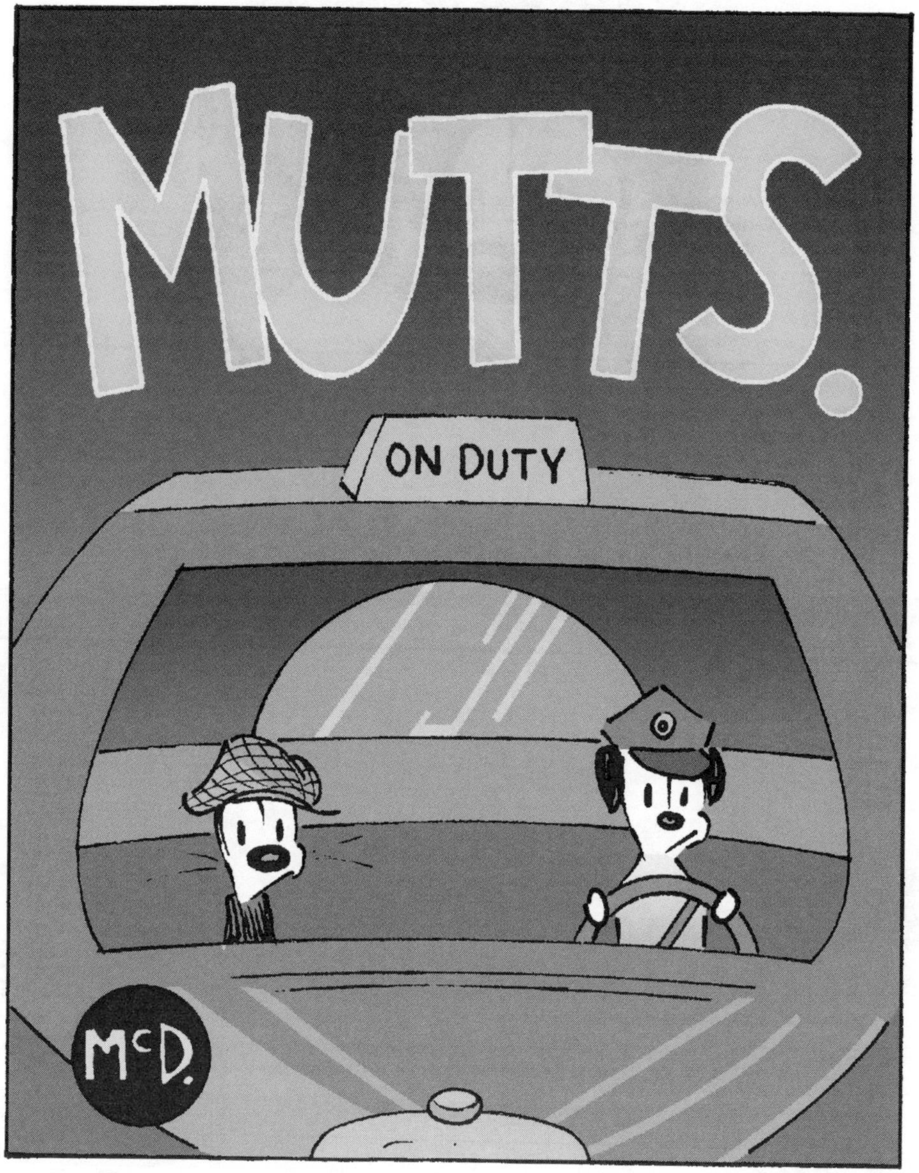
MUTTS.
ON DUTY
McD.

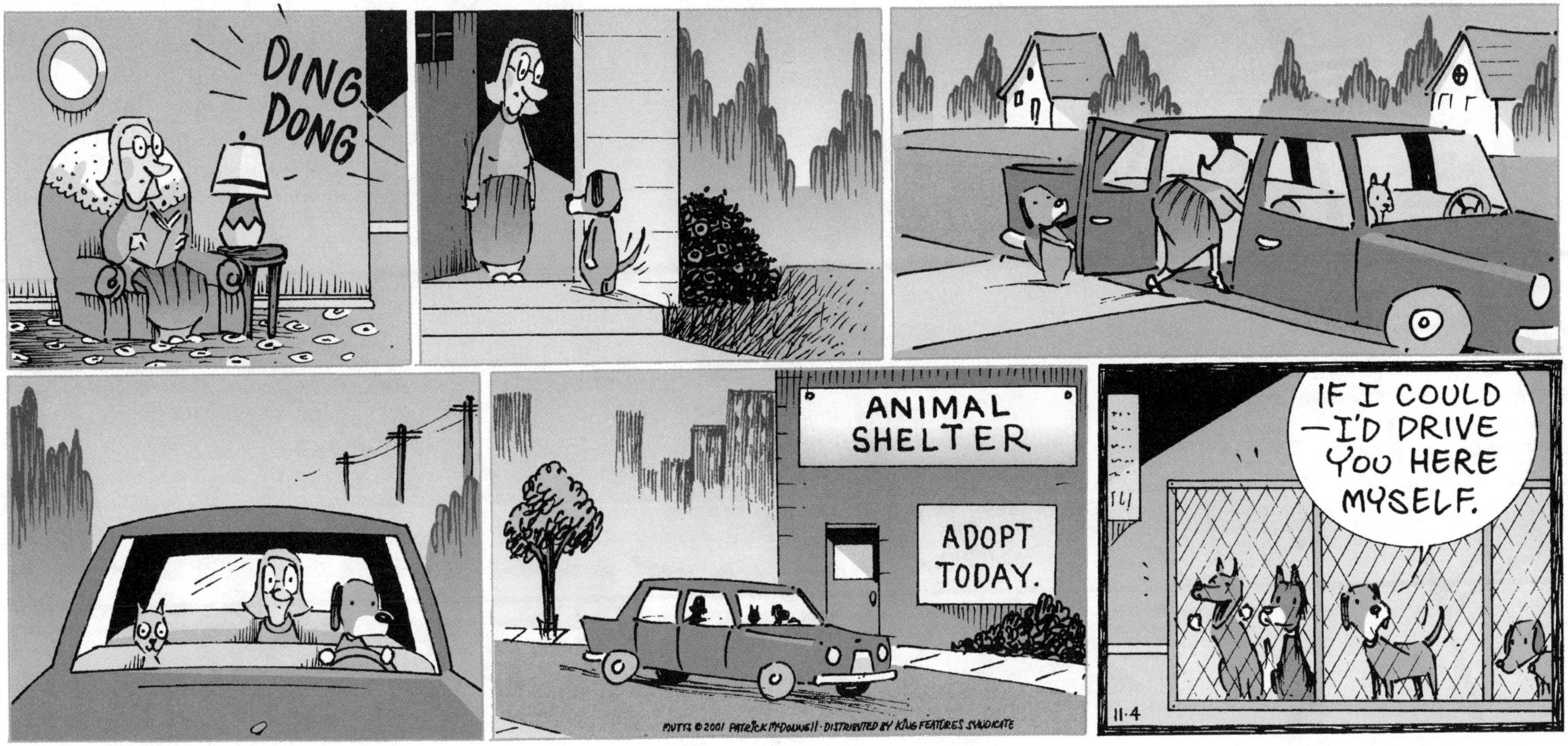
DING
DONG
ANIMAL SHELTER
ADOPT TODAY.
IF I COULD —I'D DRIVE YOU HERE MYSELF.
MUTTS © 2001 PATRICK McDONNELL · DISTRIBUTED BY KING FEATURES SYNDICATE
11·4

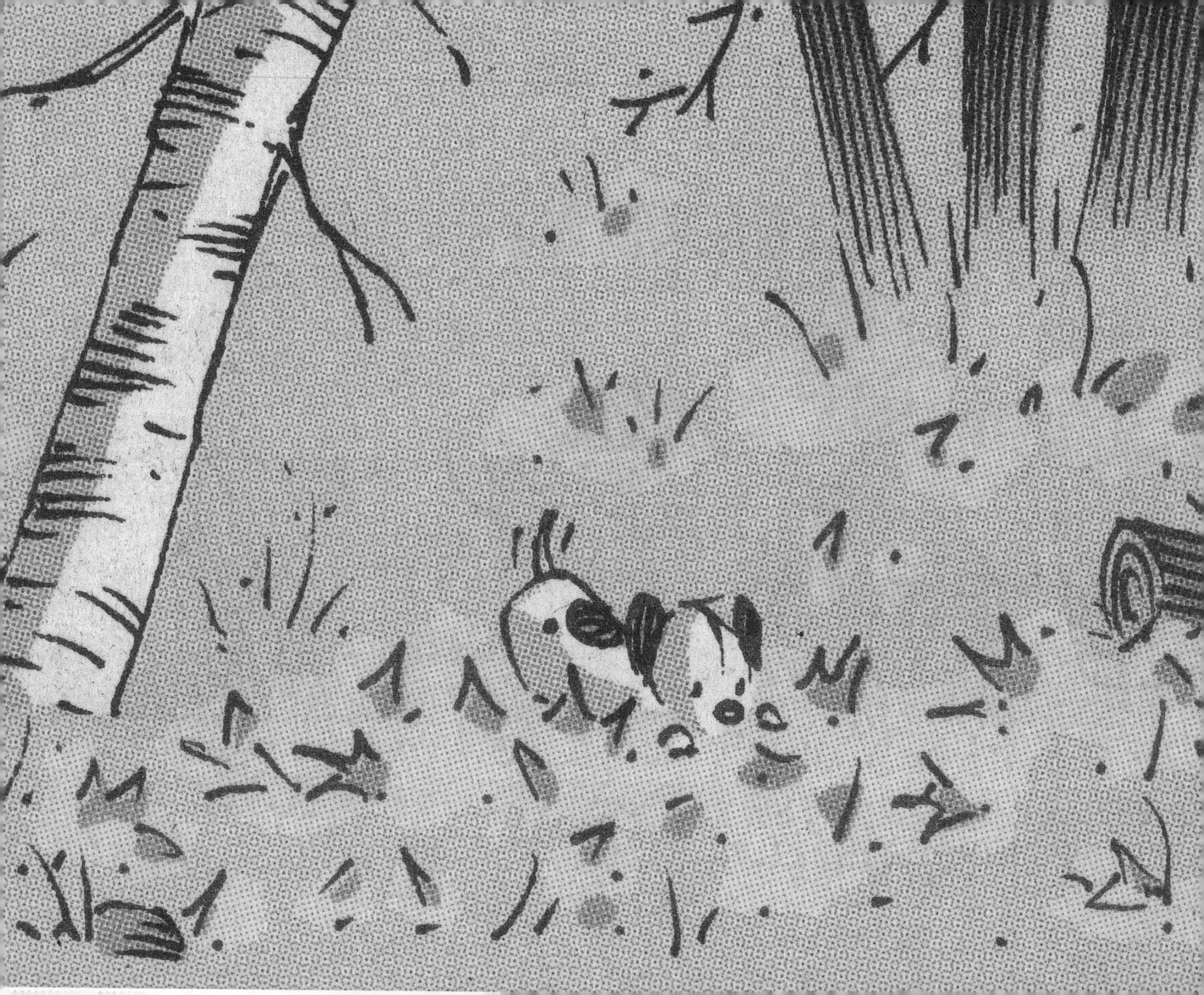

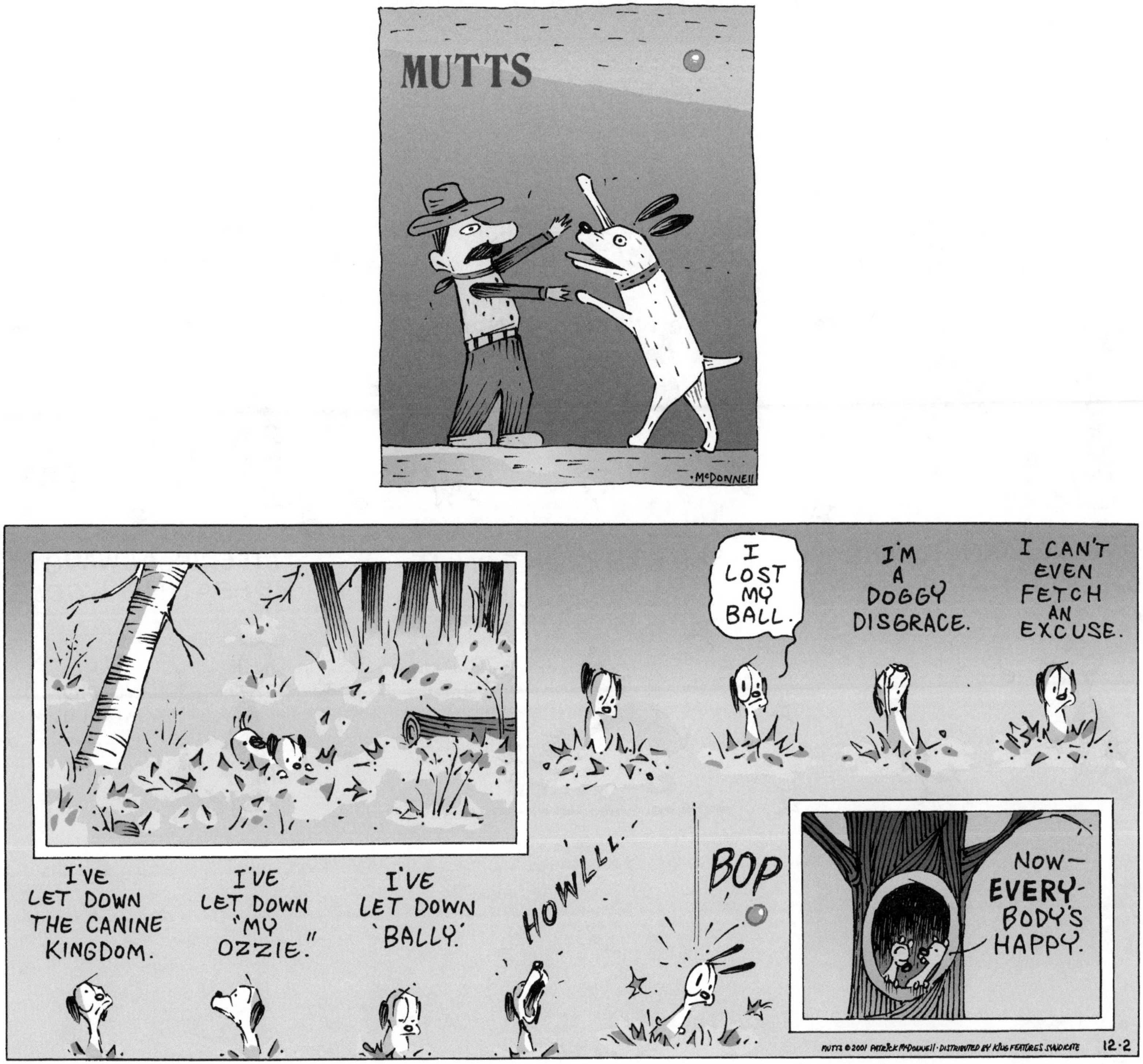
MUTTS
McDONNELL
I LOST MY BALL.
I'M A DOGGY DISGRACE.
I CAN'T EVEN FETCH AN EXCUSE.
I'VE LET DOWN THE CANINE KINGDOM.
I'VE LET DOWN "MY OZZIE."
I'VE LET DOWN 'BALLY.'
HOWLLL...
BOP
NOW— EVERY-BODY'S HAPPY.
MUTTS © 2001 PATRICK McDONNELL · DISTRIBUTED BY KING FEATURES SYNDICATE
12·2

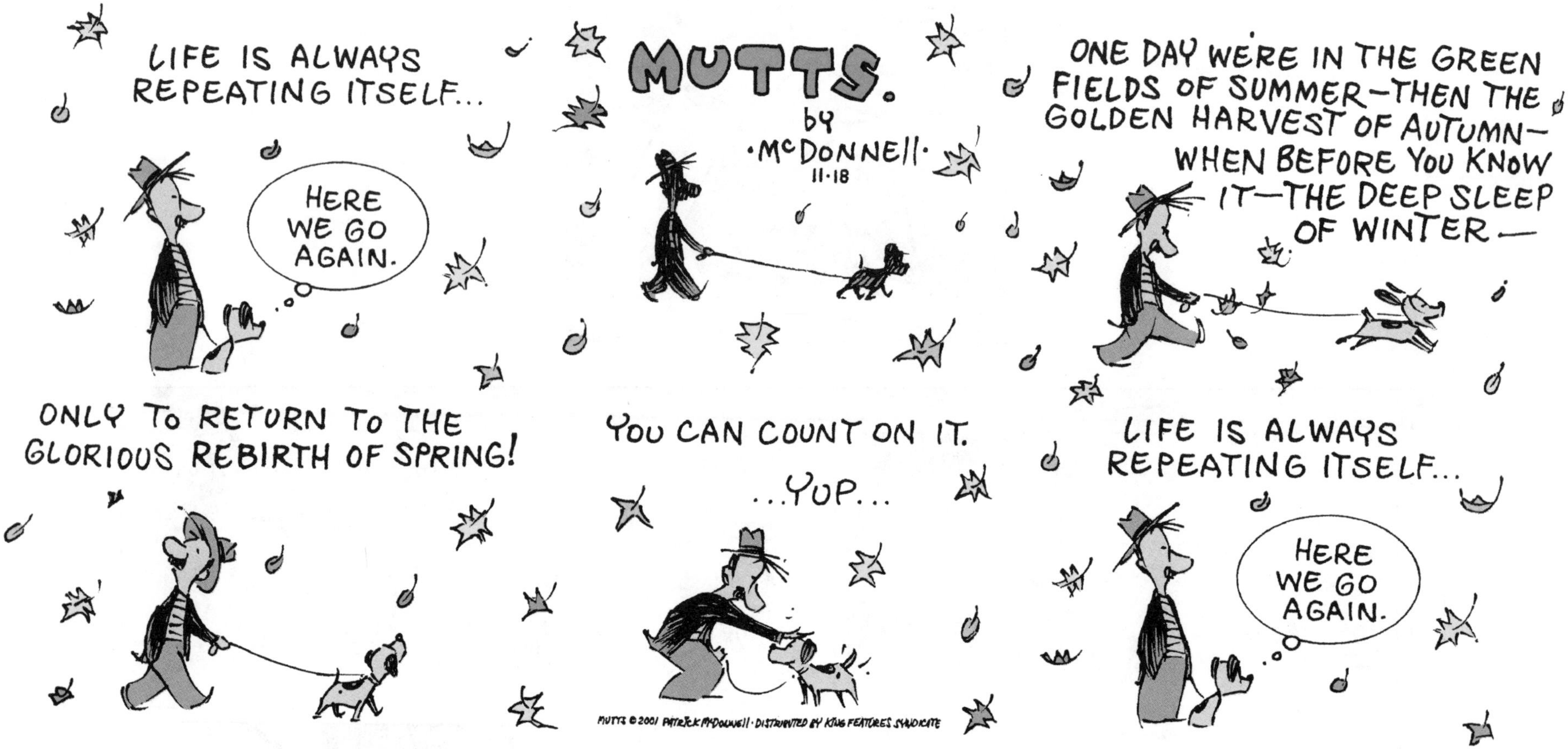
LIFE IS ALWAYS REPEATING ITSELF...
HERE WE GO AGAIN.
MUTTS.
by •McDONNELL•
11-18
ONE DAY WE'RE IN THE GREEN FIELDS OF SUMMER—THEN THE GOLDEN HARVEST OF AUTUMN—WHEN BEFORE YOU KNOW IT—THE DEEP SLEEP OF WINTER—
ONLY TO RETURN TO THE GLORIOUS REBIRTH OF SPRING!
YOU CAN COUNT ON IT.
...YUP...
MUTTS © 2001 PATRICK McDONNELL · DISTRIBUTED BY KING FEATURES SYNDICATE
LIFE IS ALWAYS REPEATING ITSELF...
HERE WE GO AGAIN.

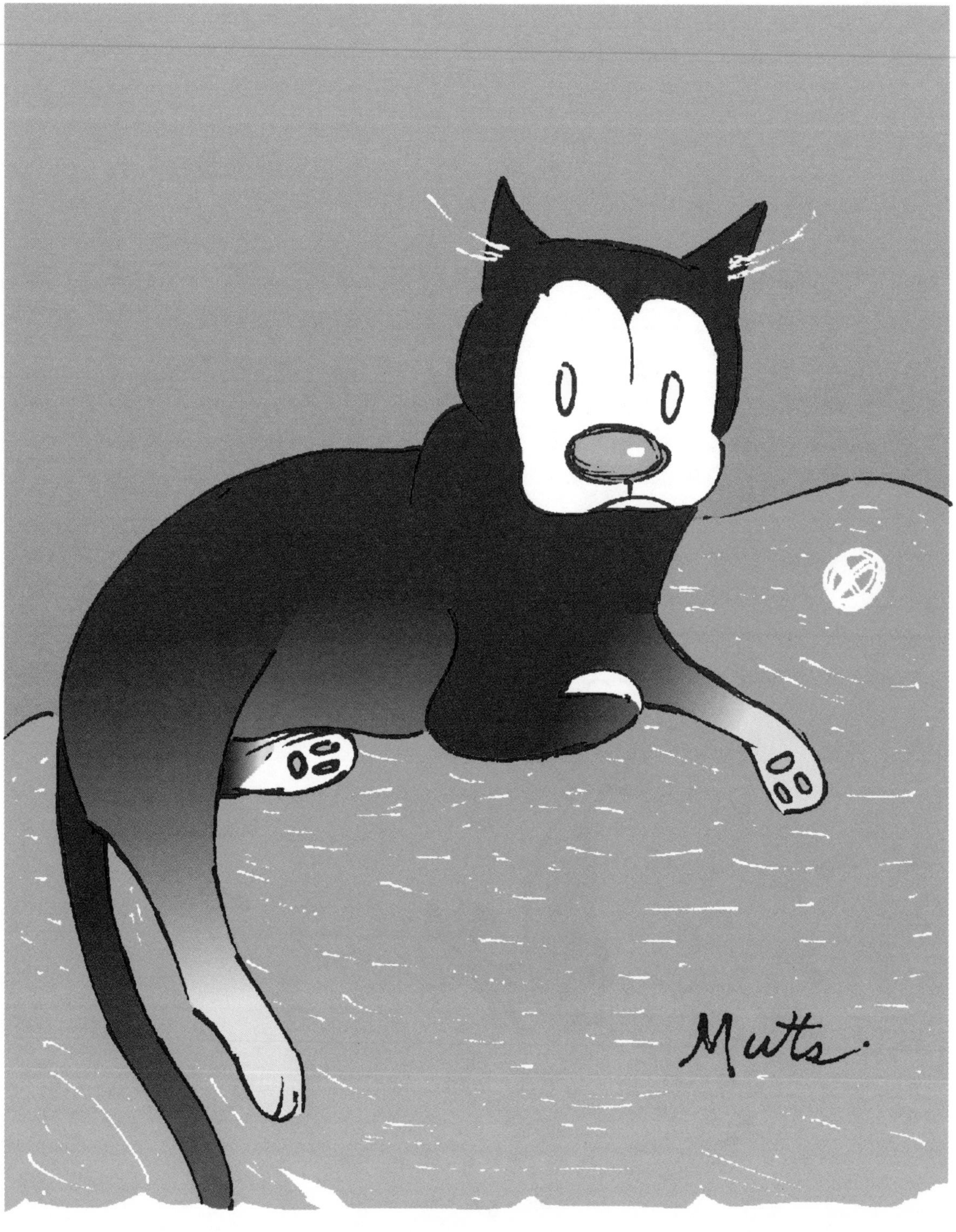
Mutts

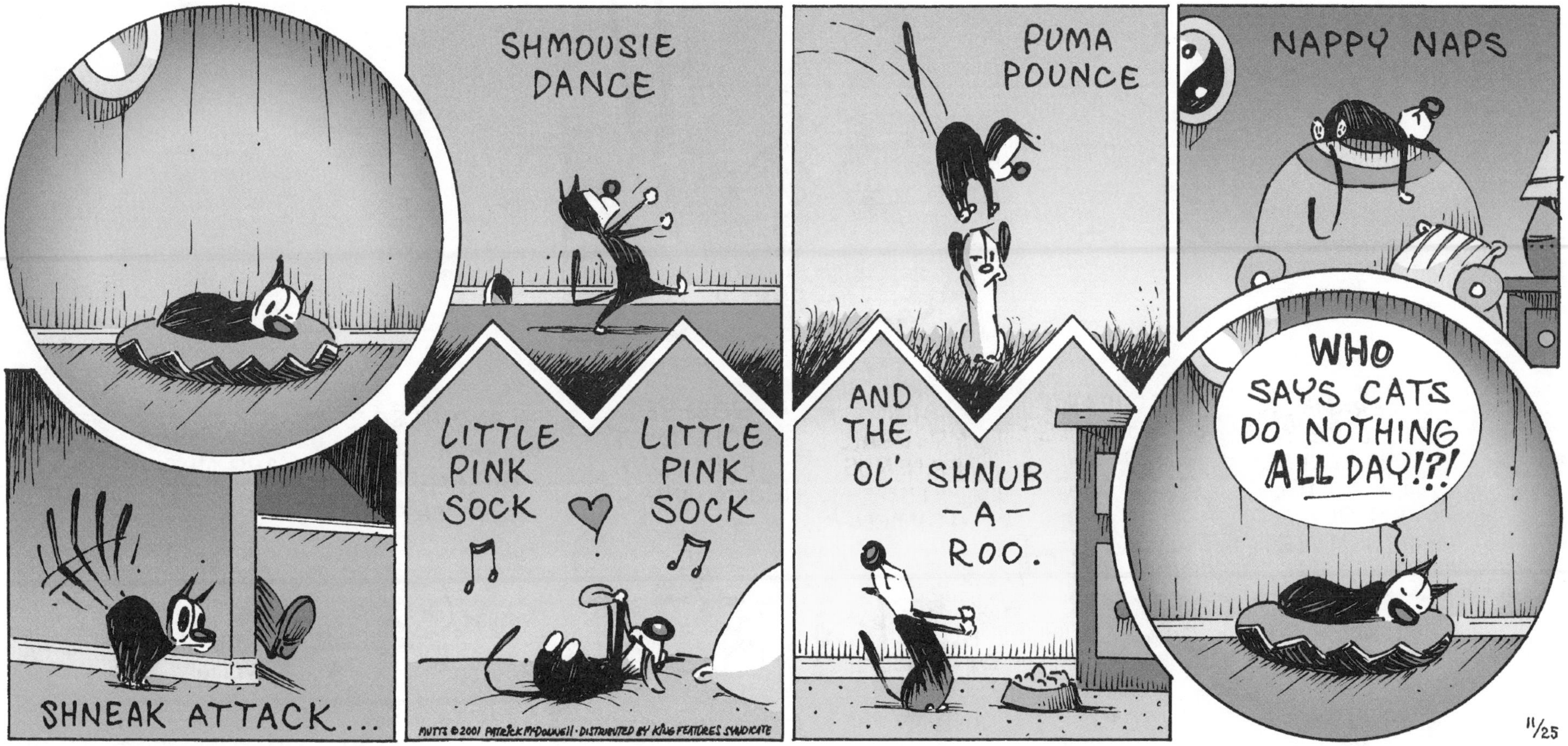
SHNEAK ATTACK...
SHMOUSIE DANCE
LITTLE PINK SOCK
LITTLE PINK SOCK
MUTTS © 2001 PATRICK McDONNELL · DISTRIBUTED BY KING FEATURES SYNDICATE
PUMA POUNCE
AND THE OL' SHNUB -A- ROO.
NAPPY NAPS
WHO SAYS CATS DO NOTHING ALL DAY!?!
11/25

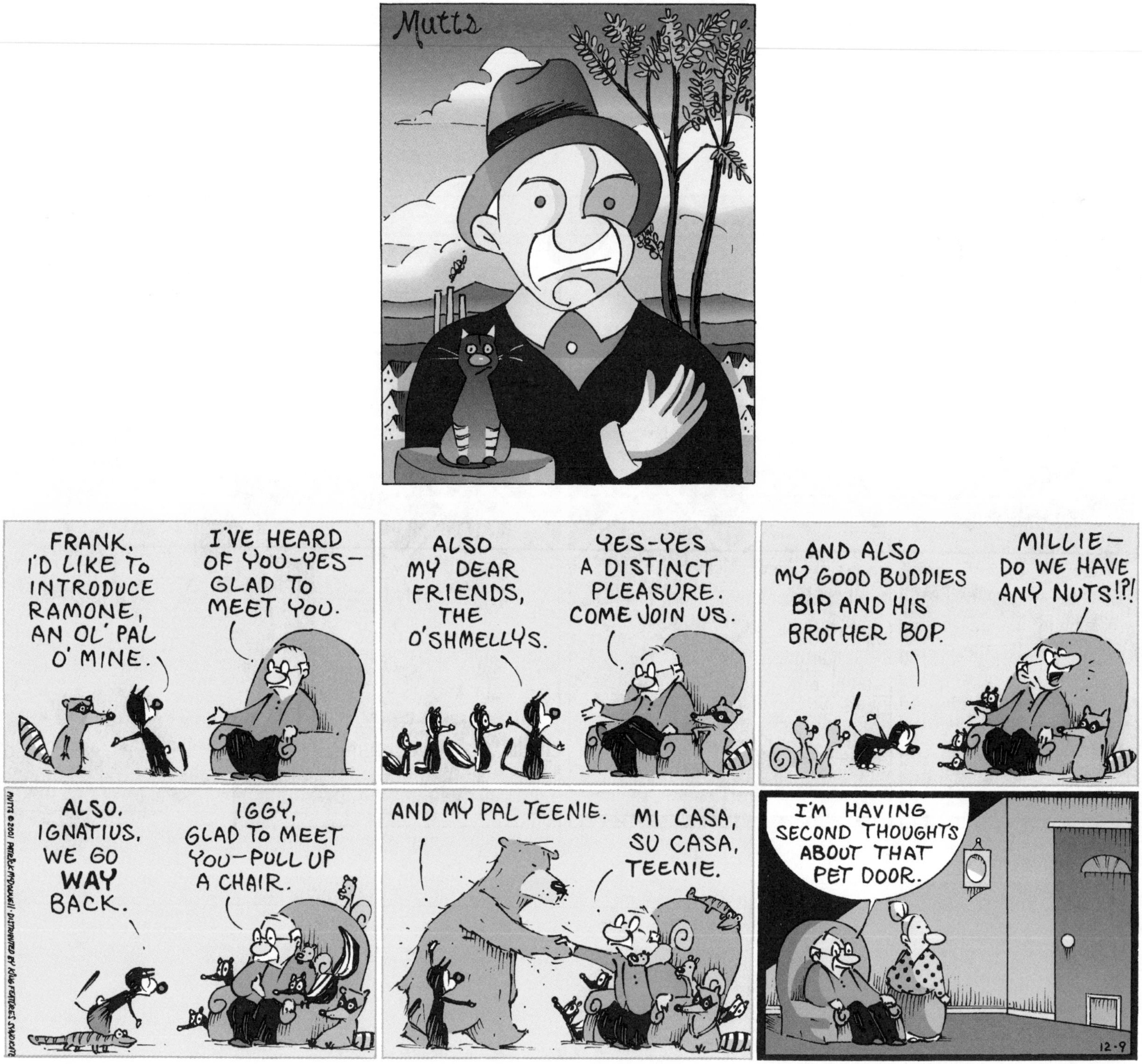
Mutts
FRANK. I'D LIKE TO INTRODUCE RAMONE, AN OL' PAL O' MINE.
I'VE HEARD OF YOU-YES-GLAD TO MEET YOU.
ALSO MY DEAR FRIENDS, THE O'SHMELLYS.
YES-YES A DISTINCT PLEASURE. COME JOIN US.
AND ALSO MY GOOD BUDDIES BIP AND HIS BROTHER BOP.
MILLIE-DO WE HAVE ANY NUTS!?!
ALSO. IGNATIUS. WE GO WAY BACK.
IGGY, GLAD TO MEET YOU-PULL UP A CHAIR.
MUTTS © 2001 PATRICK McDONNELL. DISTRIBUTED BY KING FEATURES SYNDICATE
AND MY PAL TEENIE.
MI CASA, SU CASA, TEENIE.
I'M HAVING SECOND THOUGHTS ABOUT THAT PET DOOR.
12·9

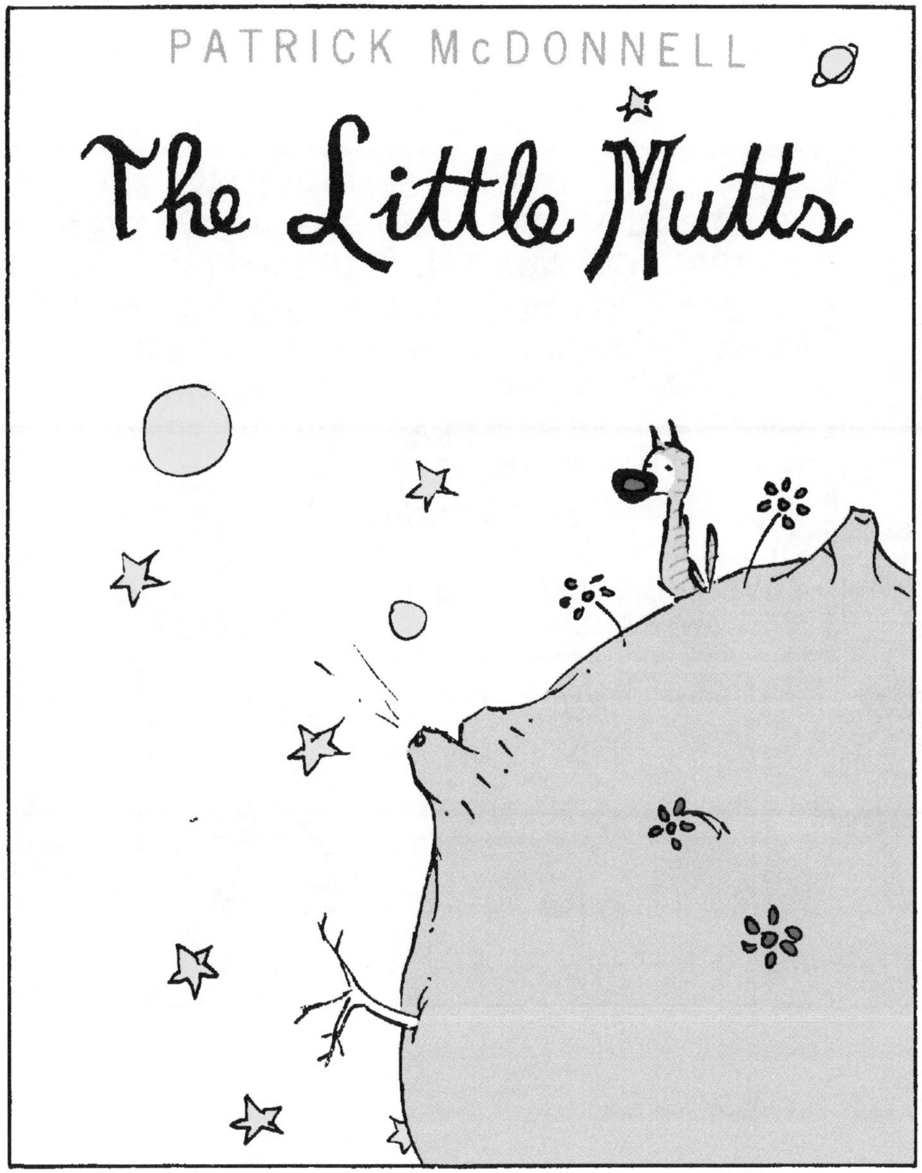
PATRICK McDONNELL
The Little Mutts

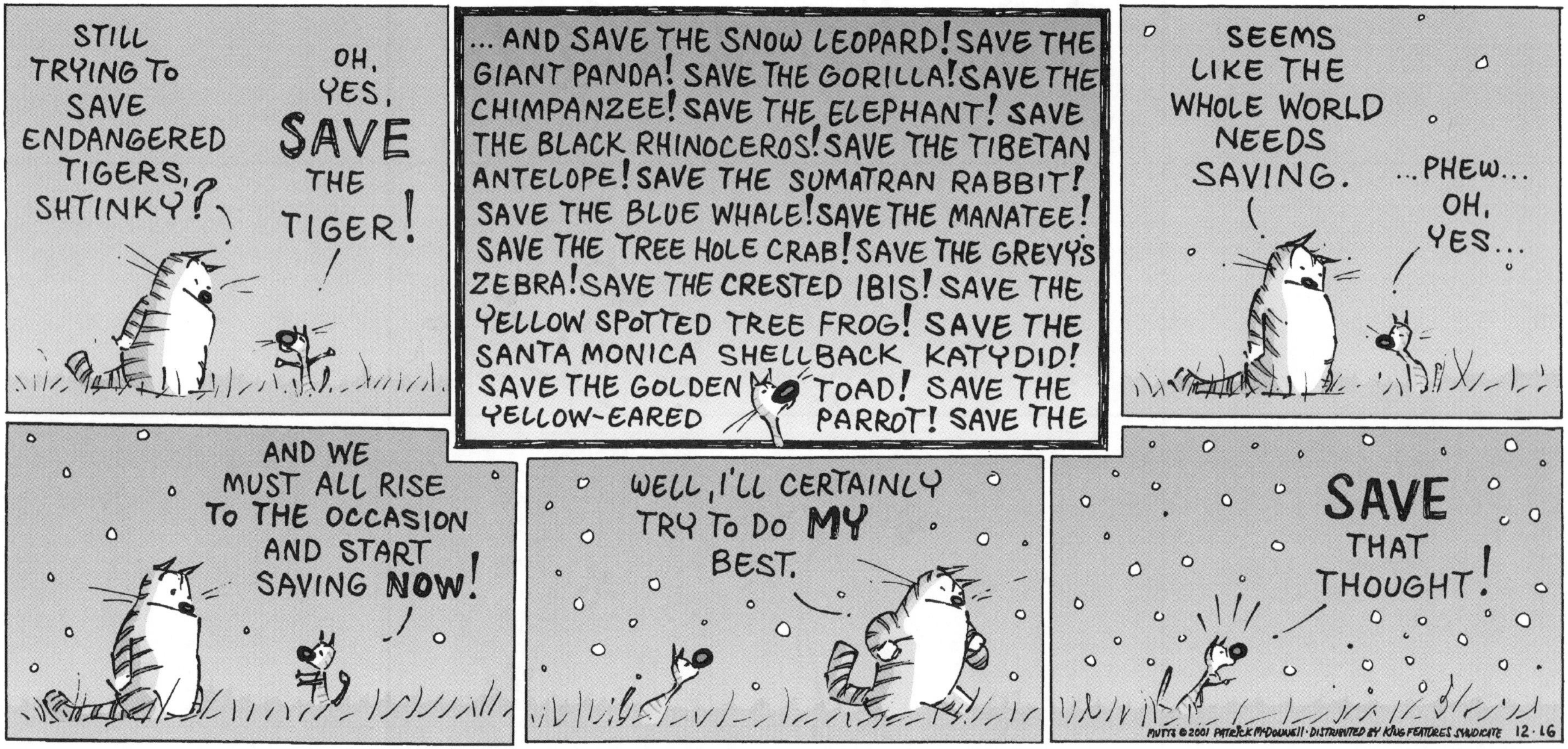

STILL TRYING TO SAVE ENDANGERED TIGERS, SHTINKY?
OH, YES, SAVE THE TIGER!
... AND SAVE THE SNOW LEOPARD! SAVE THE GIANT PANDA! SAVE THE GORILLA! SAVE THE CHIMPANZEE! SAVE THE ELEPHANT! SAVE THE BLACK RHINOCEROS! SAVE THE TIBETAN ANTELOPE! SAVE THE SUMATRAN RABBIT! SAVE THE BLUE WHALE! SAVE THE MANATEE! SAVE THE TREE HOLE CRAB! SAVE THE GREVY'S ZEBRA! SAVE THE CRESTED IBIS! SAVE THE YELLOW SPOTTED TREE FROG! SAVE THE SANTA MONICA SHELLBACK KATYDID! SAVE THE GOLDEN TOAD! SAVE THE YELLOW-EARED PARROT! SAVE THE
SEEMS LIKE THE WHOLE WORLD NEEDS SAVING.
...PHEW... OH, YES...
AND WE MUST ALL RISE TO THE OCCASION AND START SAVING NOW!
WELL, I'LL CERTAINLY TRY TO DO MY BEST.
SAVE THAT THOUGHT!
MUTTS © 2001 PATRICK McDONNELL · DISTRIBUTED BY KING FEATURES SYNDICATE 12·16

MUTTS

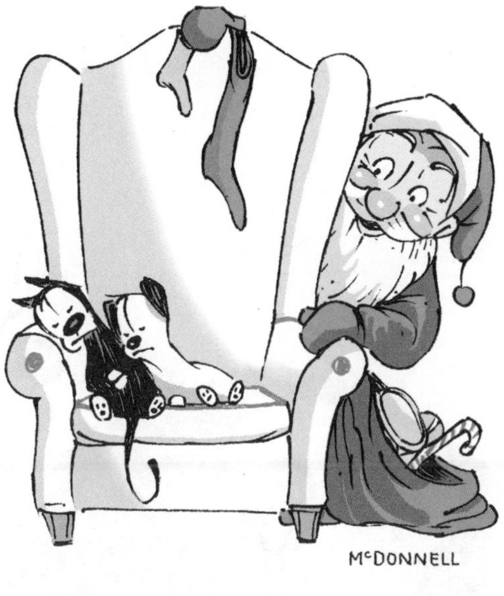
McDONNELL

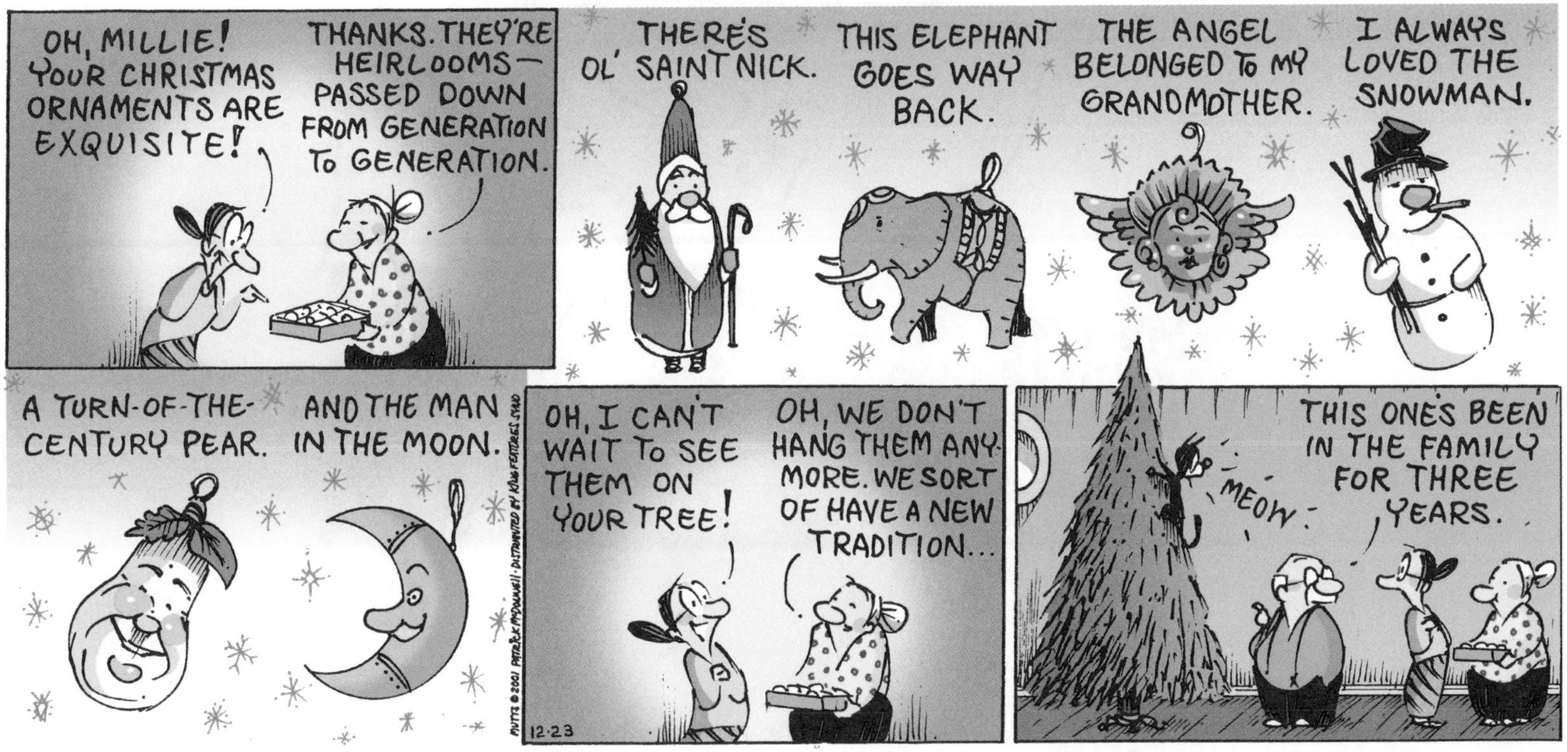
OH, MILLIE! YOUR CHRISTMAS ORNAMENTS ARE EXQUISITE!
THANKS. THEY'RE HEIRLOOMS— PASSED DOWN FROM GENERATION TO GENERATION.
THERE'S OL' SAINT NICK.
THIS ELEPHANT GOES WAY BACK.
THE ANGEL BELONGED TO MY GRANDMOTHER.
I ALWAYS LOVED THE SNOWMAN.
A TURN-OF-THE-CENTURY PEAR.
AND THE MAN IN THE MOON.
MUTTS © 2001 PATRICK McDONNELL · DISTRIBUTED BY KING FEATURES SYND.
12·23
OH, I CAN'T WAIT TO SEE THEM ON YOUR TREE!
OH, WE DON'T HANG THEM ANYMORE. WE SORT OF HAVE A NEW TRADITION...
MEOW
THIS ONE'S BEEN IN THE FAMILY FOR THREE YEARS.

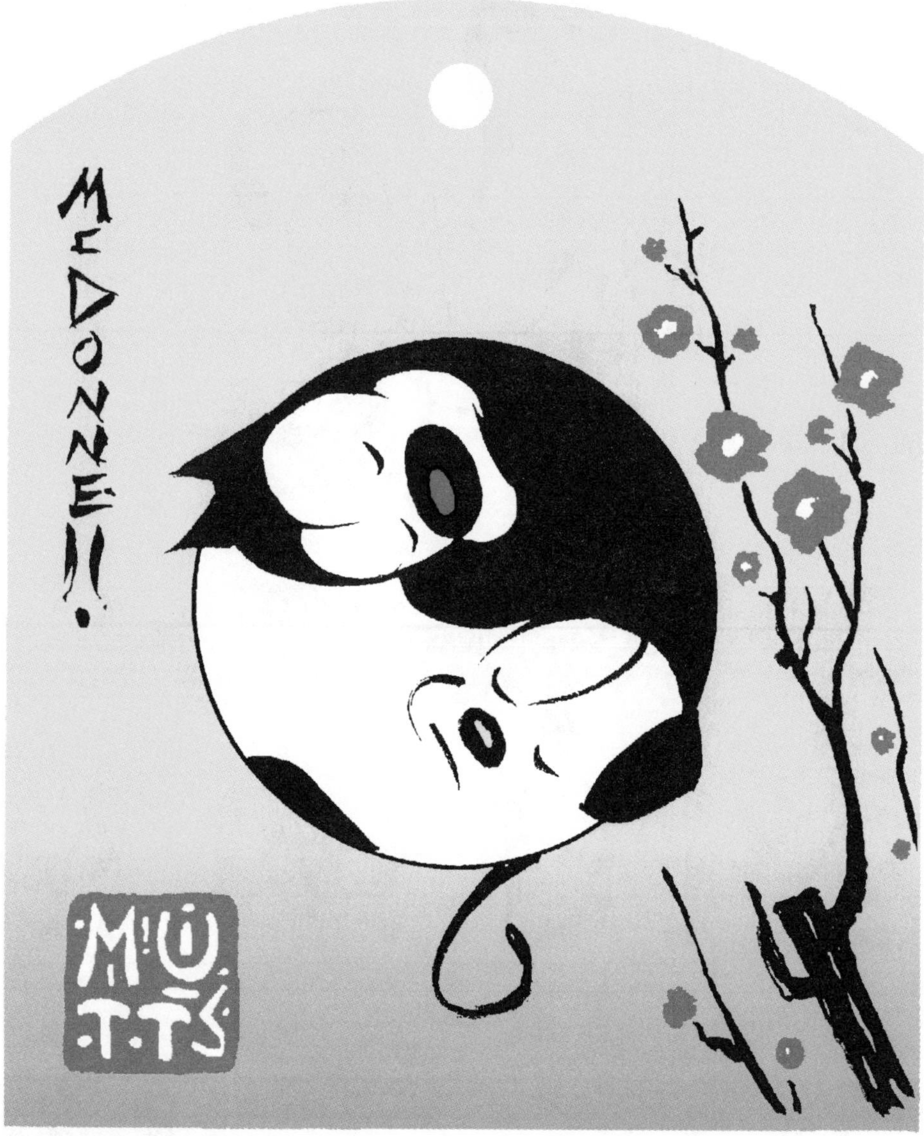
McDONNELL
MUTTS

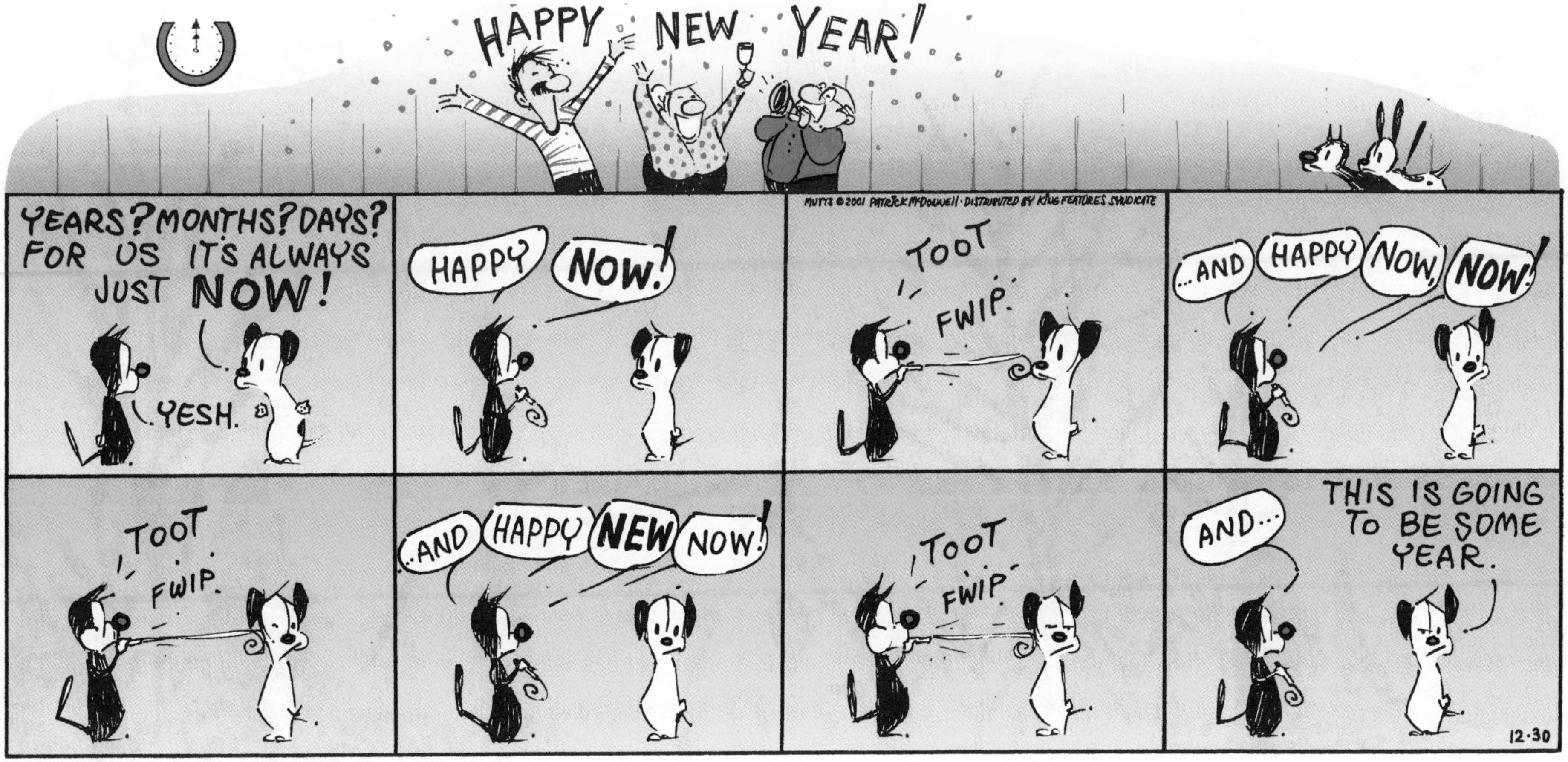
HAPPY NEW YEAR!
MUTTS © 2001 PATRICK McDONNELL · DISTRIBUTED BY KING FEATURES SYNDICATE
YEARS? MONTHS? DAYS? FOR US IT'S ALWAYS JUST NOW!
YESH.
HAPPY
NOW!
TOOT
FWIP.
...AND
HAPPY
NOW,
NOW!
TOOT
FWIP.
..AND
HAPPY
NEW
NOW!
TOOT
FWIP.
AND...
THIS IS GOING TO BE SOME YEAR.
12·30

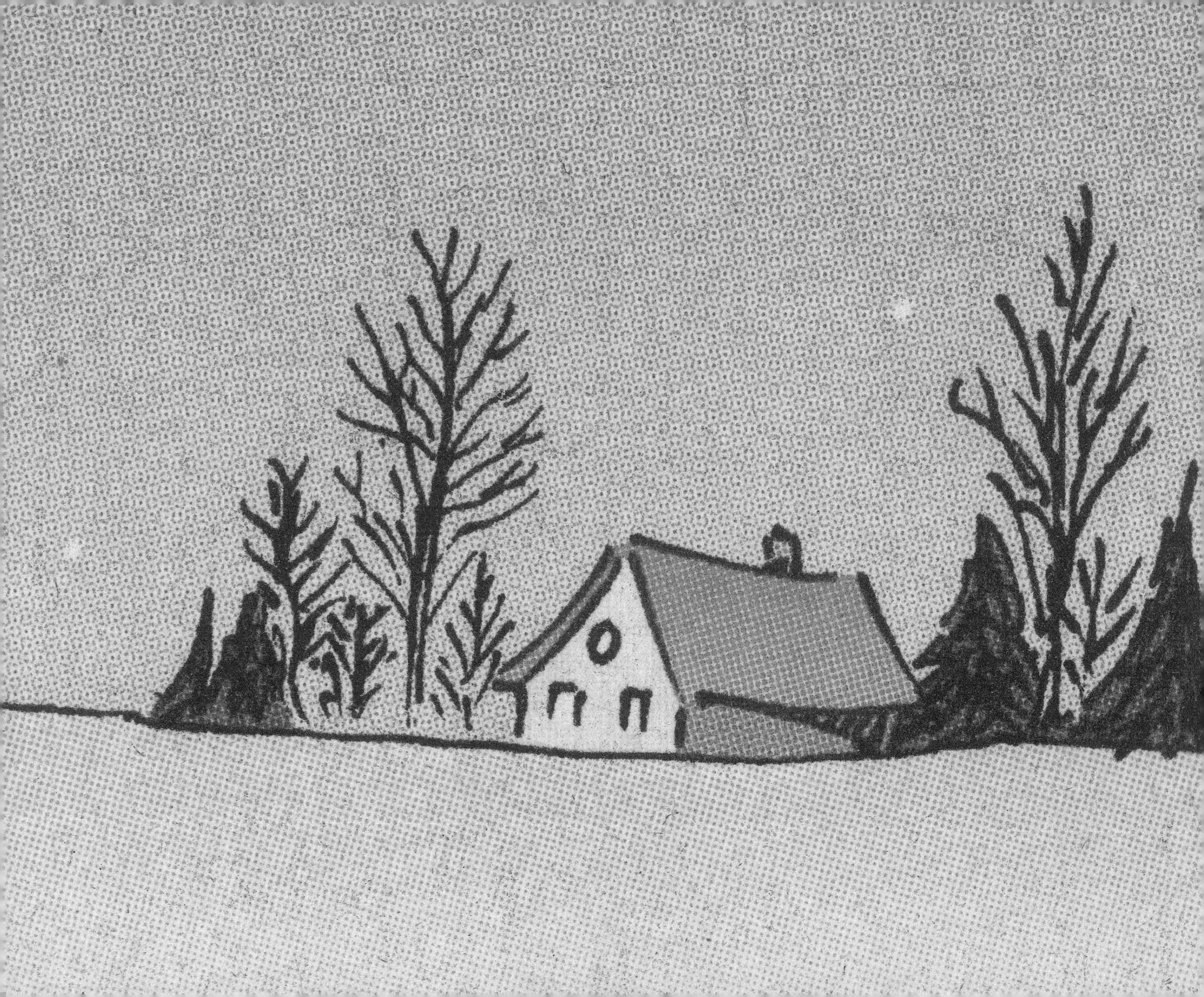

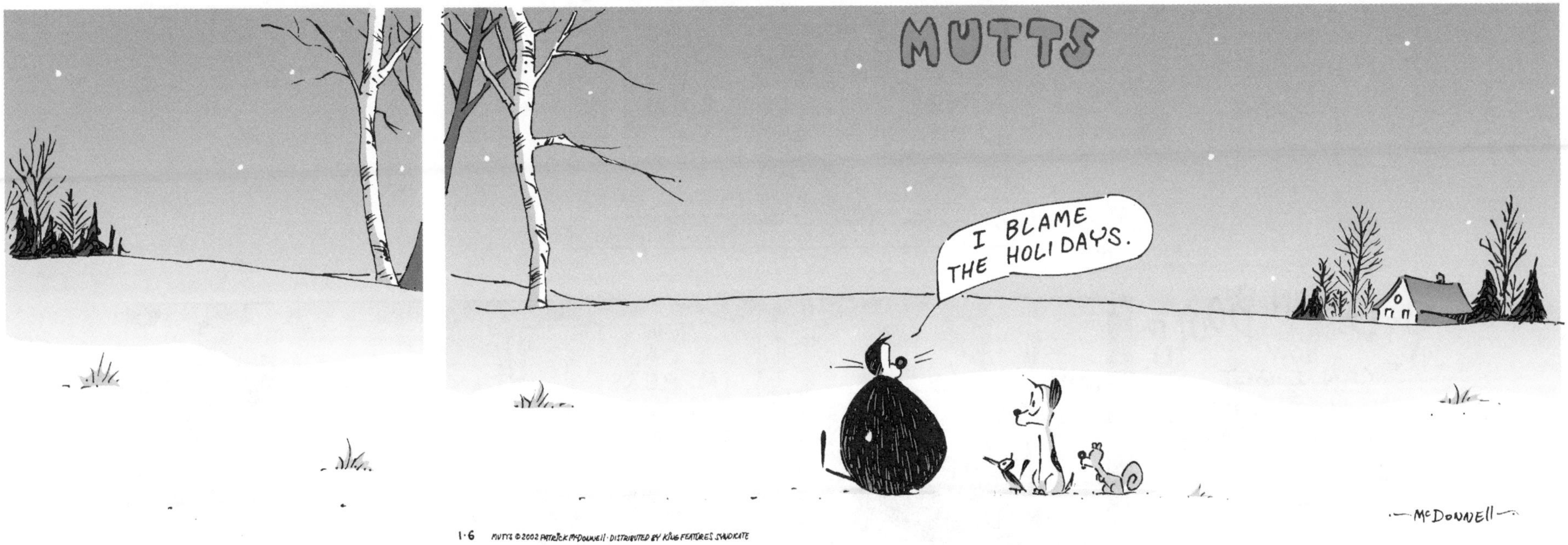
MUTTS
I BLAME THE HOLIDAYS.
McDONNELL
1·6 MUTTS © 2002 PATRICK McDONNELL · DISTRIBUTED BY KING FEATURES SYNDICATE

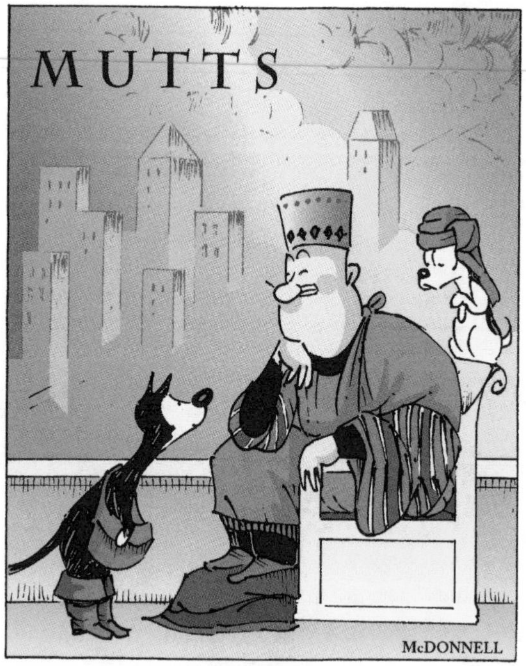
MUTTS
McDONNELL

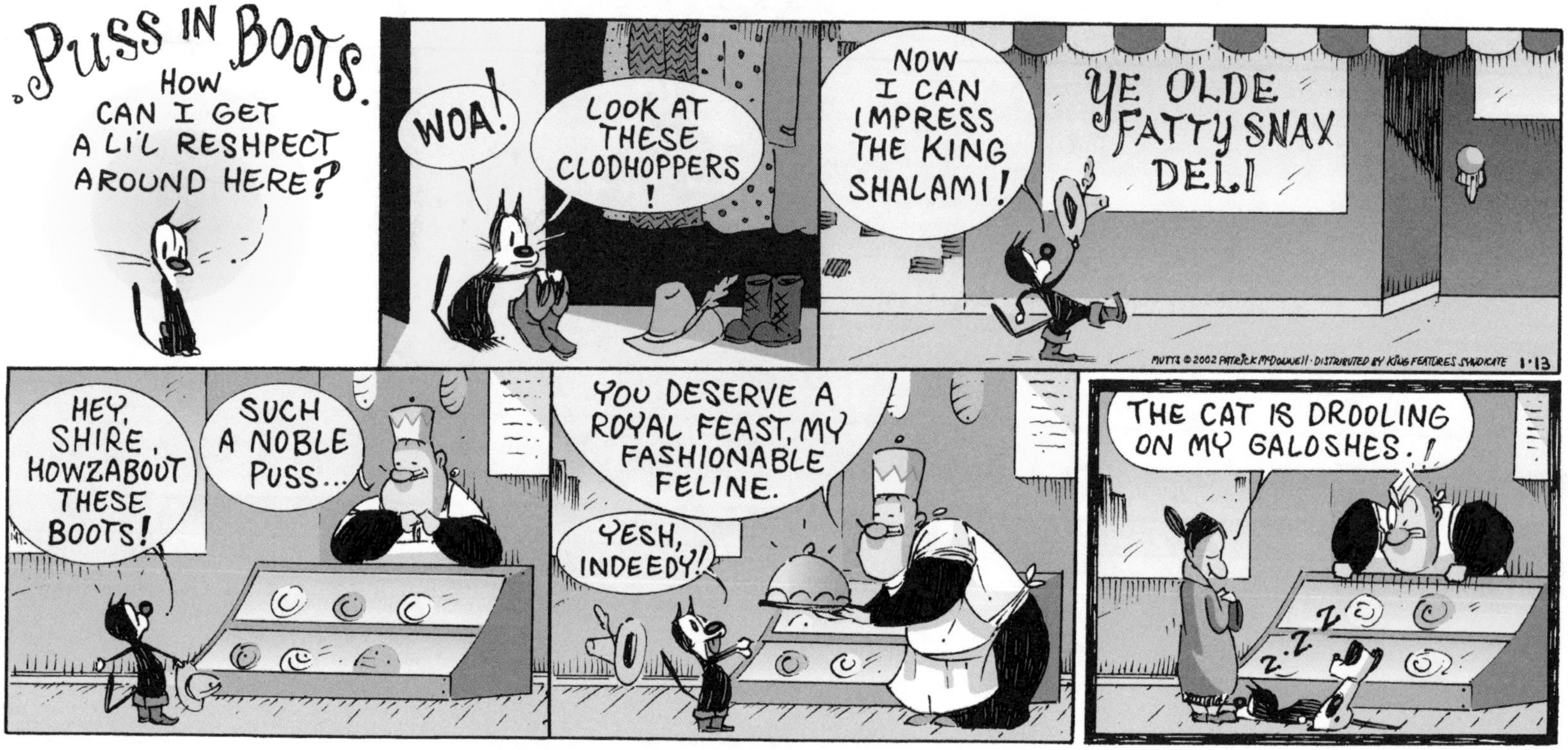
PUSS IN BOOTS.
HOW CAN I GET A LI'L RESHPECT AROUND HERE?
WOA!
LOOK AT THESE CLODHOPPERS!
NOW I CAN IMPRESS THE KING SHALAMI!
YE OLDE FATTY SNAX DELI
MUTTS © 2002 PATRICK McDONNELL · DISTRIBUTED BY KING FEATURES SYNDICATE 1·13
HEY, SHIRE, HOWZABOUT THESE BOOTS!
SUCH A NOBLE PUSS...
YOU DESERVE A ROYAL FEAST, MY FASHIONABLE FELINE.
YESH, INDEEDY!
THE CAT IS DROOLING ON MY GALOSHES.!
Z Z Z

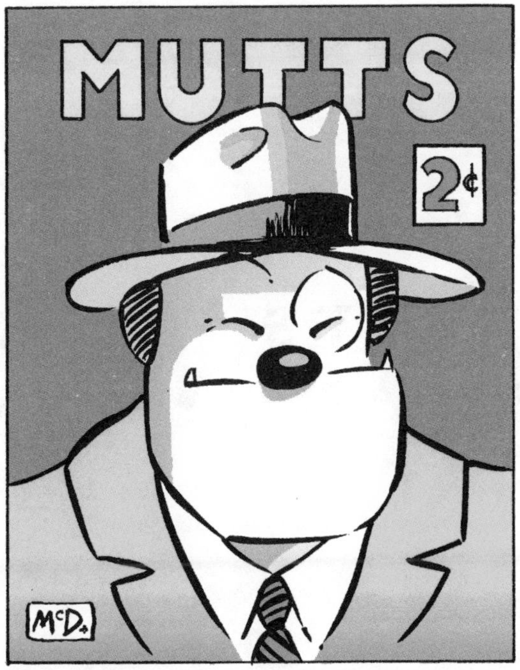
MUTTS
2¢
McD.

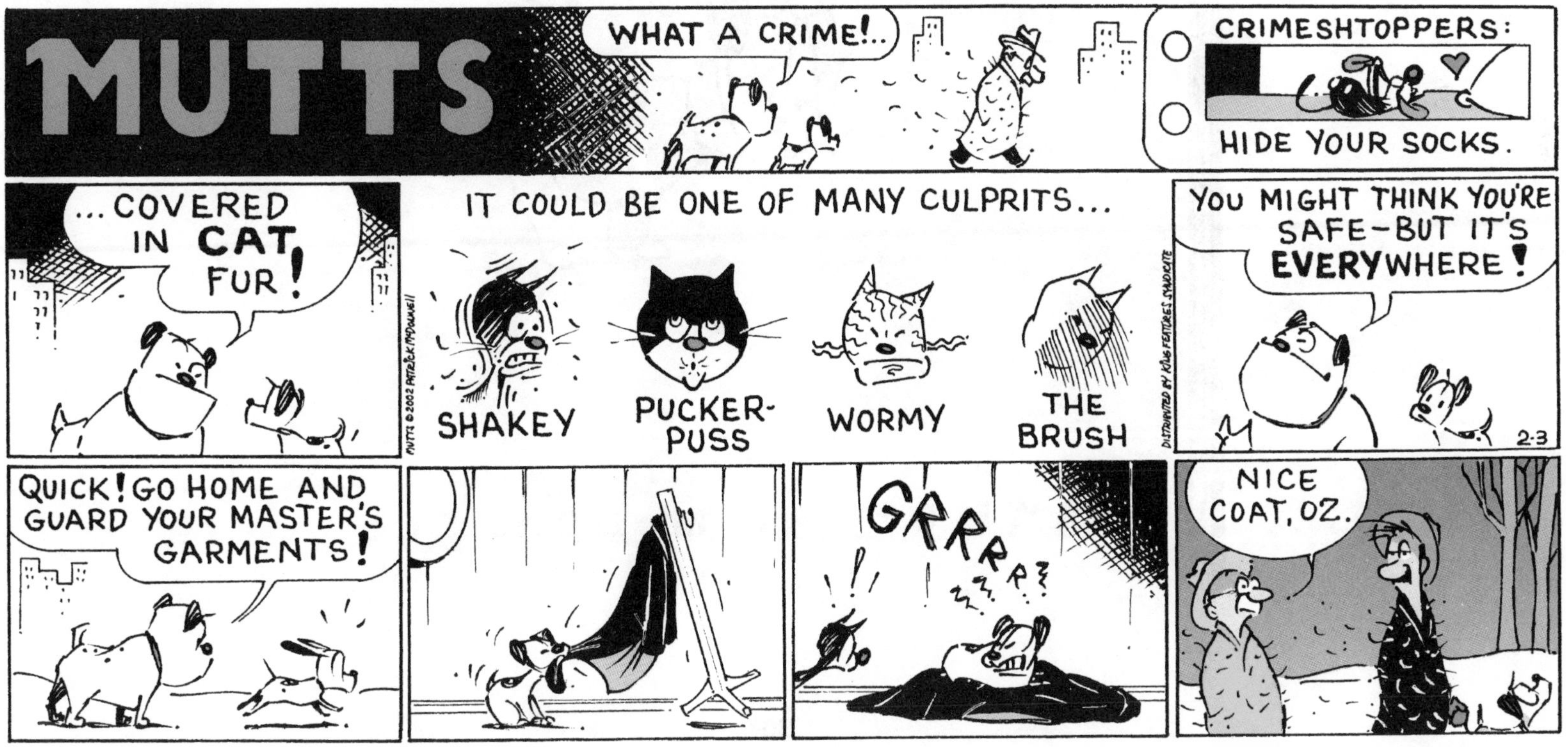
MUTTS
WHAT A CRIME!..
CRIMESHTOPPERS:
HIDE YOUR SOCKS.
...COVERED IN CAT FUR!
IT COULD BE ONE OF MANY CULPRITS...
SHAKEY
PUCKER-PUSS
WORMY
THE BRUSH
MUTTS ©2002 PATRICK McDONNELL
DISTRIBUTED BY KING FEATURES SYNDICATE
YOU MIGHT THINK YOU'RE SAFE—BUT IT'S EVERYWHERE!
2·3
QUICK! GO HOME AND GUARD YOUR MASTER'S GARMENTS!
GRRRRR
NICE COAT, OZ.

MUTTS WORLD

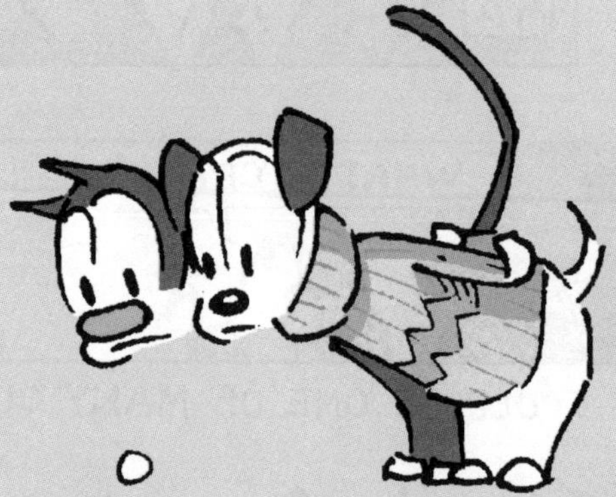

DRAWN BY P.L. McDONNELL

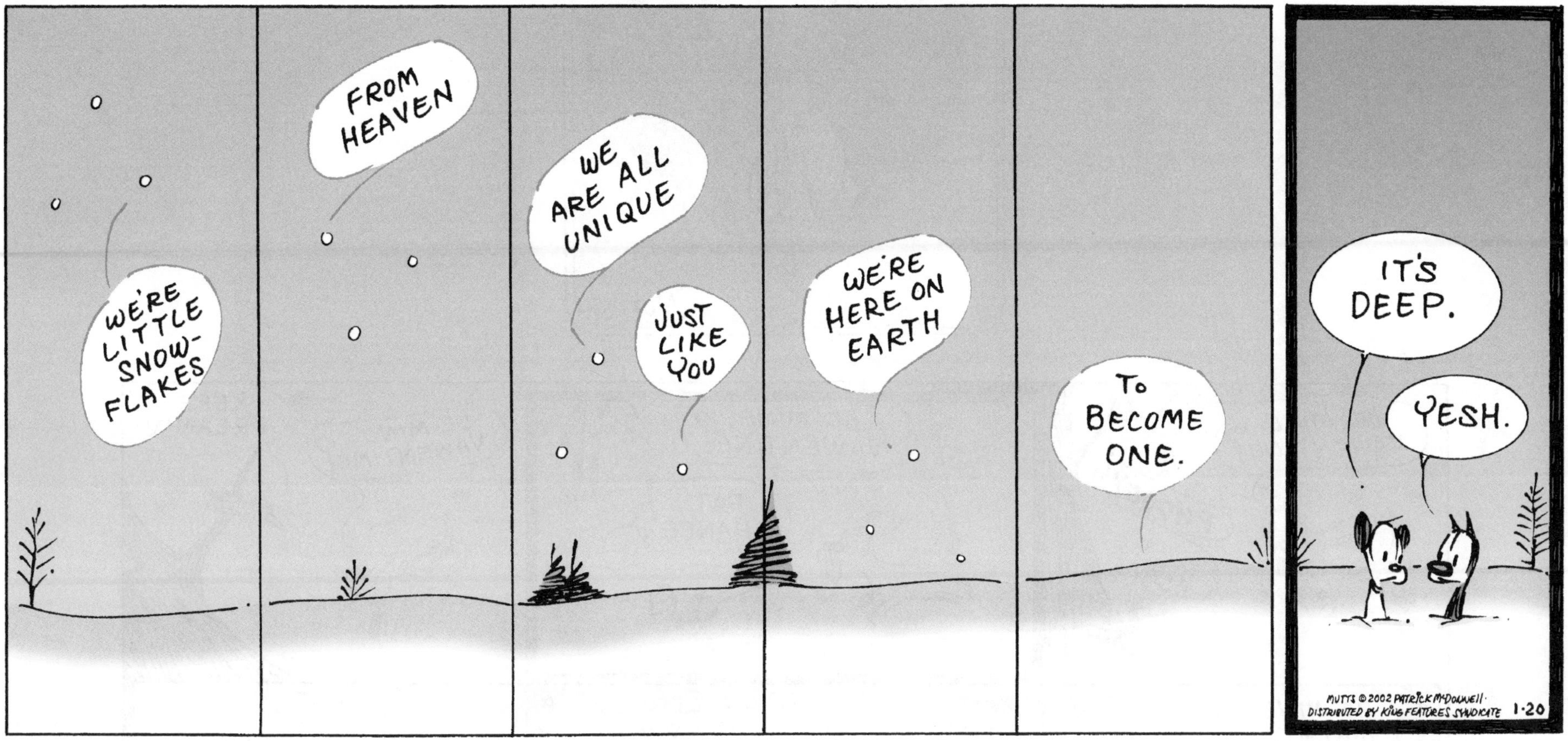
WE'RE LITTLE SNOW-FLAKES
FROM HEAVEN
WE ARE ALL UNIQUE
JUST LIKE YOU
WE'RE HERE ON EARTH
TO BECOME ONE.
IT'S DEEP.
YESH.
MUTTS © 2002 PATRICK McDONNELL · DISTRIBUTED BY KING FEATURES SYNDICATE 1·20

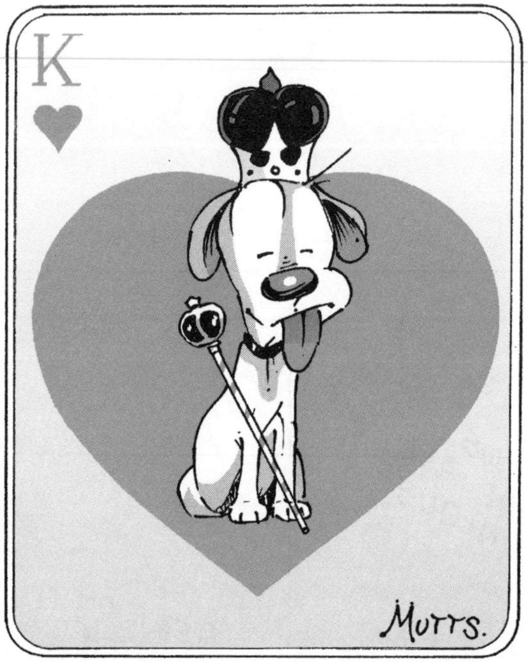
K
MUTTS.

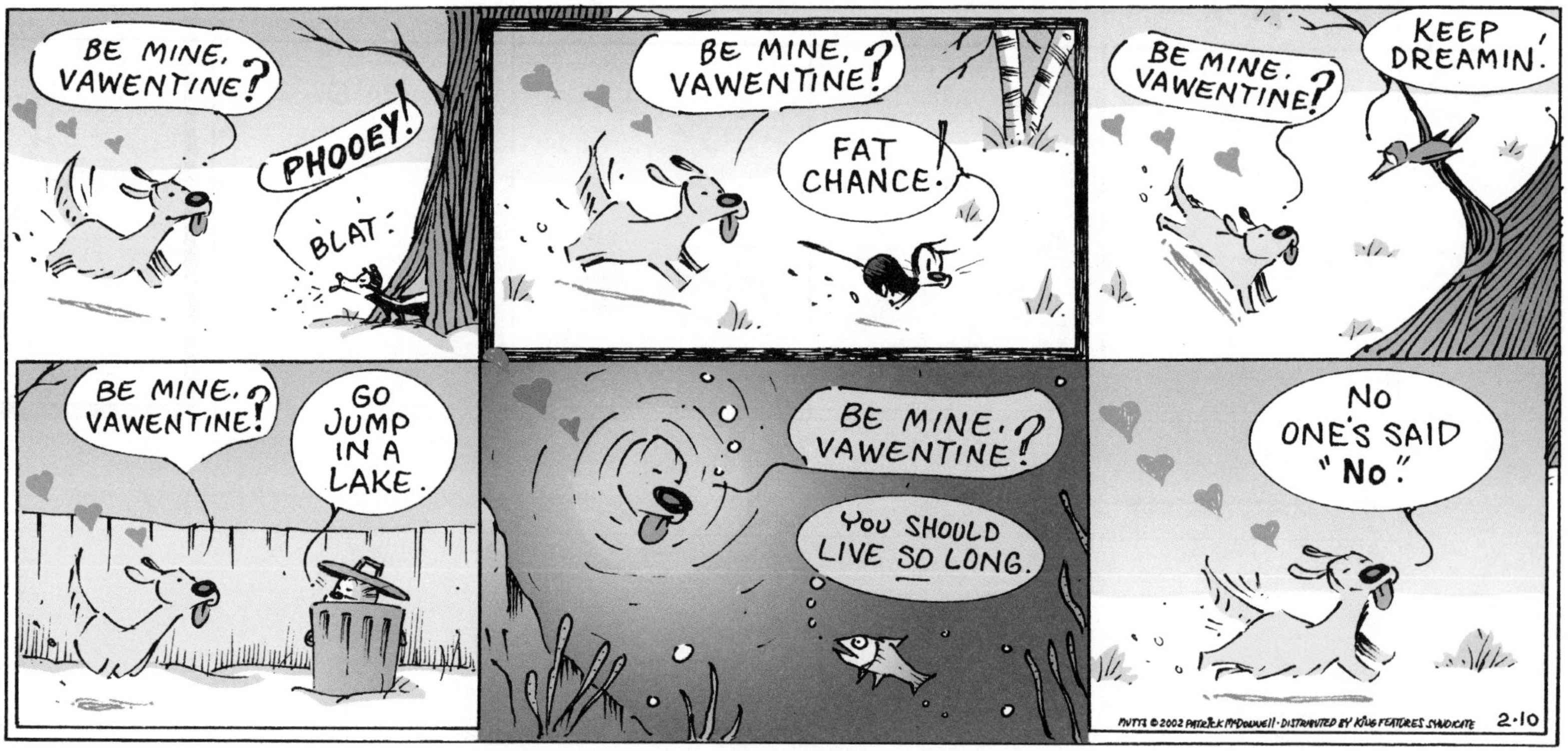
BE MINE, VAWENTINE?
PHOOEY!
BLAT!
BE MINE, VAWENTINE?
FAT CHANCE!
BE MINE, VAWENTINE?
KEEP DREAMIN'.
BE MINE, VAWENTINE?
GO JUMP IN A LAKE.
BE MINE, VAWENTINE?
YOU SHOULD LIVE SO LONG.
NO ONE'S SAID "NO."
MUTTS © 2002 PATRICK McDONNELL · DISTRIBUTED BY KING FEATURES SYNDICATE
2·10

MUTTS

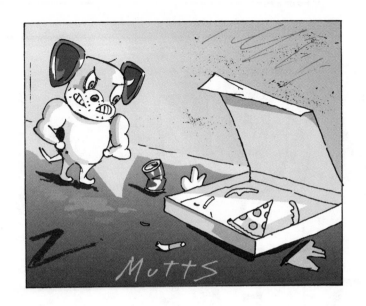

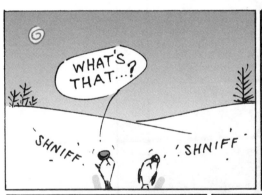

WHAT'S THAT...?
SHNIFF
SHNIFF
PIZZA!
LET ME GET MY PURSE.
THANKS, LADY.
...PIZZA...
AAAIIEEEE
IT'S COLD.
NO WONDER SHE'S UPSHET.
MUTTS © 2002 PATRICK McDONNELL · DISTRIBUTED BY KING FEATURES
2·17

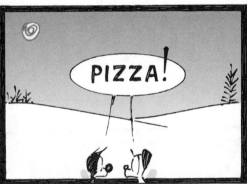

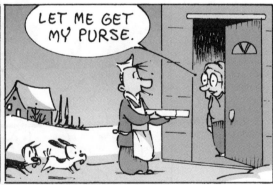

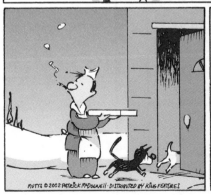

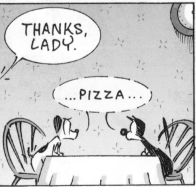

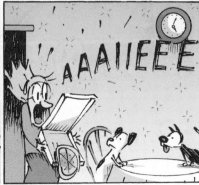

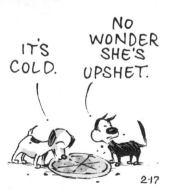

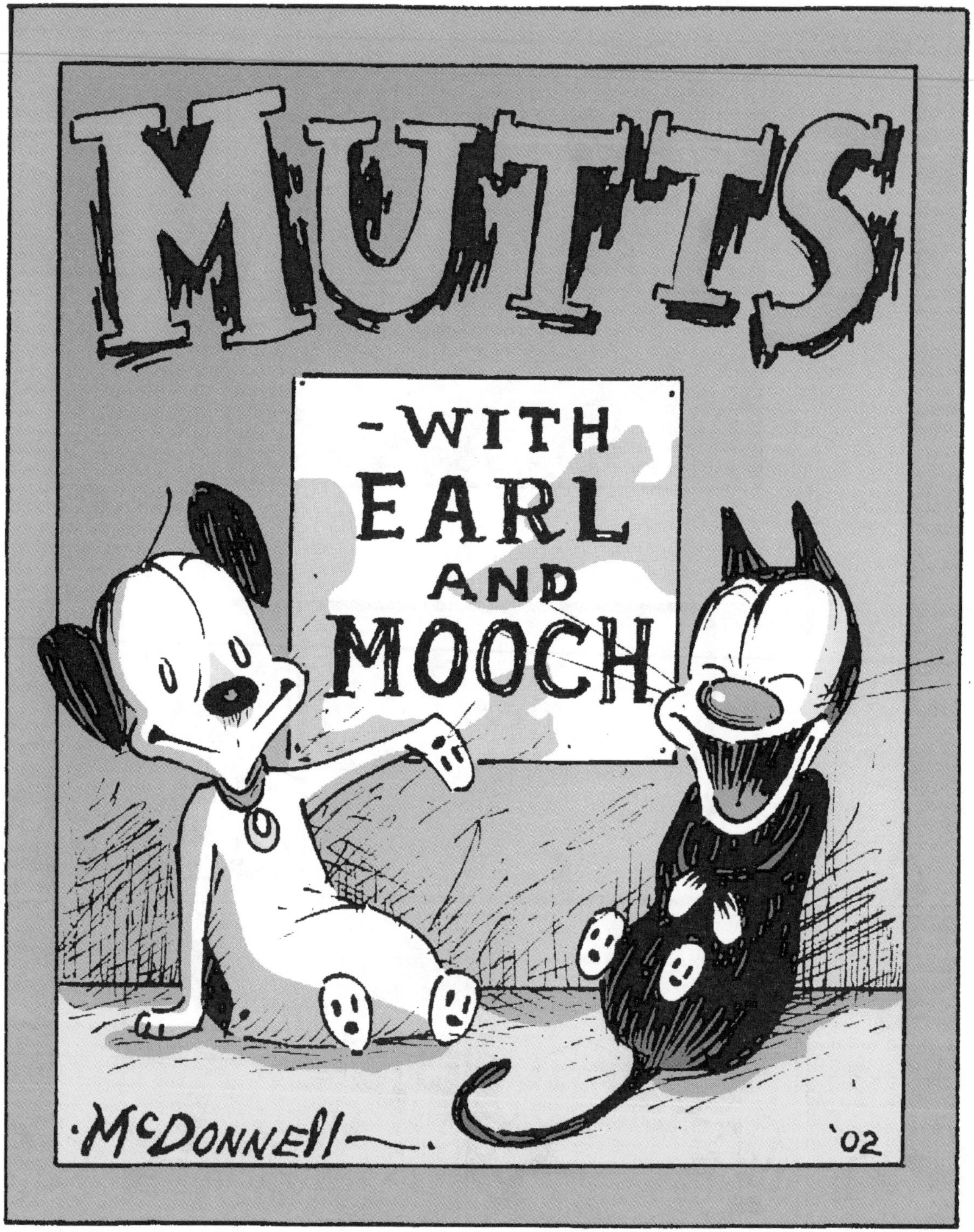
MUTTS
-WITH
EARL
AND
MOOCH
·McDONNELL—·
'02

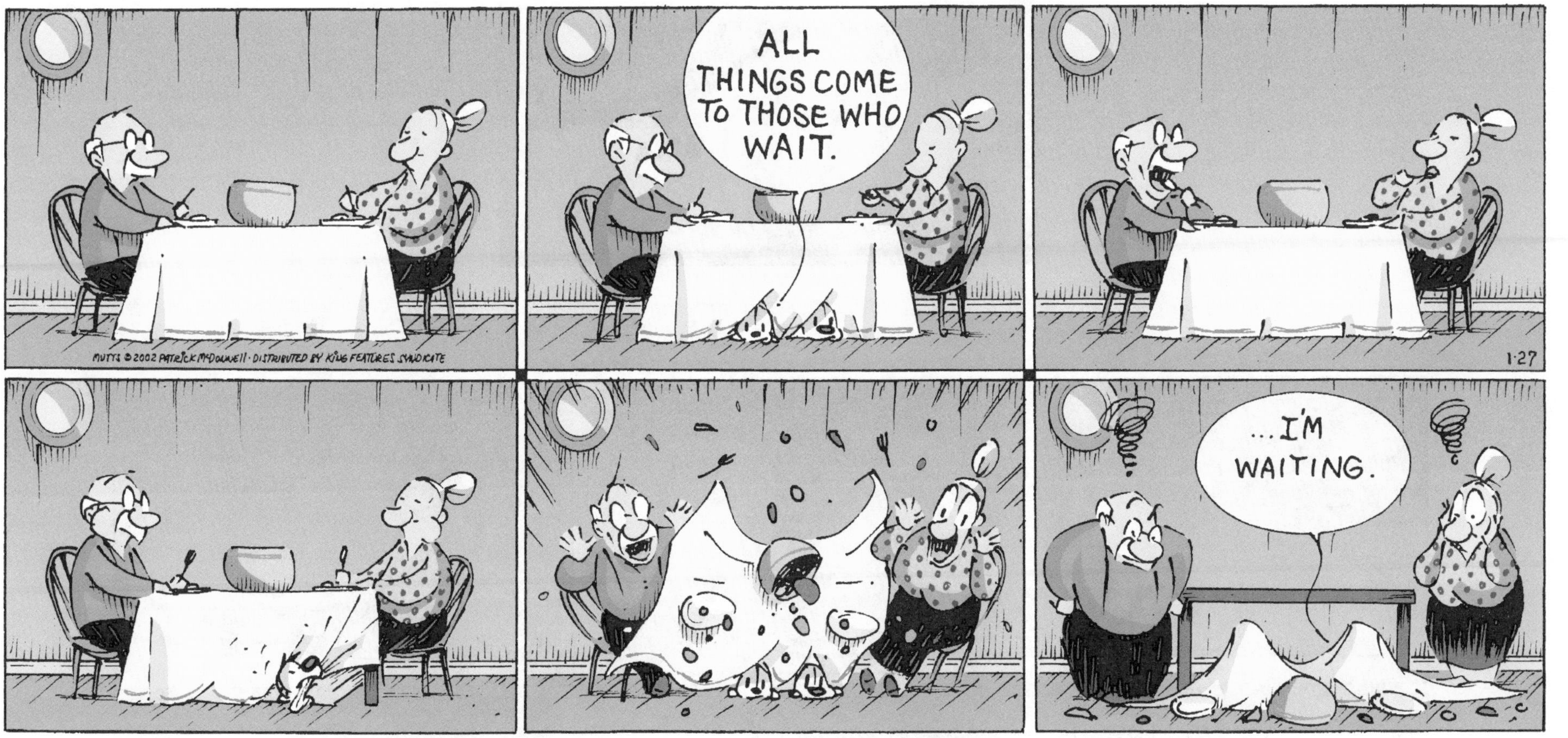
MUTTS © 2002 PATRICK McDONNELL · DISTRIBUTED BY KING FEATURES SYNDICATE
ALL THINGS COME TO THOSE WHO WAIT.
1·27
...I'M WAITING.

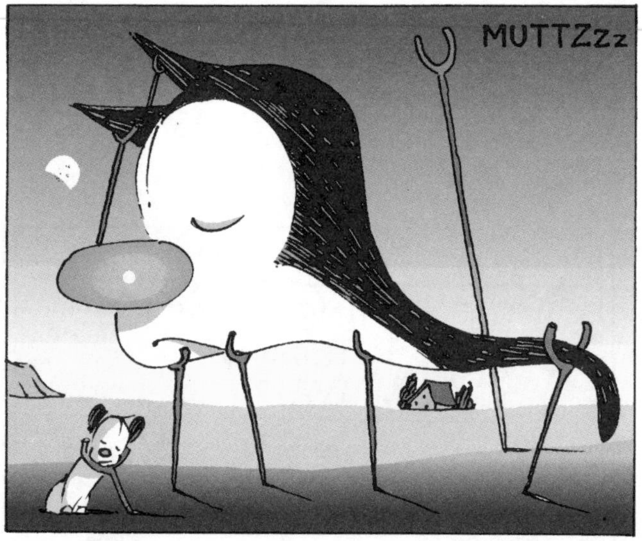
MUTTZzz

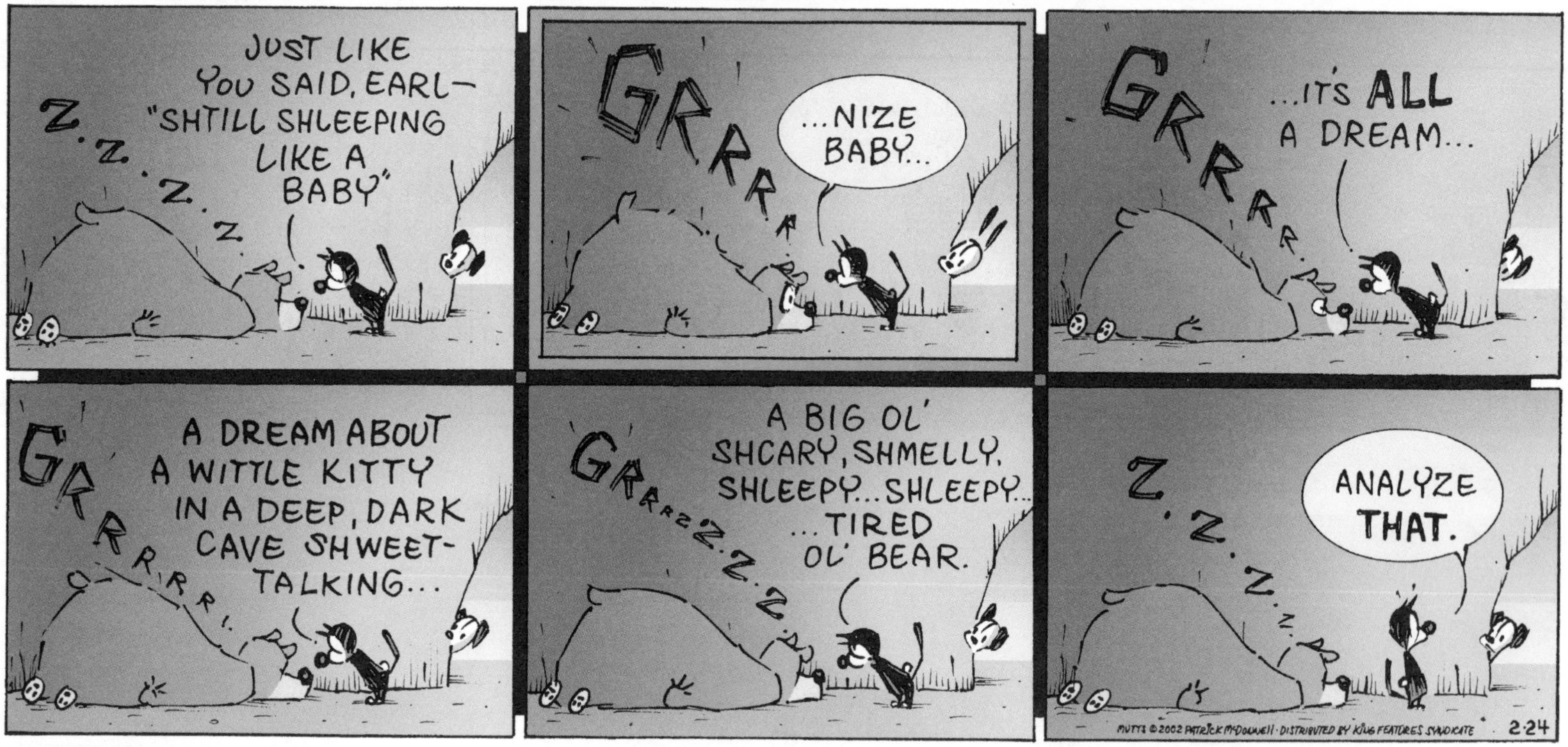
Z.Z..Z..Z
JUST LIKE YOU SAID, EARL— "SHTILL SHLEEPING LIKE A BABY"
GRRRR
...NIZE BABY...
GRRRRRR
...IT'S ALL A DREAM...
GRRRRR
A DREAM ABOUT A WITTLE KITTY IN A DEEP, DARK CAVE SHWEET-TALKING...
GRRRZZ.Z.Z
A BIG OL' SHCARY, SHMELLY, SHLEEPY...SHLEEPY... ...TIRED OL' BEAR.
Z.Z..Z..Z
ANALYZE THAT.
MUTTS © 2002 PATRICK McDONNELL · DISTRIBUTED BY KING FEATURES SYNDICATE
2·24

MUTTS.
by
PATRICK McDONNELL
C'MON SPRING!
MUTTS © 2002 PATRICK McDONNELL · DISTRIBUTED BY KING FEATURES SYNDICATE
3·3

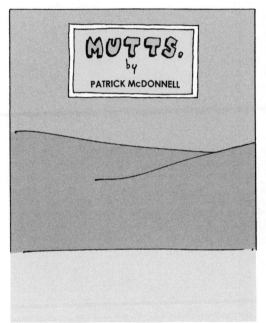

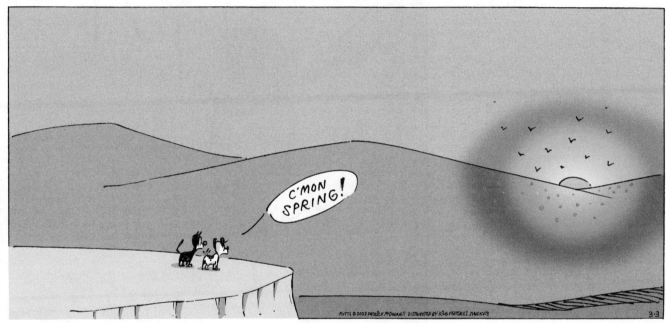

PATRICK McDONNELL
Mutts

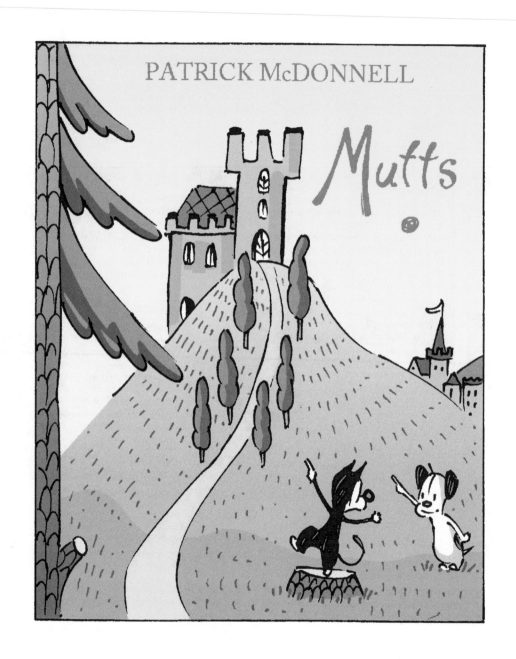

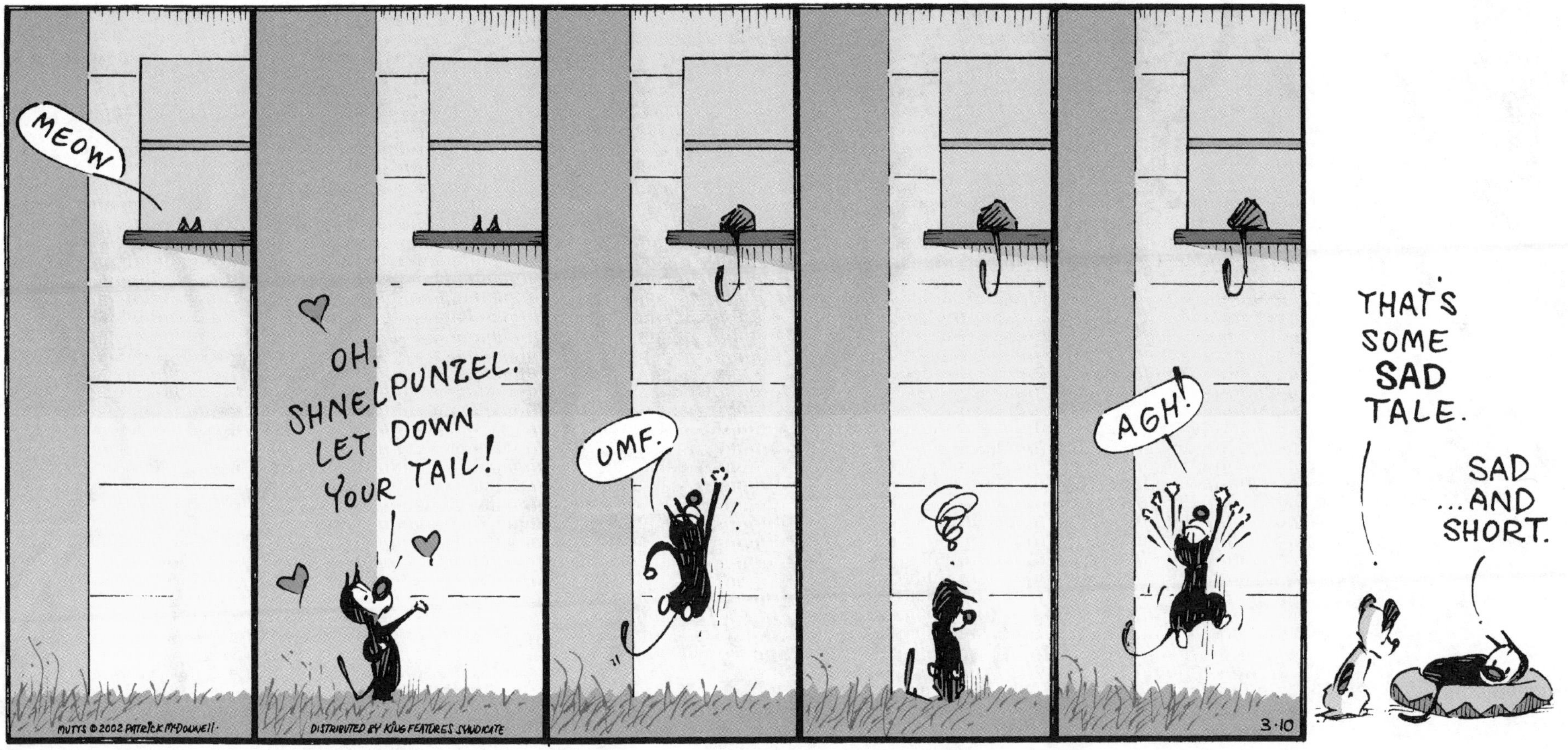
MEOW
OH, SHNELPUNZEL. LET DOWN YOUR TAIL!
UMF.
AGH!
THAT'S SOME SAD TALE.
SAD ...AND SHORT.
MUTTS © 2002 PATRICK McDONNELL
DISTRIBUTED BY KING FEATURES SYNDICATE
3·10

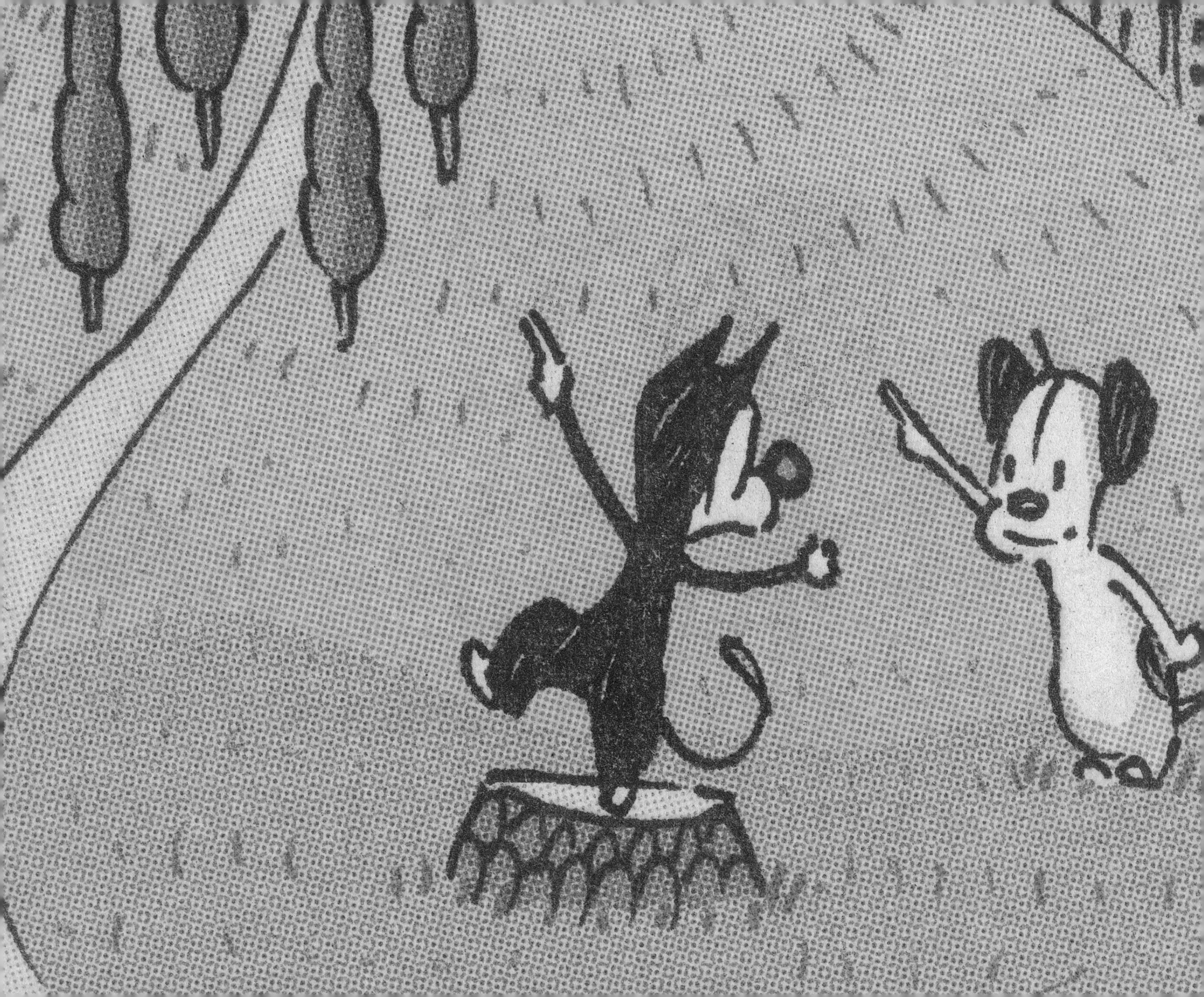

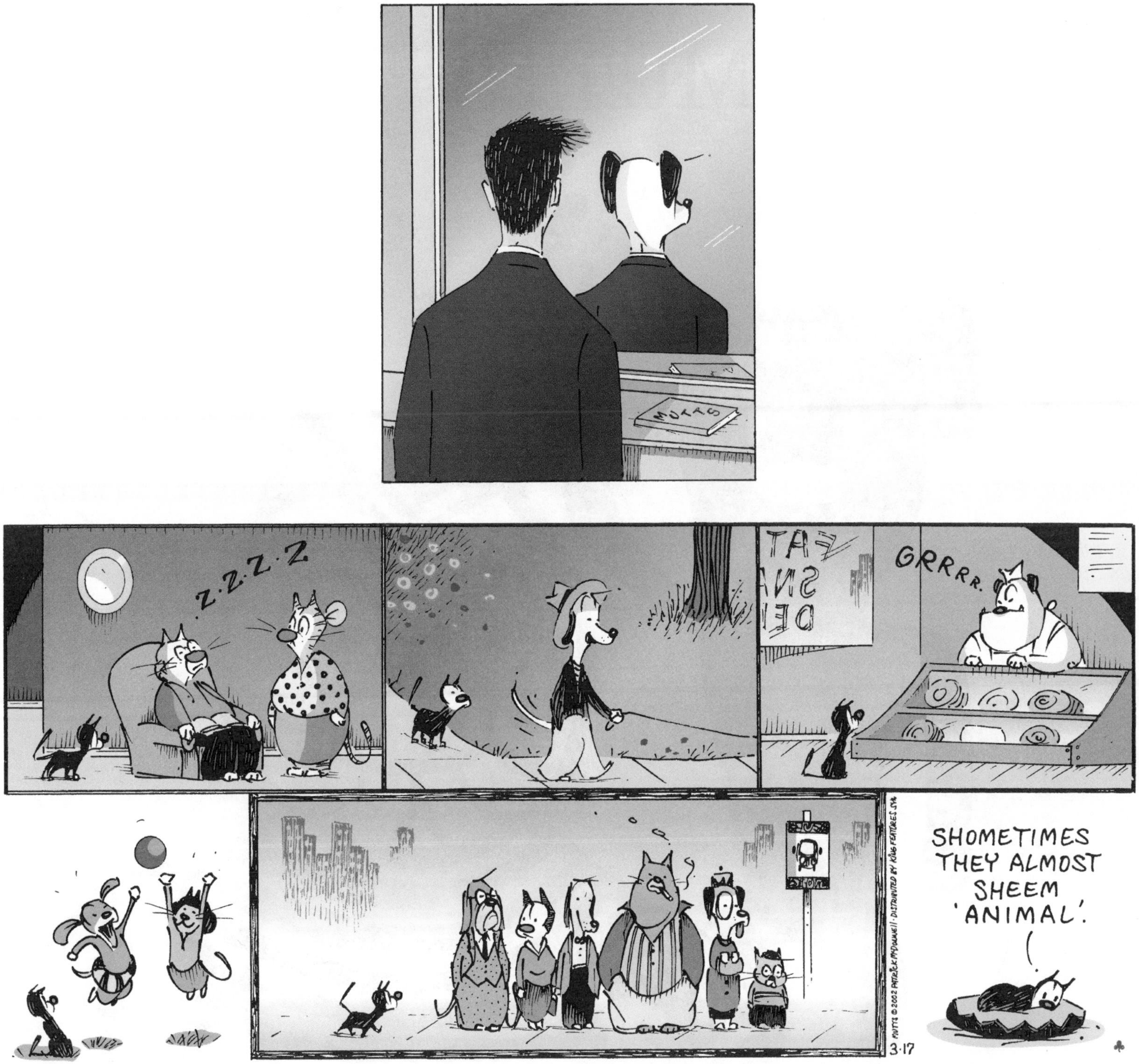
MUTAS
Z.Z.Z.Z
GRRRR.
SHOMETIMES THEY ALMOST SHEEM 'ANIMAL'.
MUTTS ©2002 PATRICK McDONNELL · DISTRIBUTED BY KING FEATURES SYN.
3·17

MUTTS

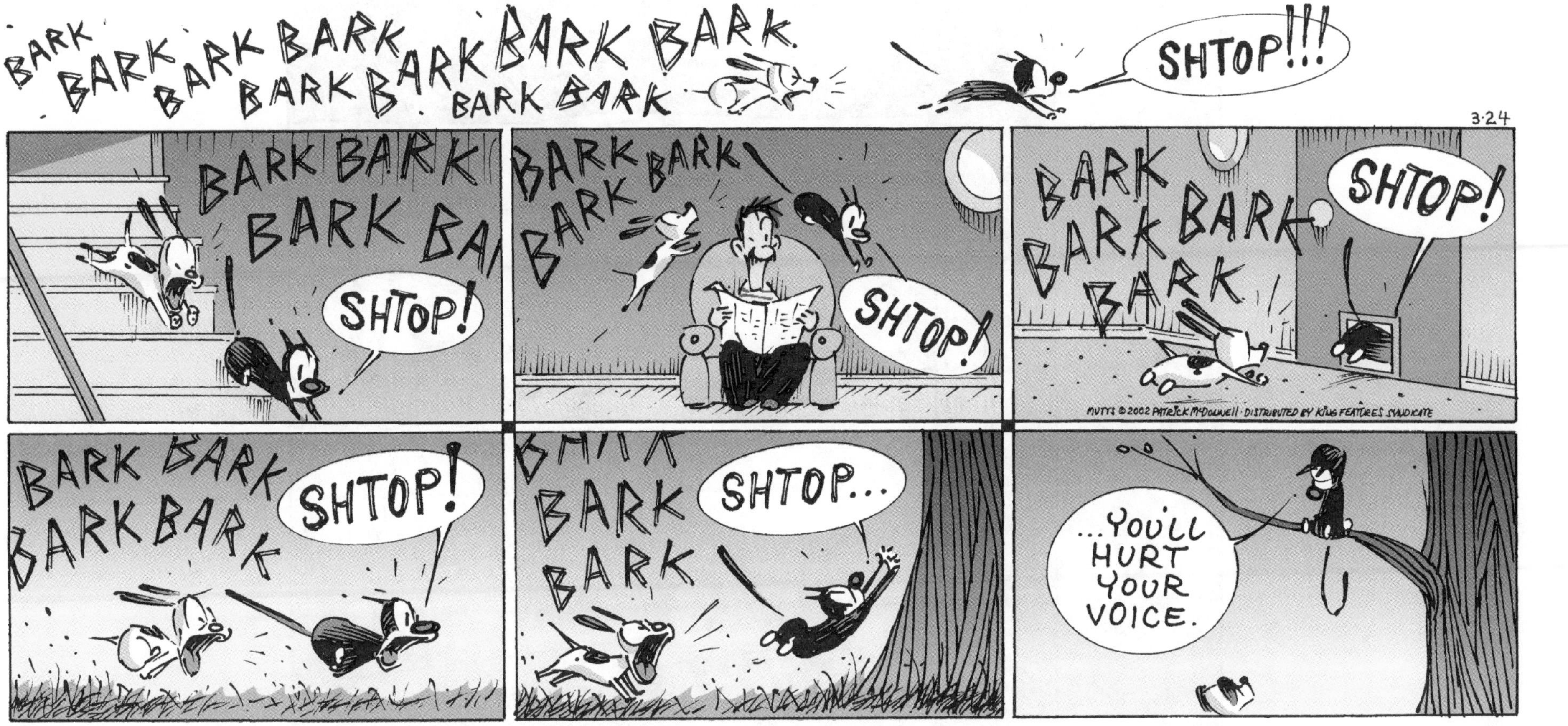

BARK BARK BARK BARK BARK BARK BARK BARK BARK BARK BARK
SHTOP!!!
3·24
BARK BARK BARK
SHTOP!
BARK BARK BARK
SHTOP!
BARK BARK BARK BARK
SHTOP!
MUTTS © 2002 PATRICK McDONNELL · DISTRIBUTED BY KING FEATURES SYNDICATE
BARK BARK BARK BARK
SHTOP!
BARK BARK
SHTOP...
...YOU'LL HURT YOUR VOICE.

HEY, MOOCH! WHAT'CHA DOIN'?
3·31
MUTTS ©2002 PATRICK McDONNELL · DISTRIBUTED BY KING FEATURES SYNDICATE
I'M SHMAKING FACES AT THE NEW NEIGHBORS DOG.
THE NEW NEIGHBORS DON'T HAVE A DOG.
... BUT WE'RE SURE THINKING ABOUT GETTING ONE.

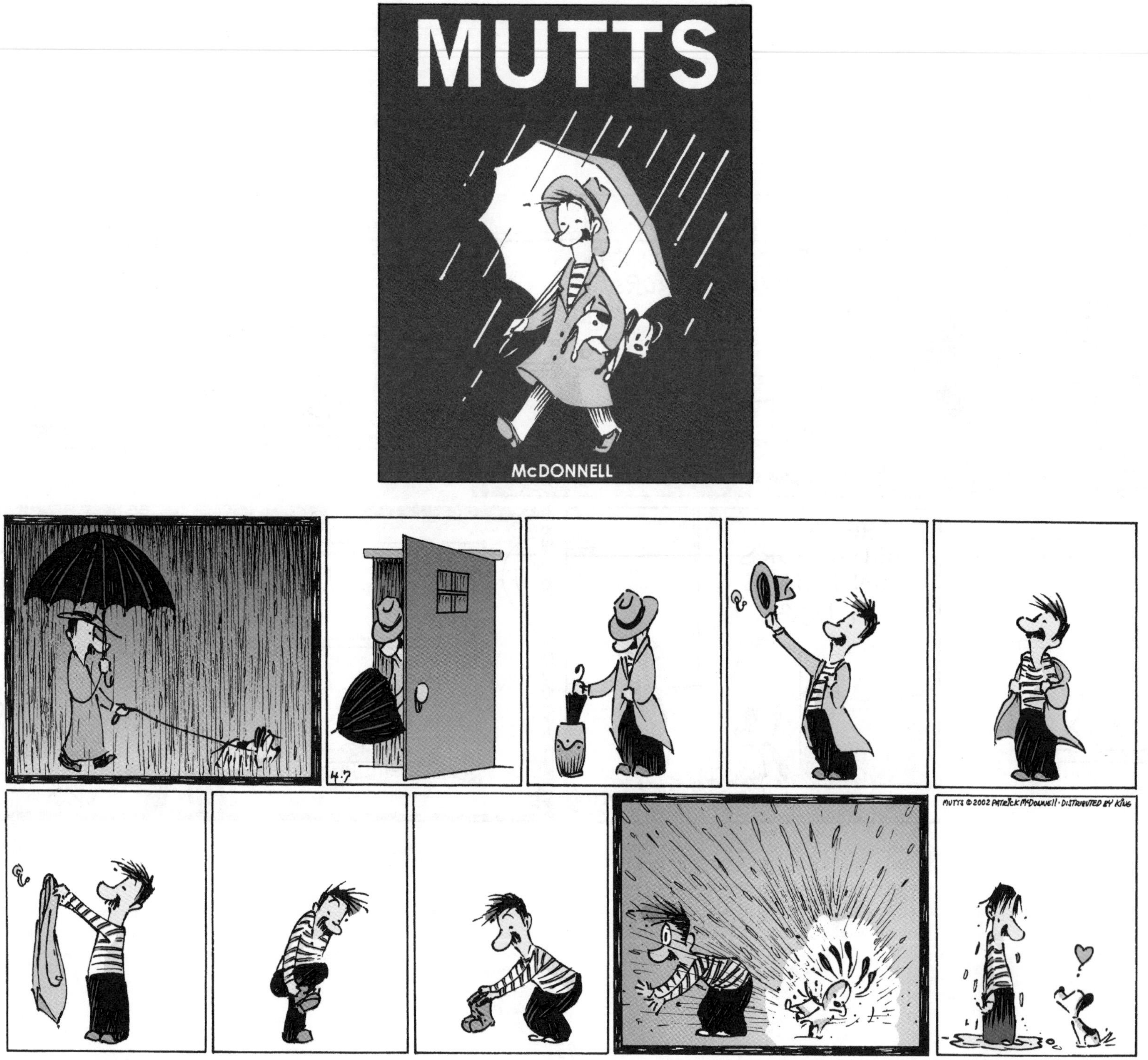
MUTTS
McDONNELL
4-7
MUTTS © 2002 PATRICK McDONNELL · DISTRIBUTED BY KING

The Mutts.

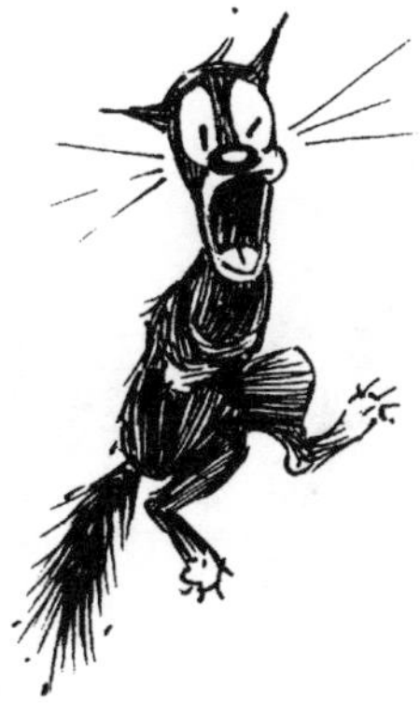

·Patrick McDonnell·

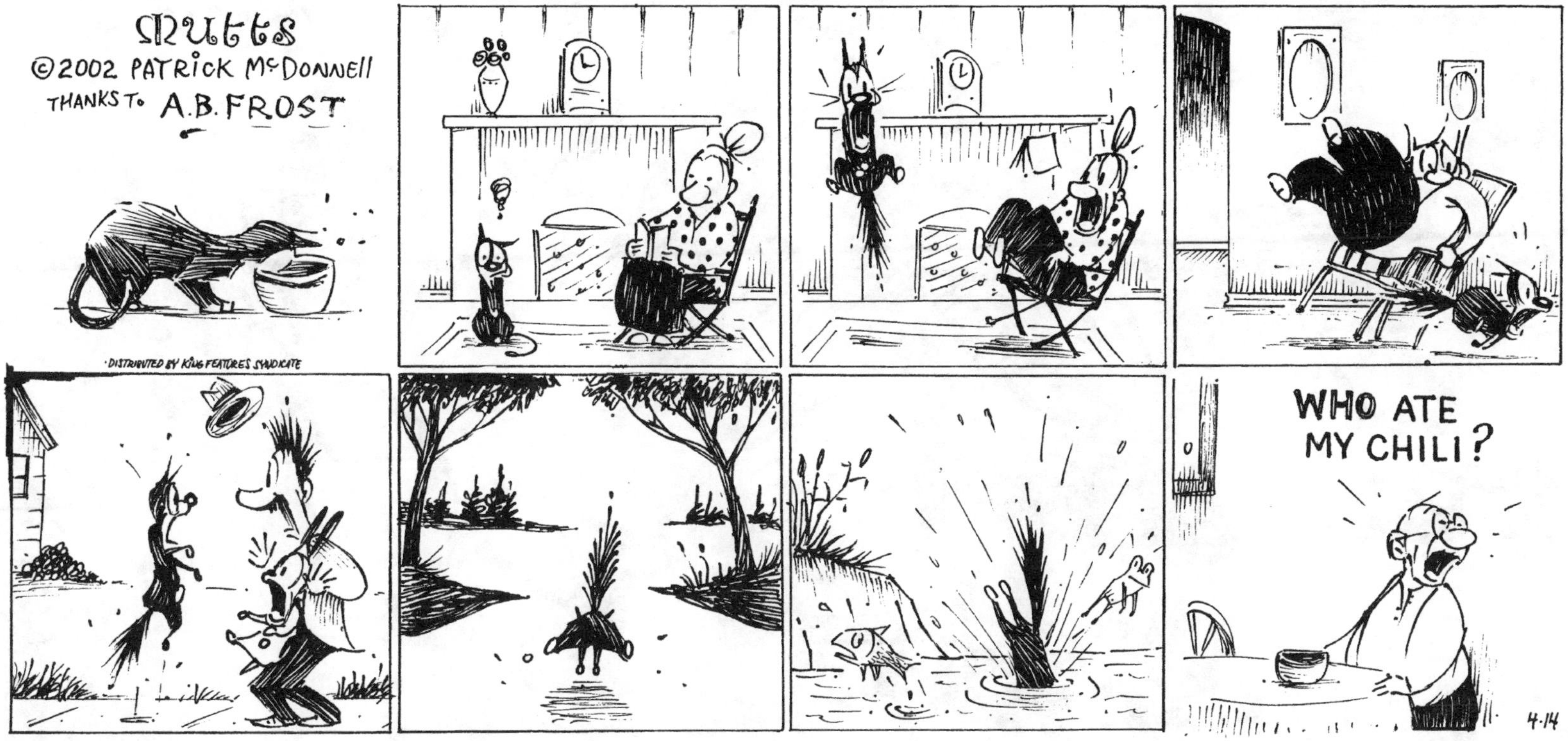
MUTTS
©2002 PATRICK McDONNELL
THANKS TO A.B. FROST
·DISTRIBUTED BY KING FEATURES SYNDICATE
WHO ATE MY CHILI?
4·14

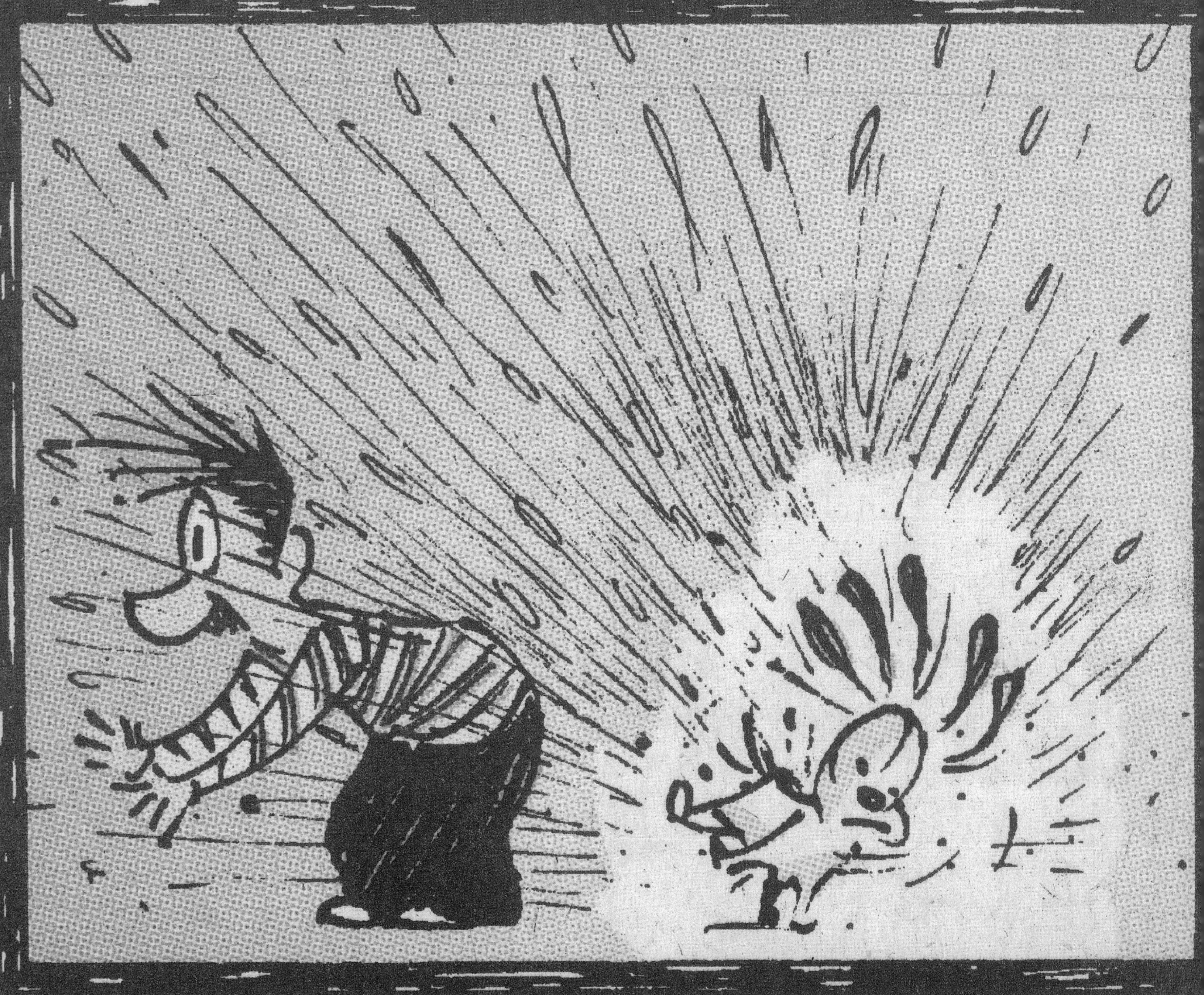

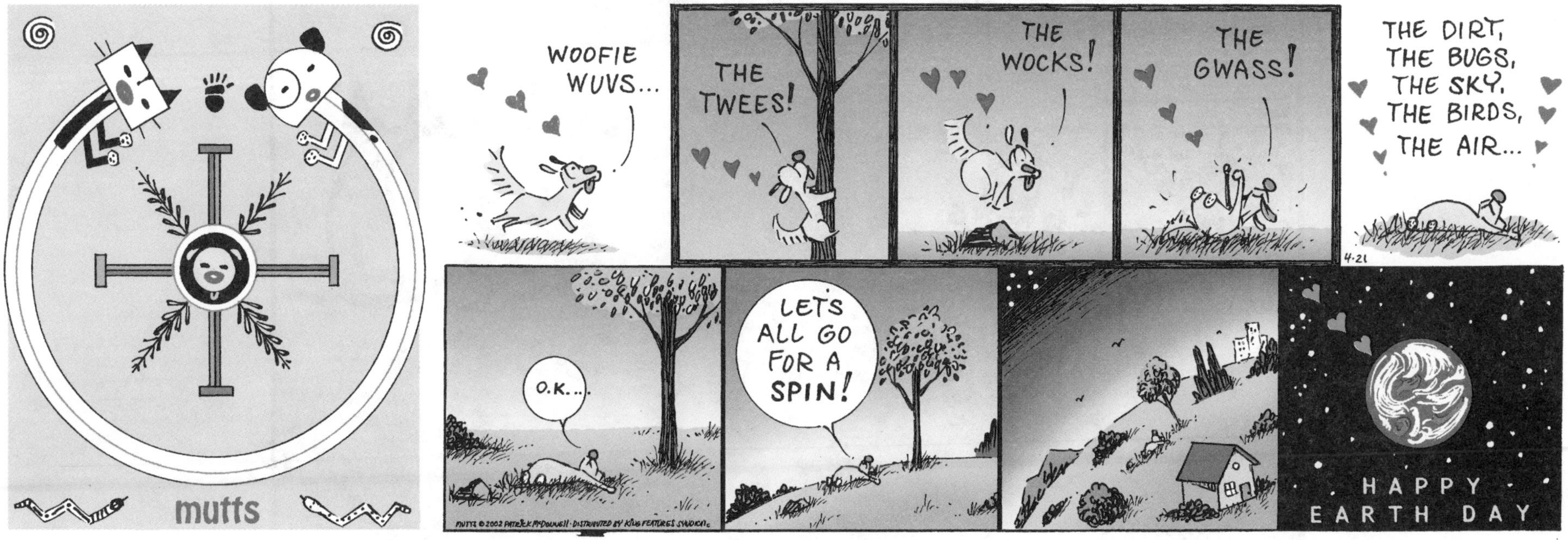
mutts
WOOFIE WUVS...
THE TWEES!
THE WOCKS!
THE GWASS!
THE DIRT, THE BUGS, THE SKY, THE BIRDS, THE AIR...
4.21
O.K....
LET'S ALL GO FOR A SPIN!
HAPPY EARTH DAY

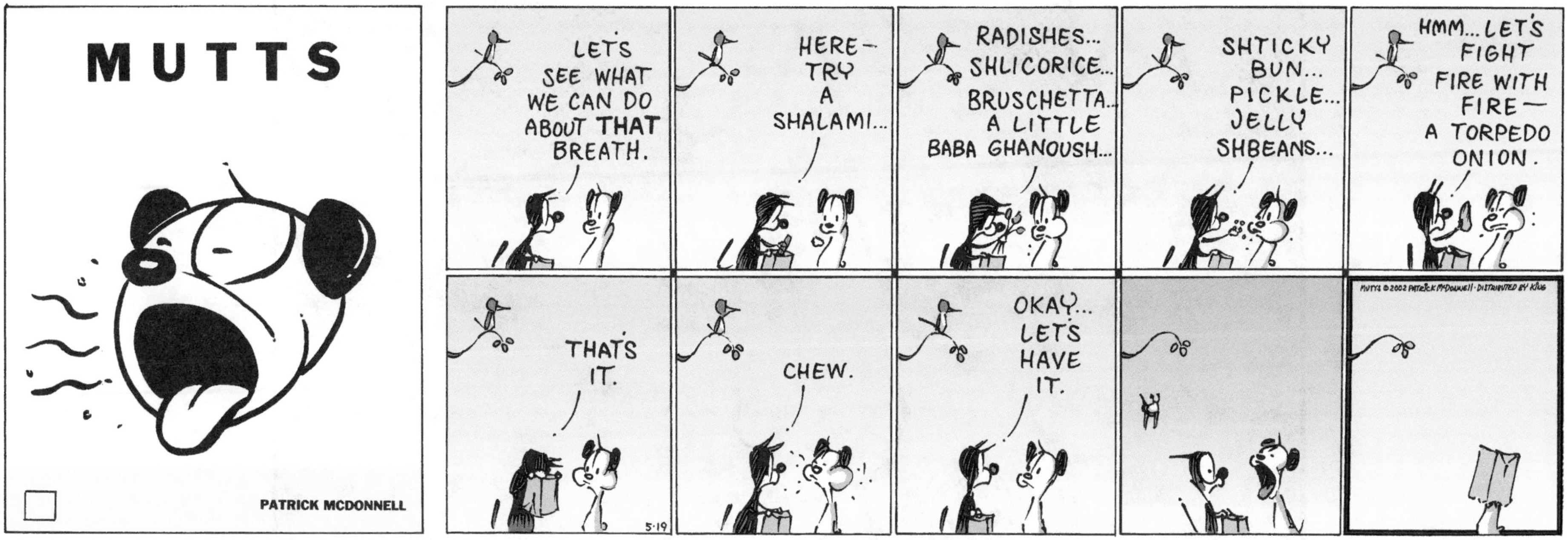
MUTTS
PATRICK MCDONNELL
LET'S SEE WHAT WE CAN DO ABOUT THAT BREATH.
HERE- TRY A SHALAMI...
RADISHES... SHLICORICE... BRUSCHETTA... A LITTLE BABA GHANOUSH...
SHTICKY BUN... PICKLE... JELLY SHBEANS...
HMM... LET'S FIGHT FIRE WITH FIRE- A TORPEDO ONION.
THAT'S IT.
5.19
CHEW.
OKAY... LET'S HAVE IT.

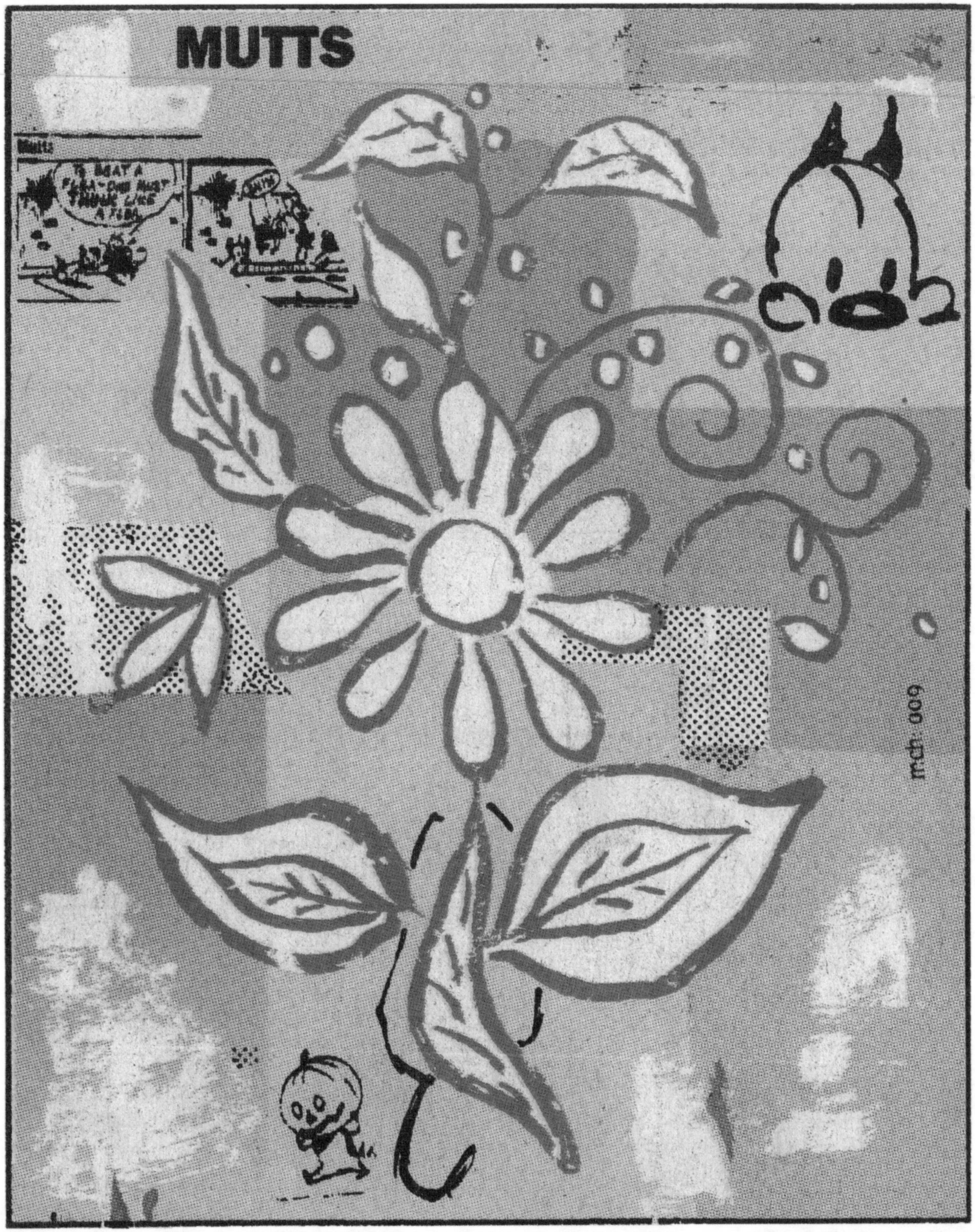
MUTTS
mch 009

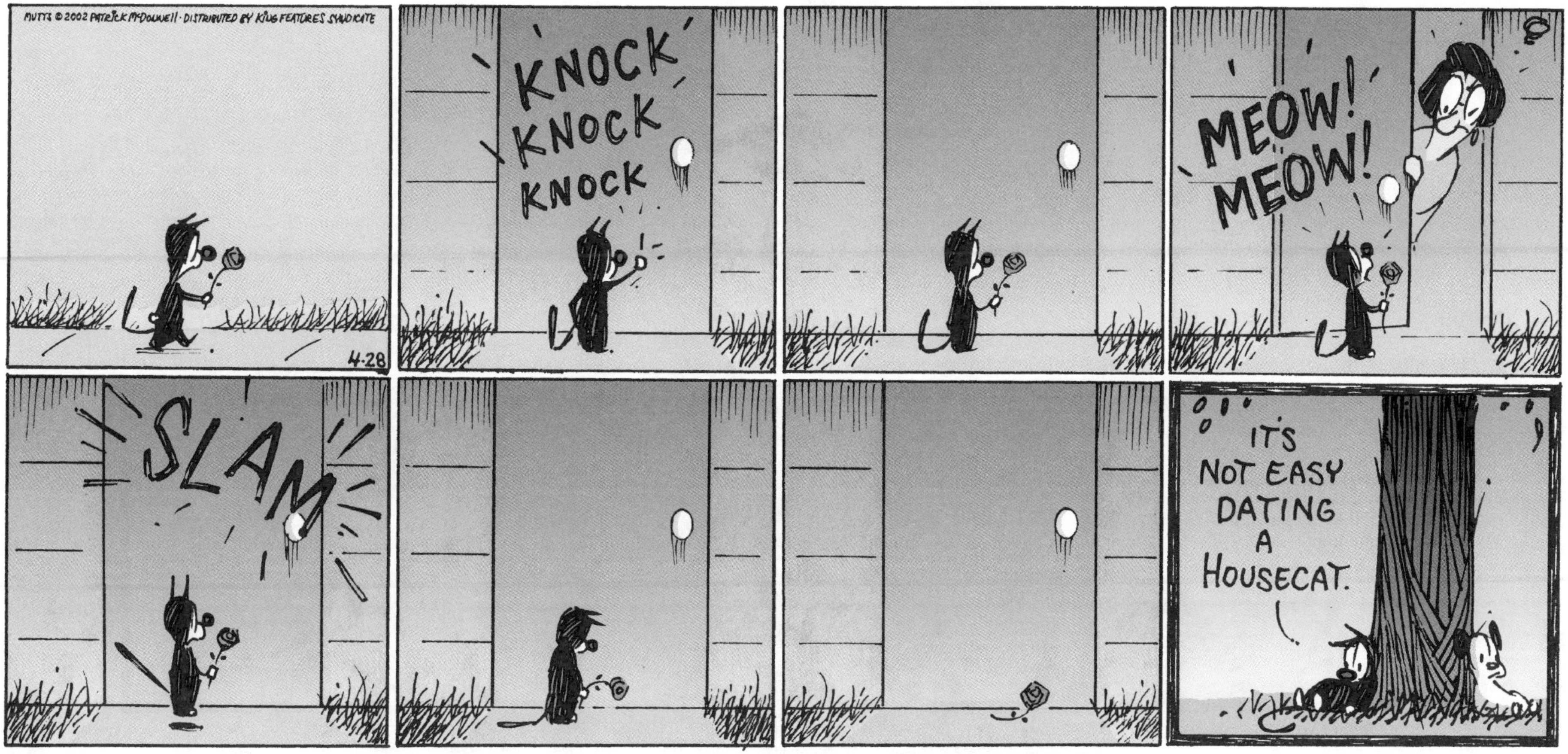

MUTTS © 2002 PATRICK McDONNELL · DISTRIBUTED BY KING FEATURES SYNDICATE
4-28
KNOCK KNOCK KNOCK
MEOW! MEOW!
SLAM
IT'S NOT EASY DATING A HOUSECAT.

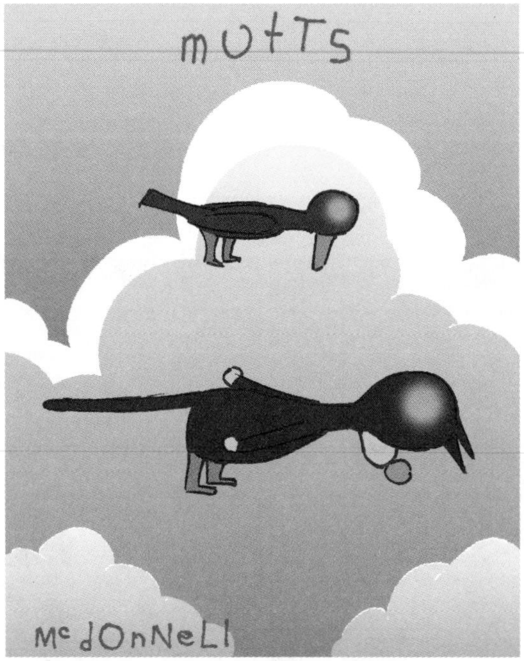
MUTTS
McDONNELL

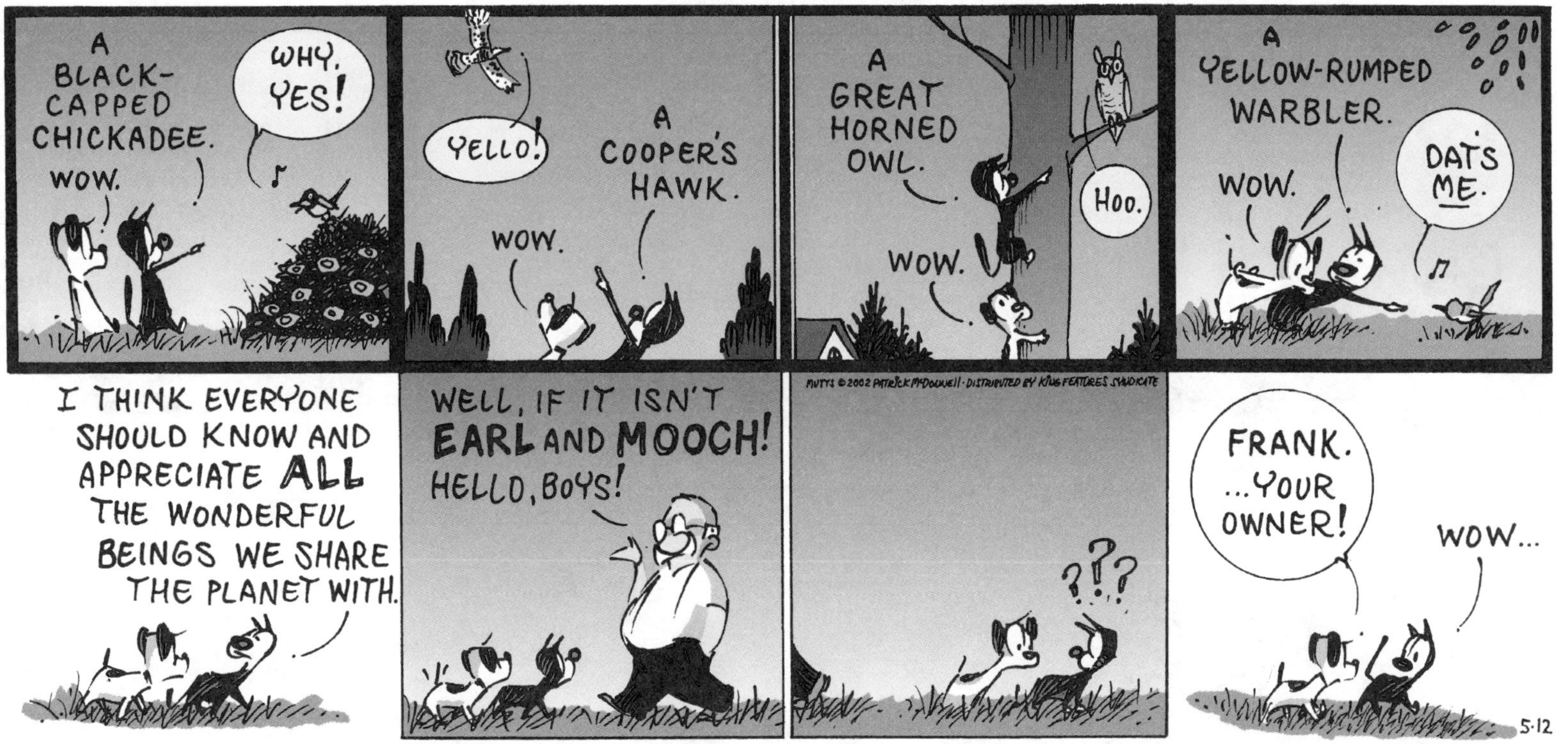
A BLACK-CAPPED CHICKADEE.
WOW.
WHY, YES!
YELLO!
A COOPER'S HAWK.
WOW.
A GREAT HORNED OWL.
WOW.
HOO.
A YELLOW-RUMPED WARBLER.
WOW.
DAT'S ME.
I THINK EVERYONE SHOULD KNOW AND APPRECIATE ALL THE WONDERFUL BEINGS WE SHARE THE PLANET WITH.
WELL, IF IT ISN'T EARL AND MOOCH! HELLO, BOYS!
MUTTS © 2002 PATRICK McDONNELL · DISTRIBUTED BY KING FEATURES SYNDICATE
?!?
FRANK. ...YOUR OWNER!
WOW...
5·12

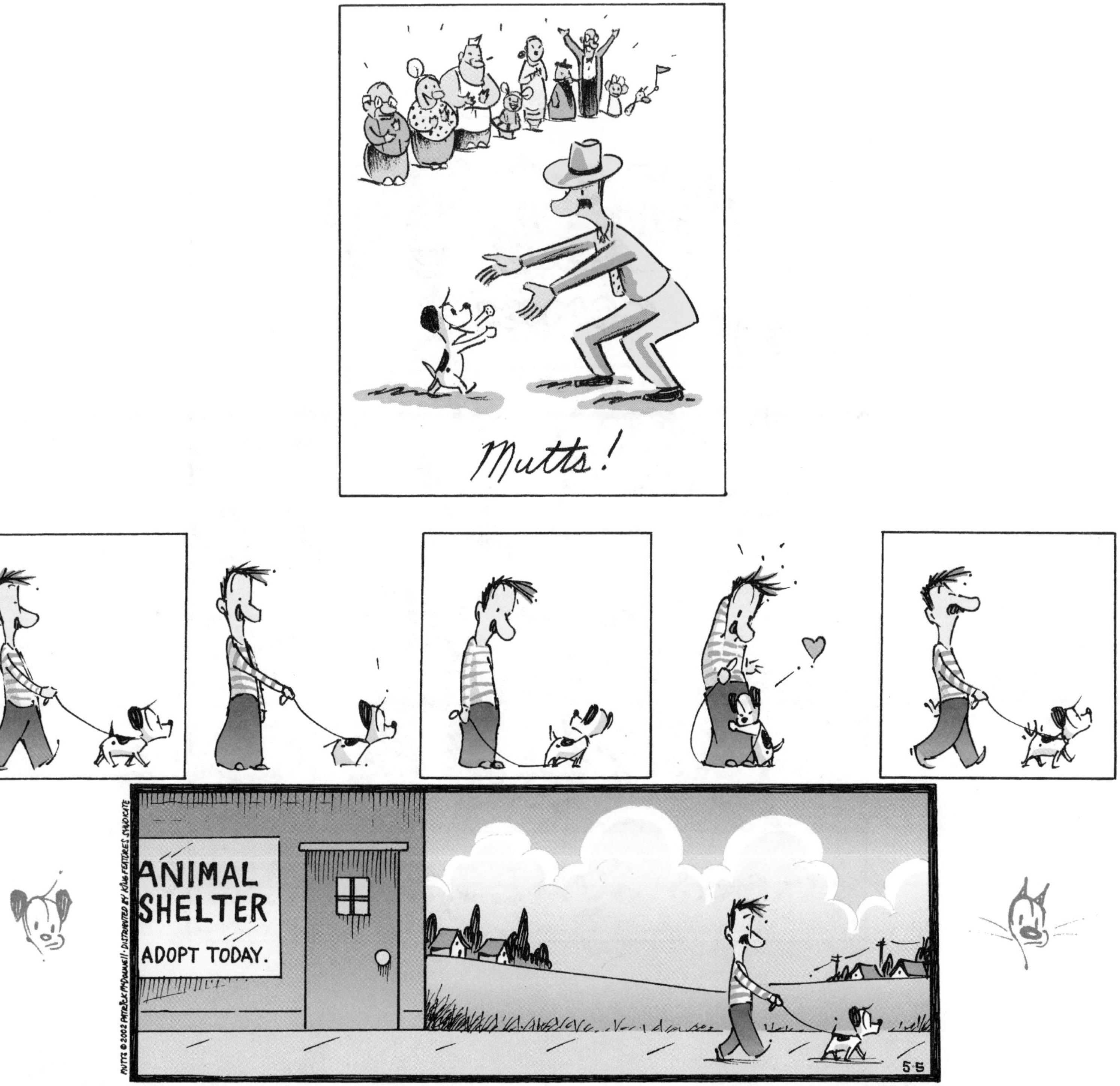

Mutts!
ANIMAL SHELTER
ADOPT TODAY.
MUTTS © 2002 PATRICK McDONNELL · DISTRIBUTED BY KING FEATURES SYNDICATE
5·5

MUTTS
2¢
COMIX
NO. 1
. GAGS, JOKES, SHTUFF

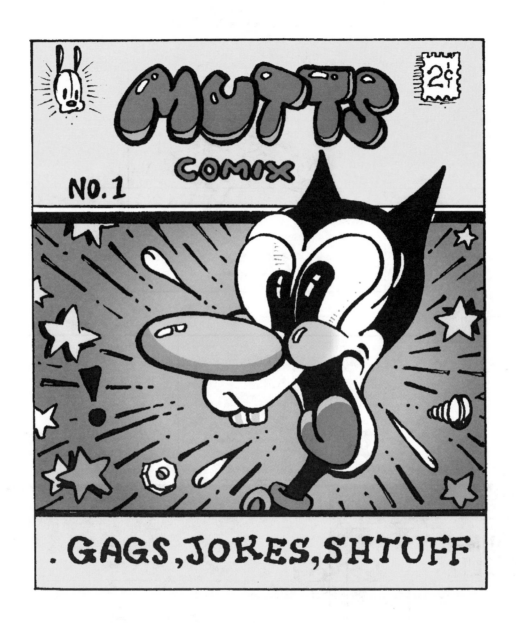

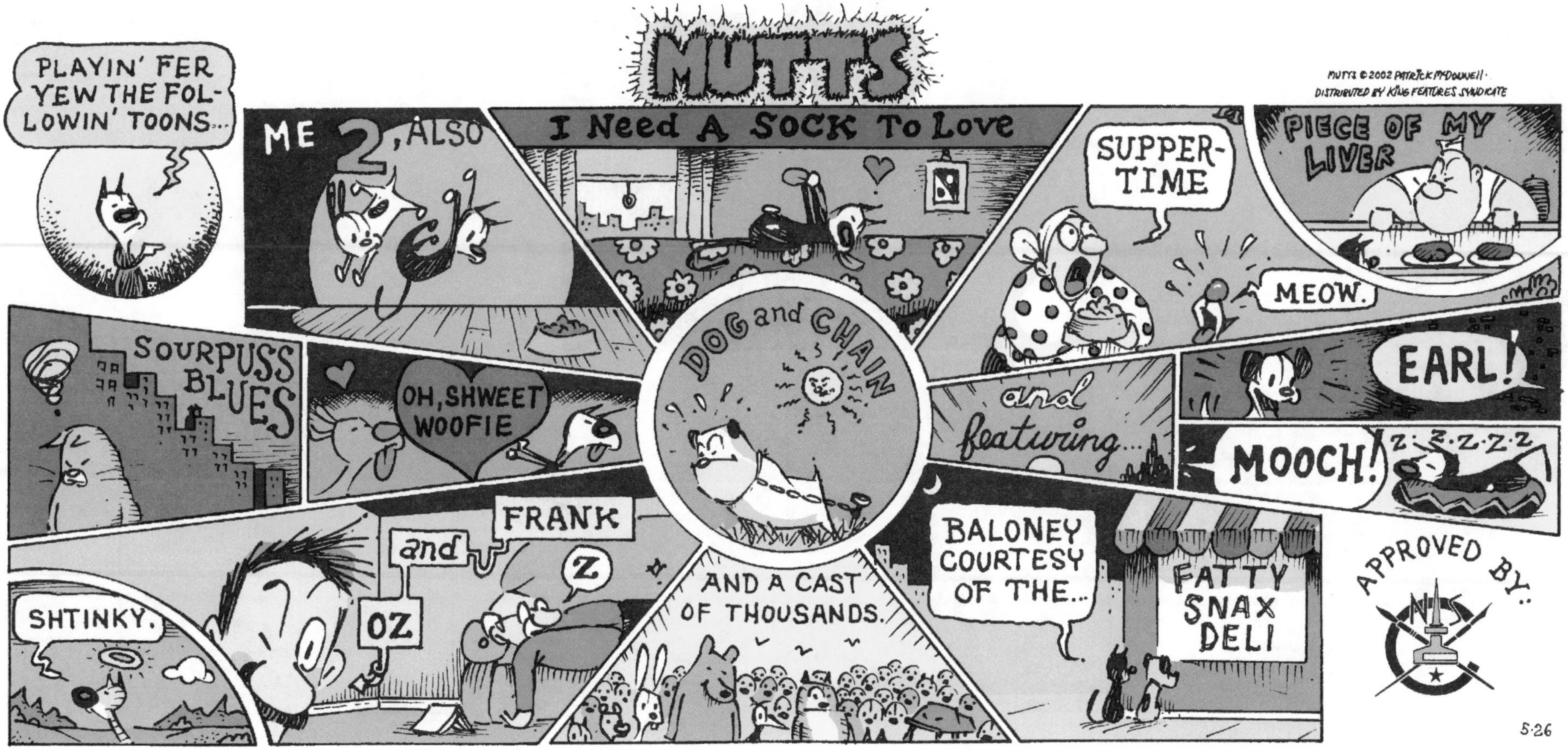
MUTTS
MUTTS © 2002 PATRICK McDONNELL · DISTRIBUTED BY KING FEATURES SYNDICATE
PLAYIN' FER YEW THE FOL-LOWIN' TOONS...
ME 2, ALSO
I Need A SOCK To Love
SUPPER-TIME
PIECE OF MY LIVER
MEOW.
SOURPUSS BLUES
OH, SHWEET WOOFIE
DOG and CHAIN
and featuring...
EARL!
MOOCH!
Z·Z·Z·Z·Z
FRANK
and
OZ
Z
SHTINKY.
AND A CAST OF THOUSANDS.
BALONEY COURTESY OF THE...
FATTY SNAX DELI
APPROVED BY:
NCS
5·26

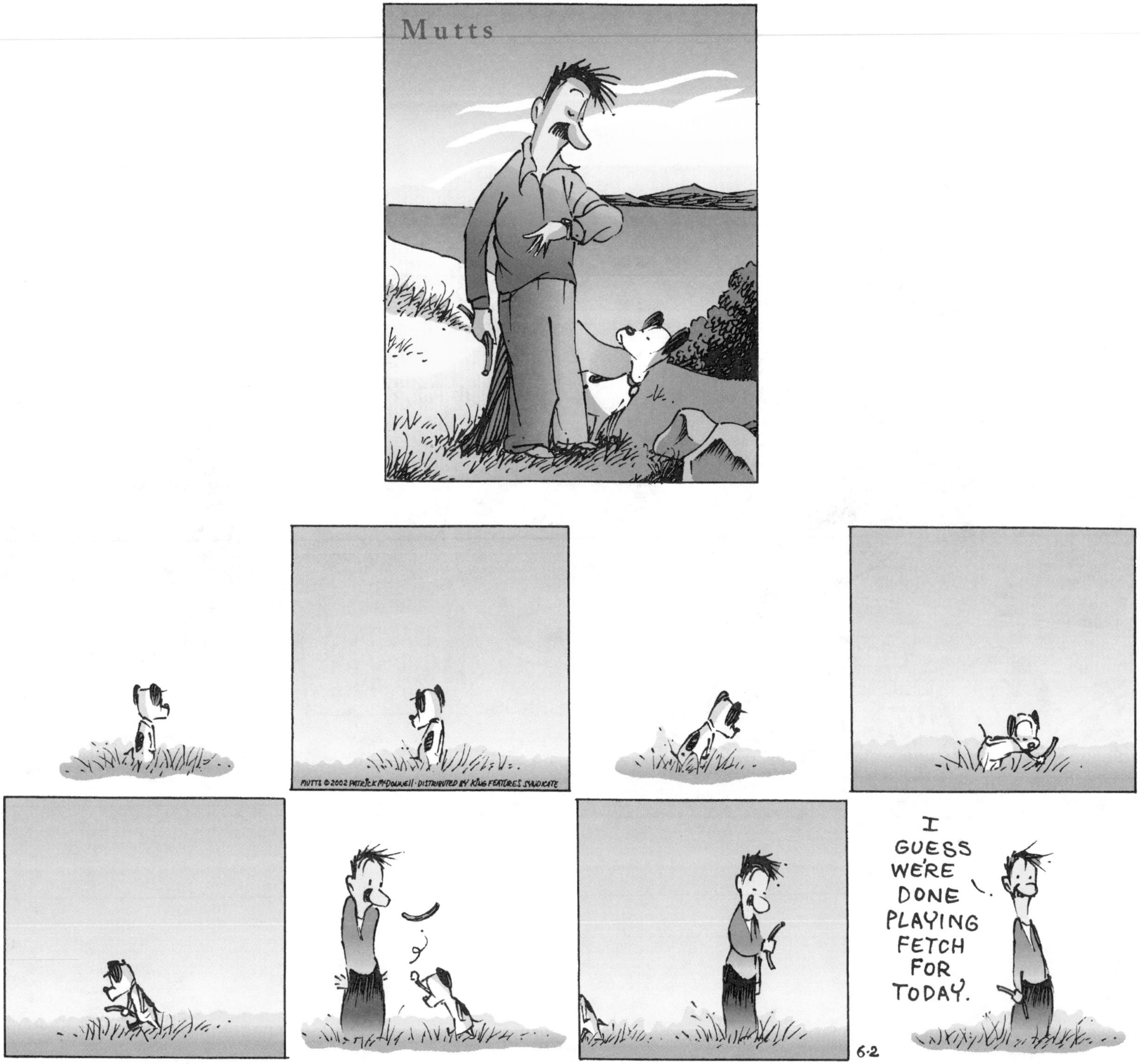
Mutts
MUTTS © 2002 PATRICK McDONNELL · DISTRIBUTED BY KING FEATURES SYNDICATE
I GUESS WE'RE DONE PLAYING FETCH FOR TODAY.
6·2

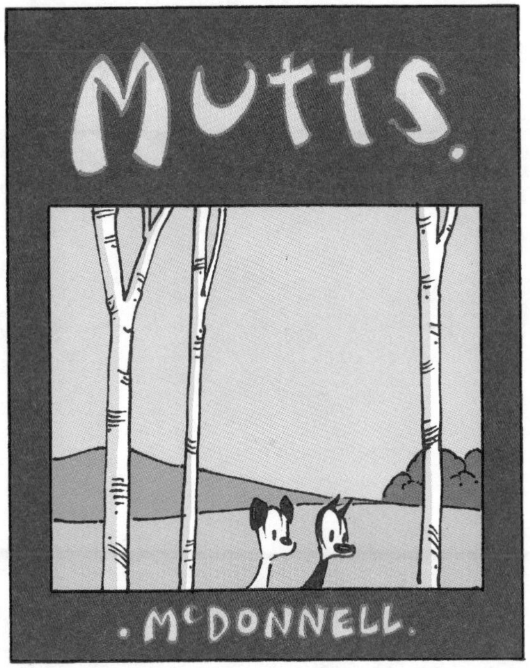
MUTTS.
.McDONNELL.

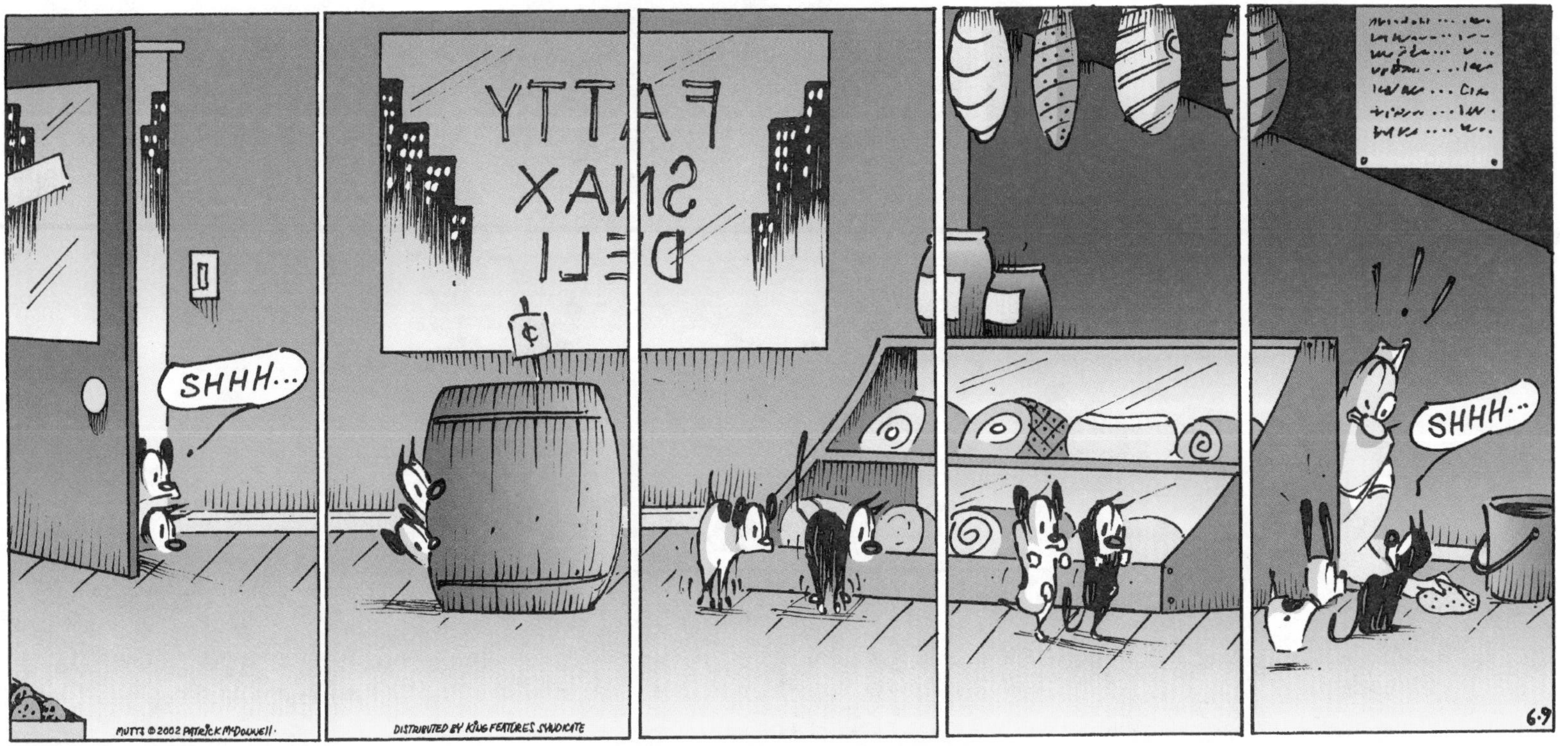
SHHH...
FATTY
SNAX
DELI
¢
!!!
SHHH...
MUTTS © 2002 PATRICK McDONNELL
DISTRIBUTED BY KING FEATURES SYNDICATE
6·9

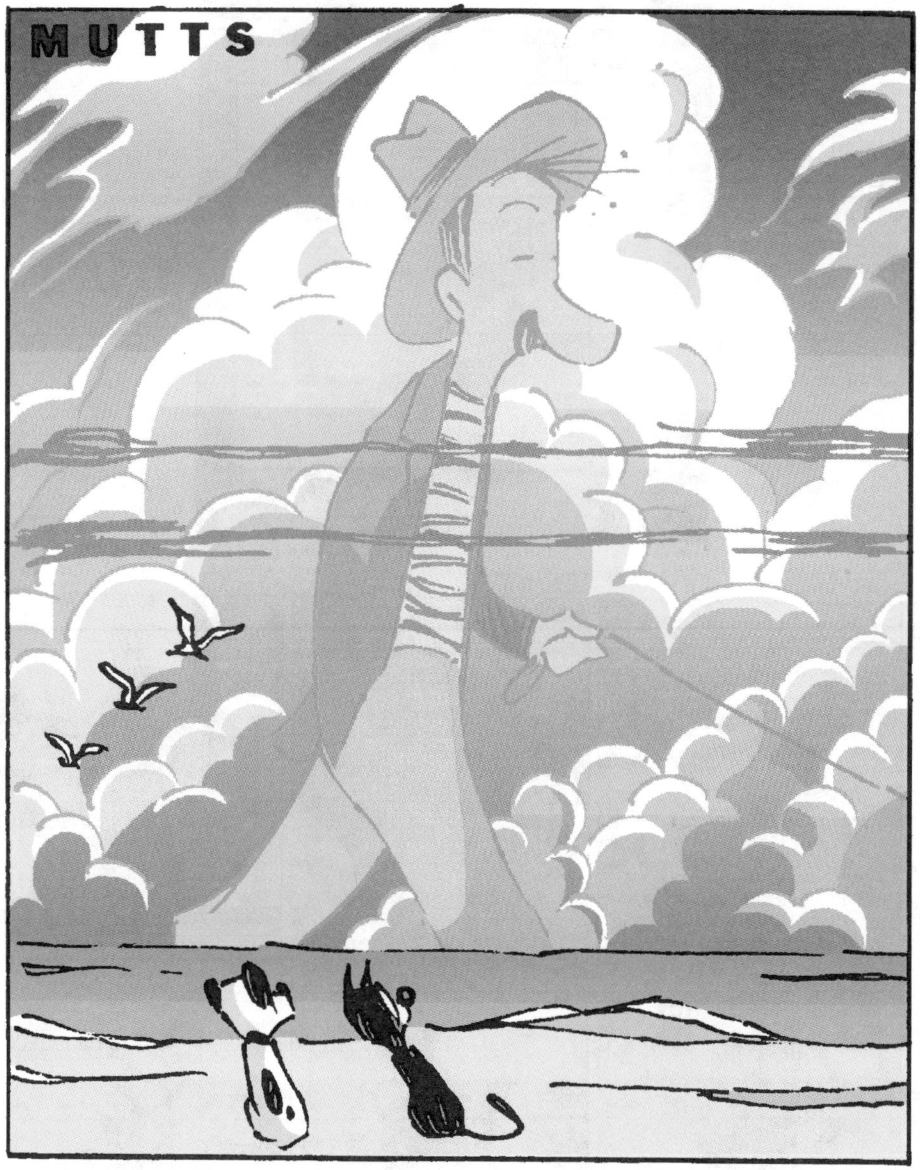
MUTTS

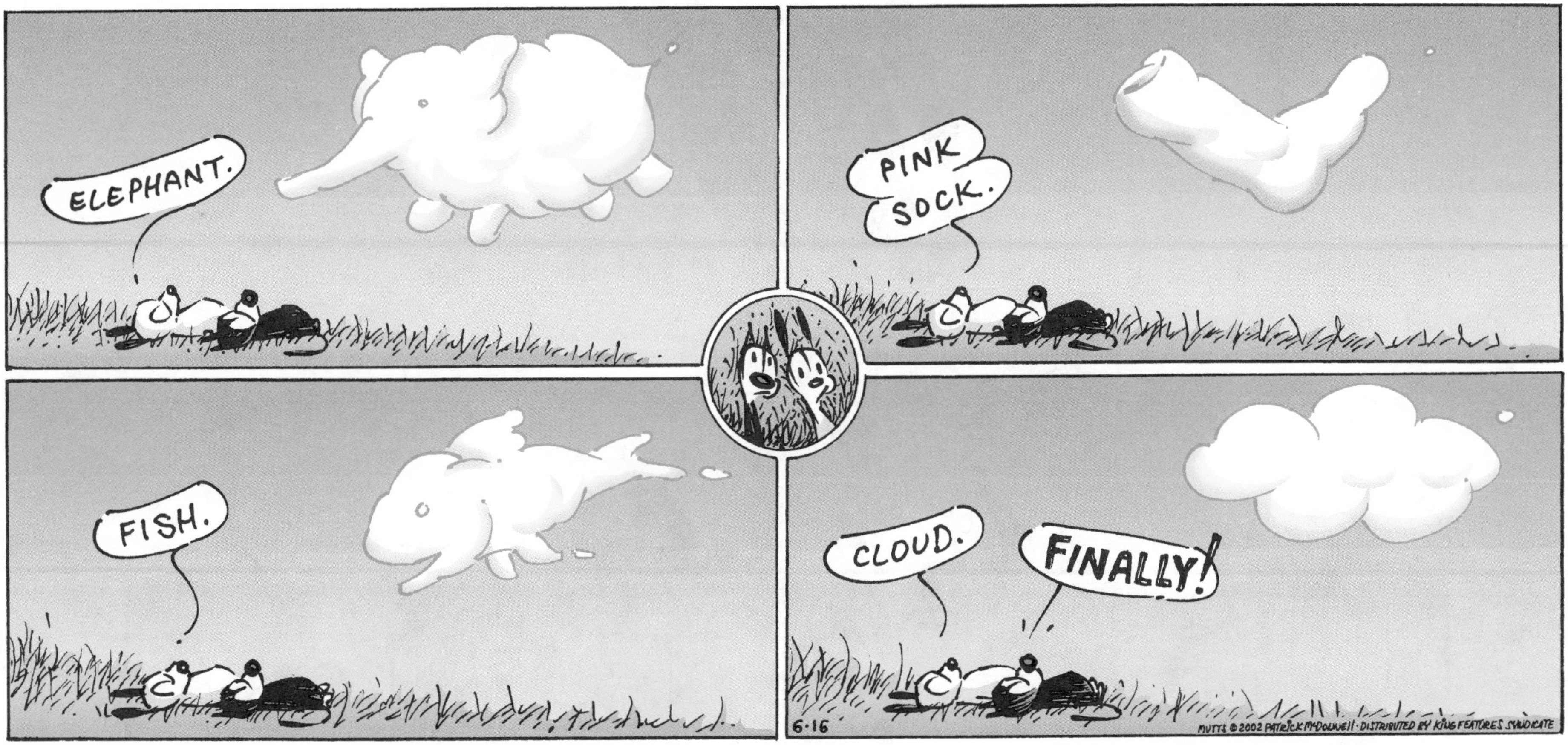
ELEPHANT.
PINK SOCK.
FISH.
CLOUD.
FINALLY!
6·16
MUTTS © 2002 PATRICK McDONNELL · DISTRIBUTED BY KING FEATURES SYNDICATE

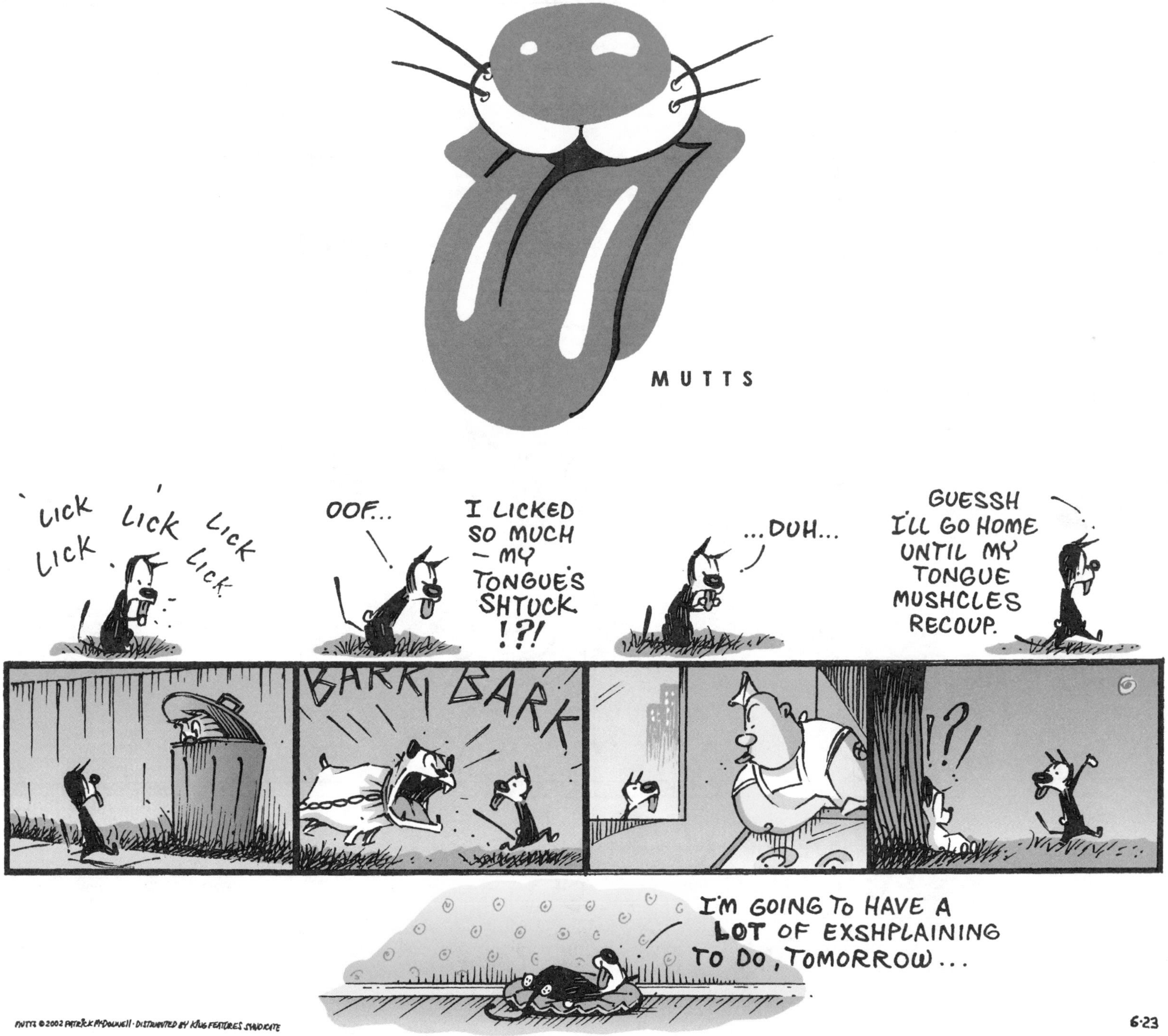
MUTTS
LICK LICK LICK LICK LICK LICK
OOF...
I LICKED SO MUCH — MY TONGUE'S SHTUCK !?!
...DUH...
GUESSH I'LL GO HOME UNTIL MY TONGUE MUSHCLES RECOUP.
BARK BARK
!?!
I'M GOING TO HAVE A LOT OF EXSHPLAINING TO DO, TOMORROW...
MUTTS © 2002 PATRICK McDONNELL · DISTRIBUTED BY KING FEATURES SYNDICATE
6·23

The Mutts Weekly
Patrick McDonnell

EARL, LET'S PLAY HIDE-AND-SHEEK!
O.K.
...7...6...5...
...4...3...
...2...1!
READY OR NOT HERE I COME!
HEY! WHERE'S MY FOOD?
IT'S HIDING.
7·7
MUTTS © 2002 PATRICK McDONNELL · DISTRIBUTED BY KING FEATURES SYNDICATE

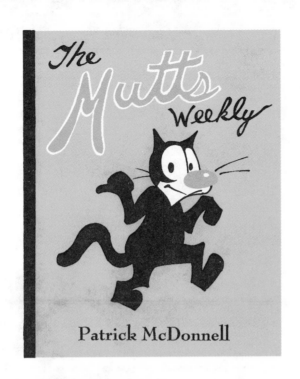

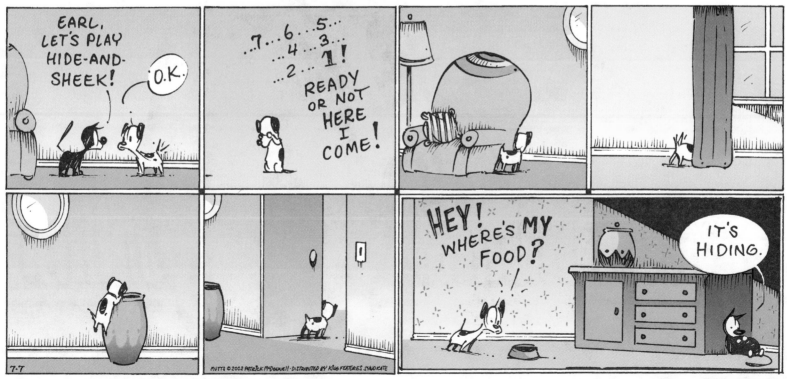

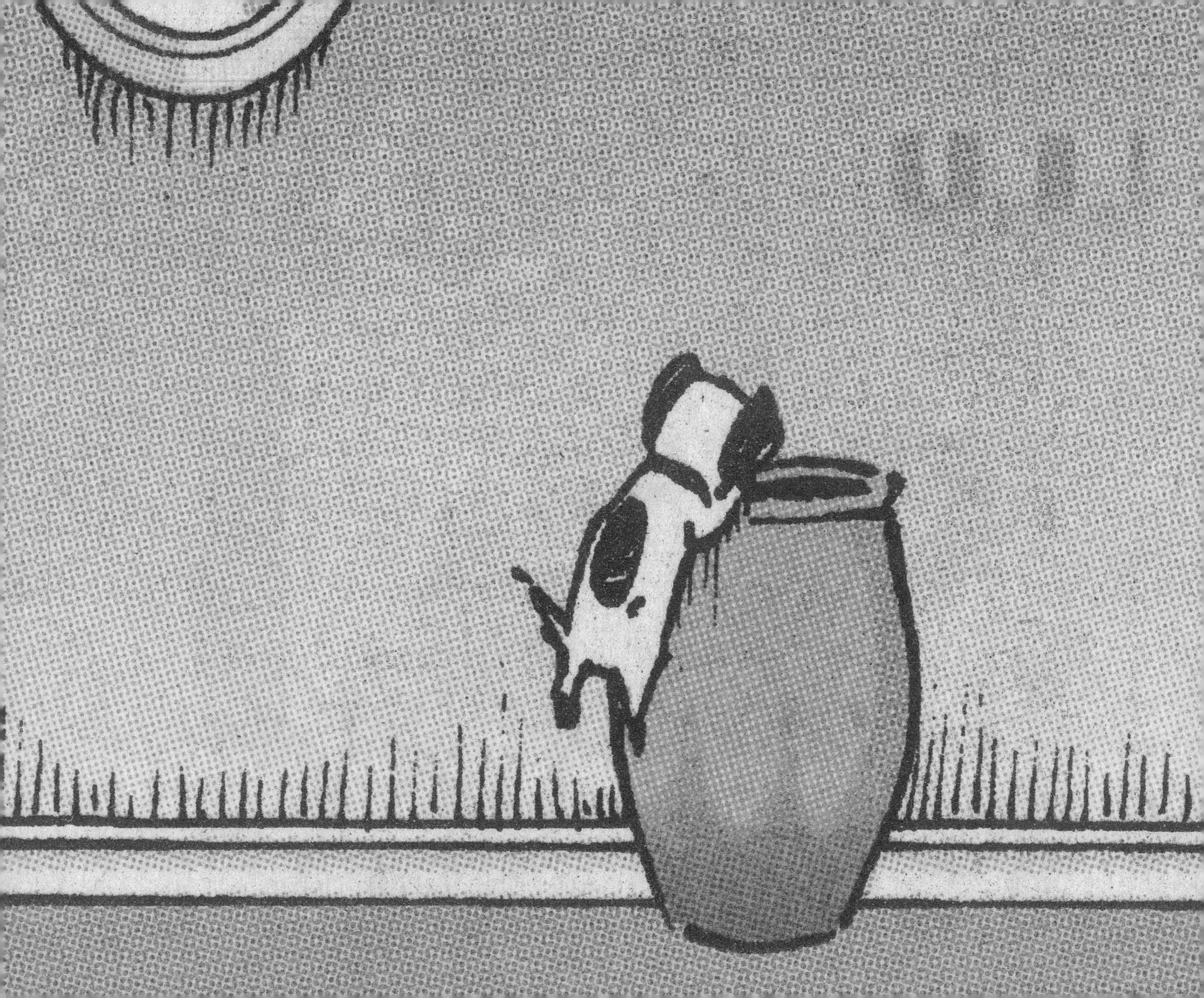

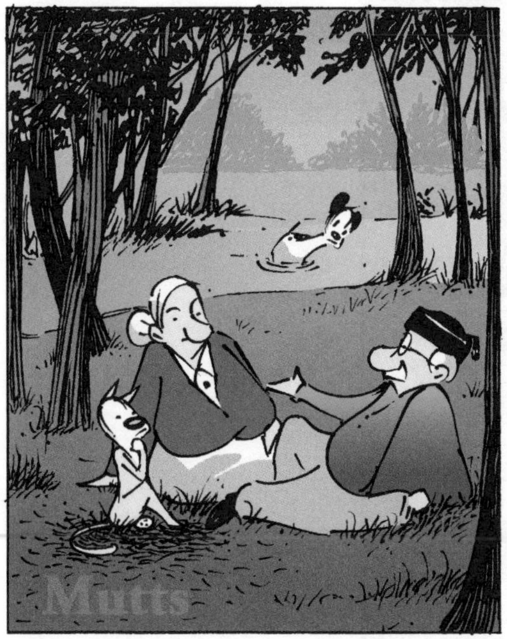
Mutts

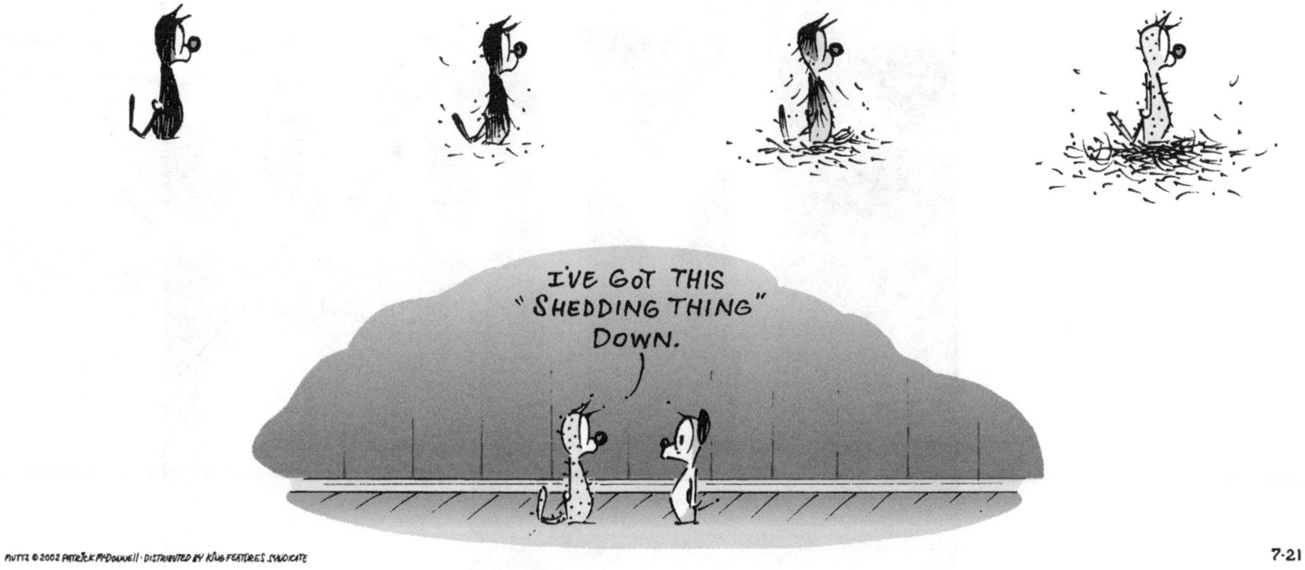
I'VE GOT THIS "SHEDDING THING" DOWN.
MUTTS © 2002 PATRICK McDONNELL · DISTRIBUTED BY KING FEATURES SYNDICATE
7-21

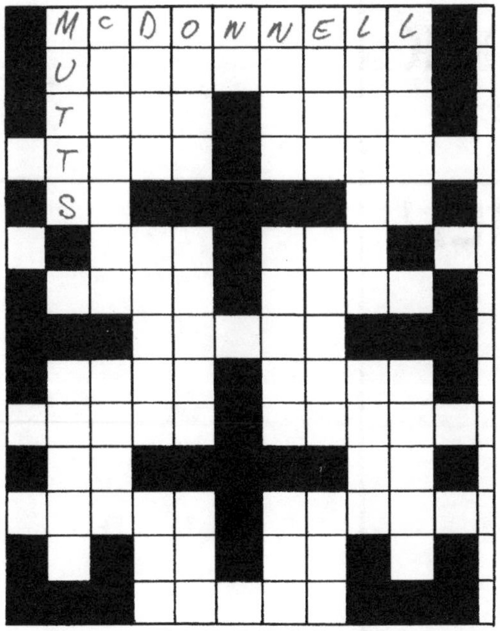
McDONNELL
MUTTS

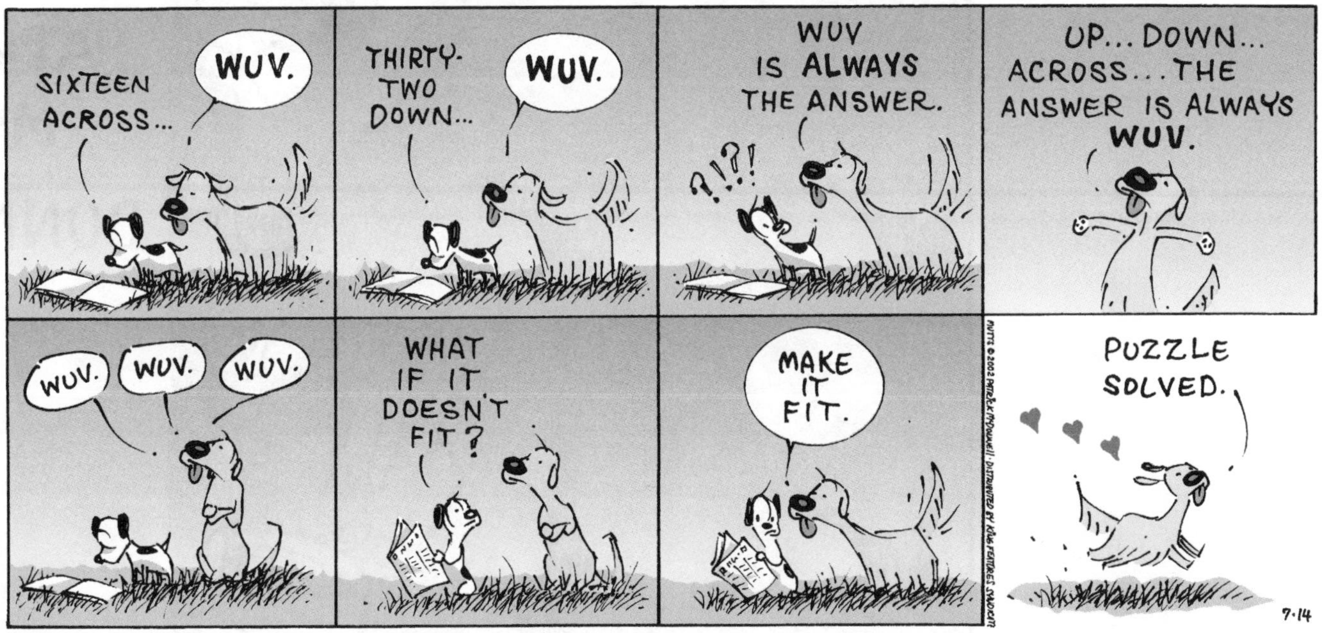
SIXTEEN ACROSS...
WUV.
THIRTY-TWO DOWN...
WUV.
?!?!
WUV IS ALWAYS THE ANSWER.
UP... DOWN... ACROSS... THE ANSWER IS ALWAYS WUV.
WUV.
WUV.
WUV.
WHAT IF IT DOESN'T FIT?
MAKE IT FIT.
MUTTS © 2002 PATRICK McDONNELL · DISTRIBUTED BY KING FEATURES SYNDICATE
PUZZLE SOLVED.
7-14

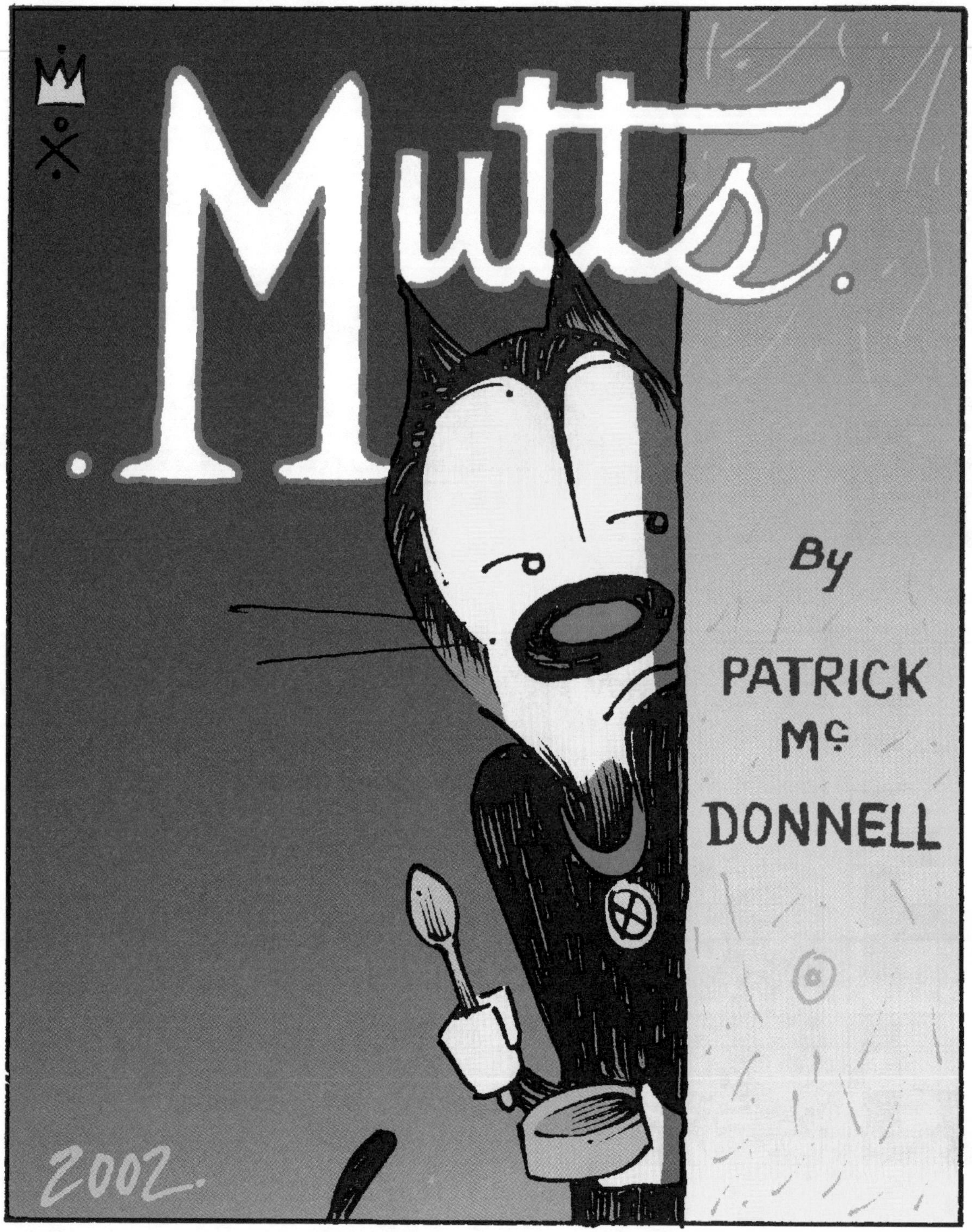

Mutts.
By
PATRICK
Mc
DONNELL
2002.

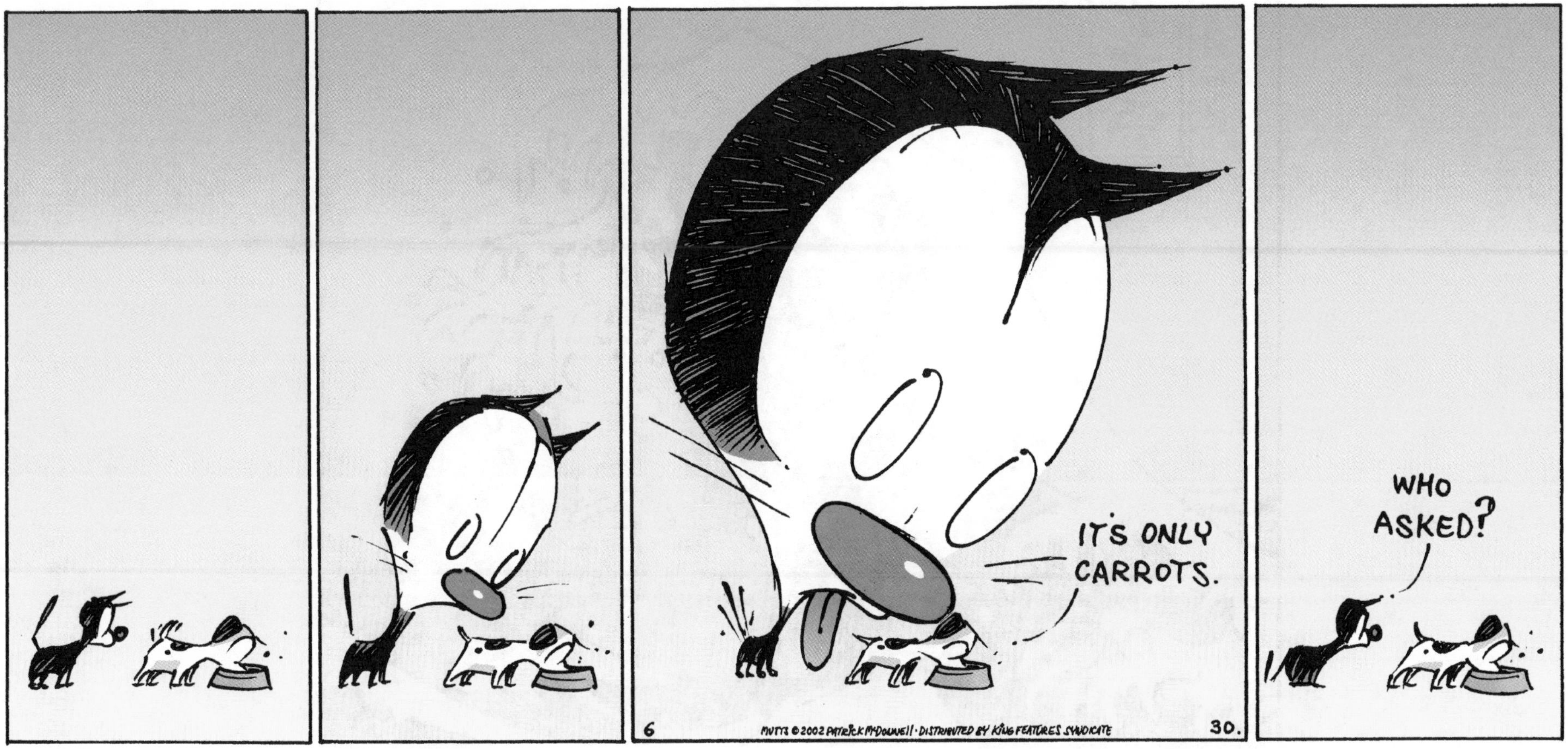
IT'S ONLY CARROTS.
MUTTS © 2002 PATRICK McDONNELL · DISTRIBUTED BY KING FEATURES SYNDICATE
WHO ASKED?

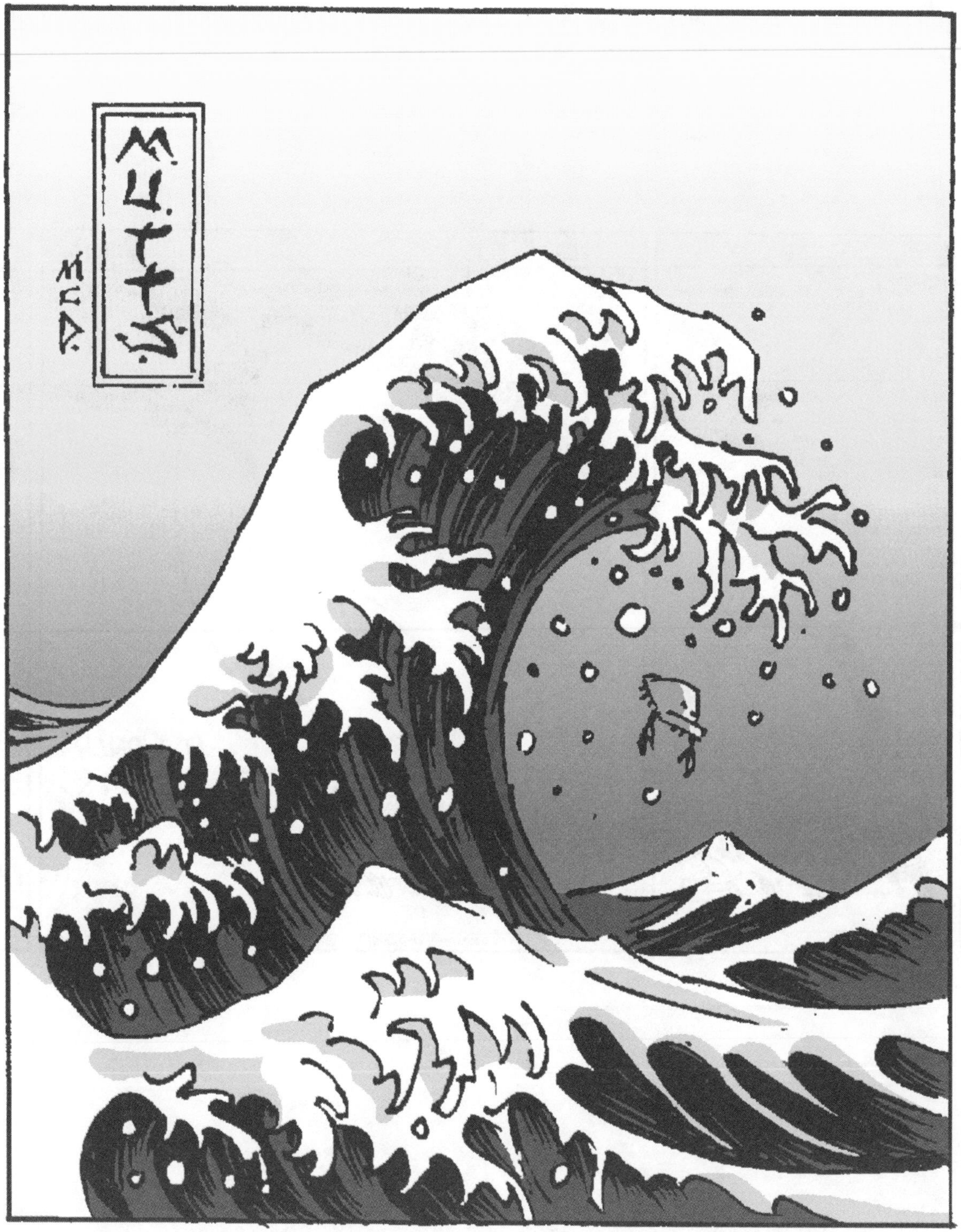
MUTTS
MCD.

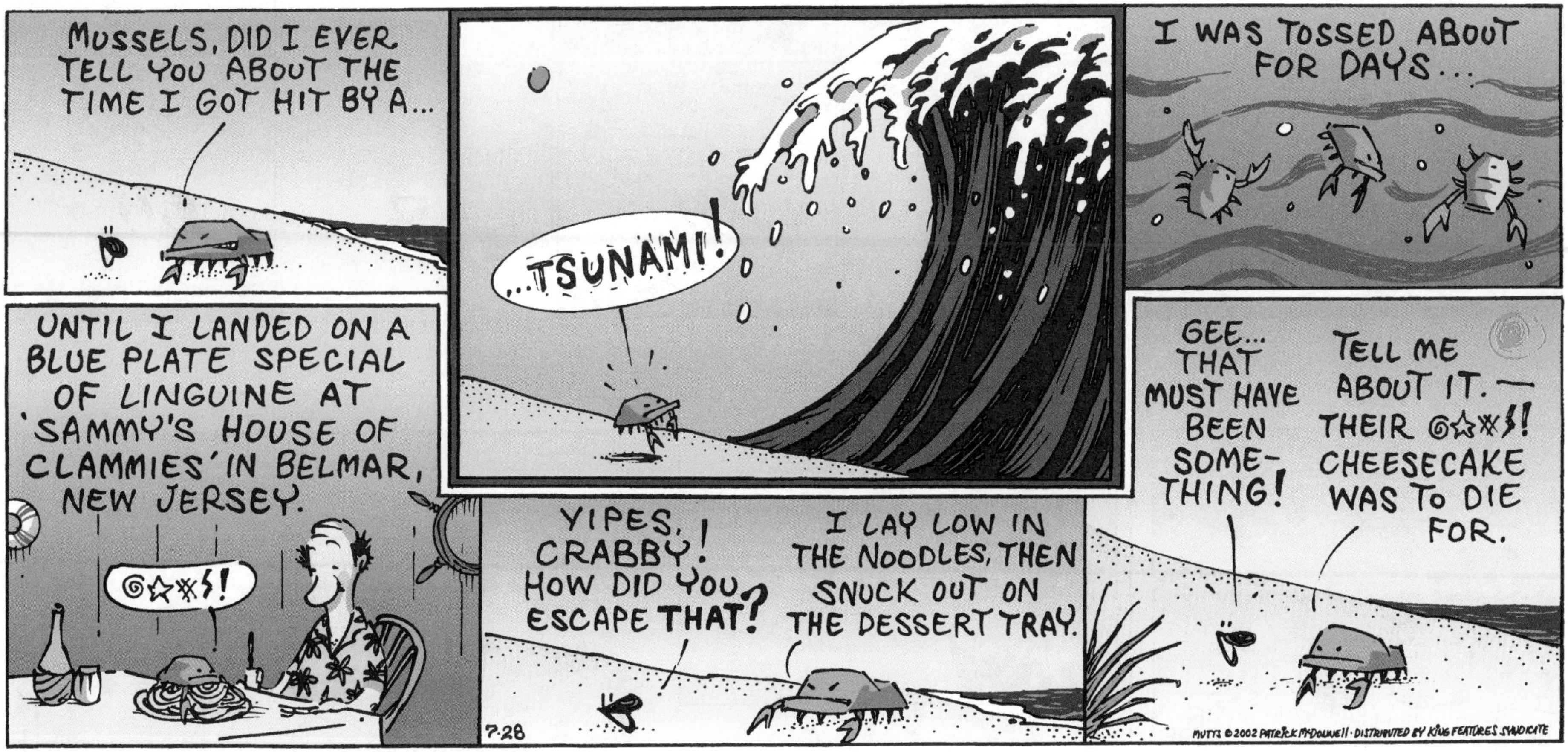
MUSSELS, DID I EVER TELL YOU ABOUT THE TIME I GOT HIT BY A...
...TSUNAMI!
I WAS TOSSED ABOUT FOR DAYS...
UNTIL I LANDED ON A BLUE PLATE SPECIAL OF LINGUINE AT 'SAMMY'S HOUSE OF CLAMMIES' IN BELMAR, NEW JERSEY.
YIPES, CRABBY! HOW DID YOU ESCAPE THAT?
I LAY LOW IN THE NOODLES, THEN SNUCK OUT ON THE DESSERT TRAY.
GEE... THAT MUST HAVE BEEN SOME-THING!
TELL ME ABOUT IT. — THEIR CHEESECAKE WAS TO DIE FOR.
7-28
MUTTS © 2002 PATRICK McDONNELL · DISTRIBUTED BY KING FEATURES SYNDICATE

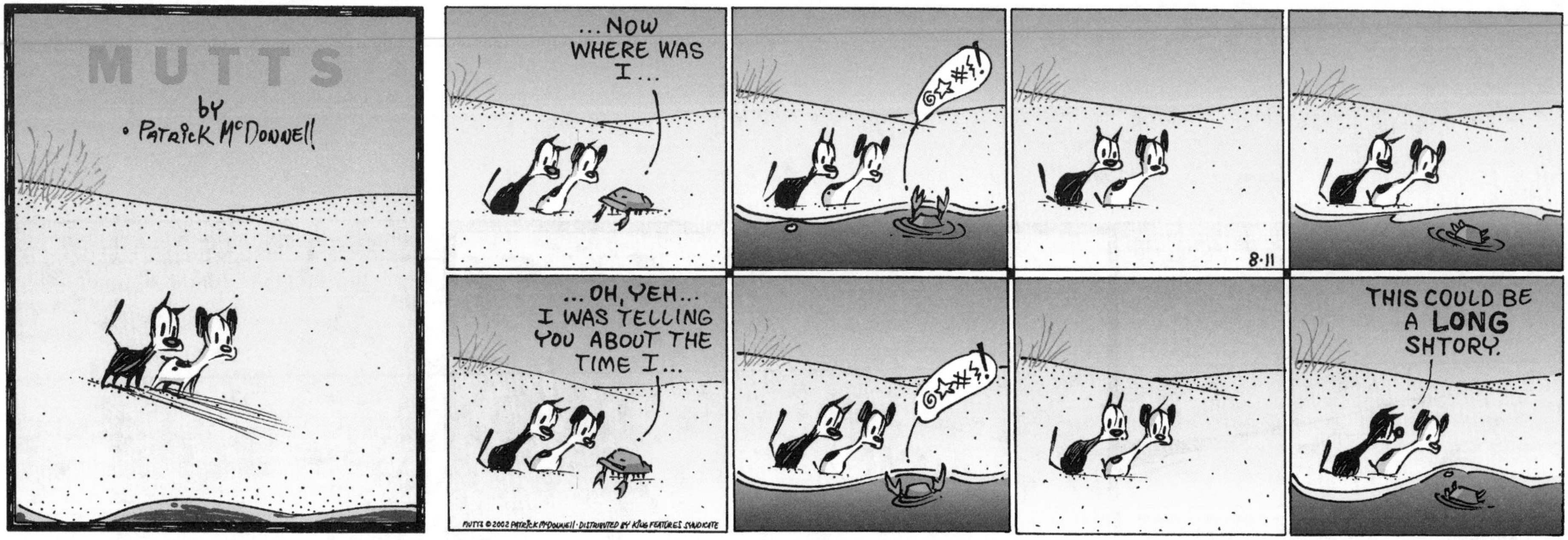
MUTTS
by
Patrick McDonnell
...NOW WHERE WAS I...
8·11
...OH, YEH... I WAS TELLING YOU ABOUT THE TIME I...
THIS COULD BE A **LONG** SHTORY.
MUTTS © 2002 PATRICK McDONNELL · DISTRIBUTED BY KING FEATURES SYNDICATE

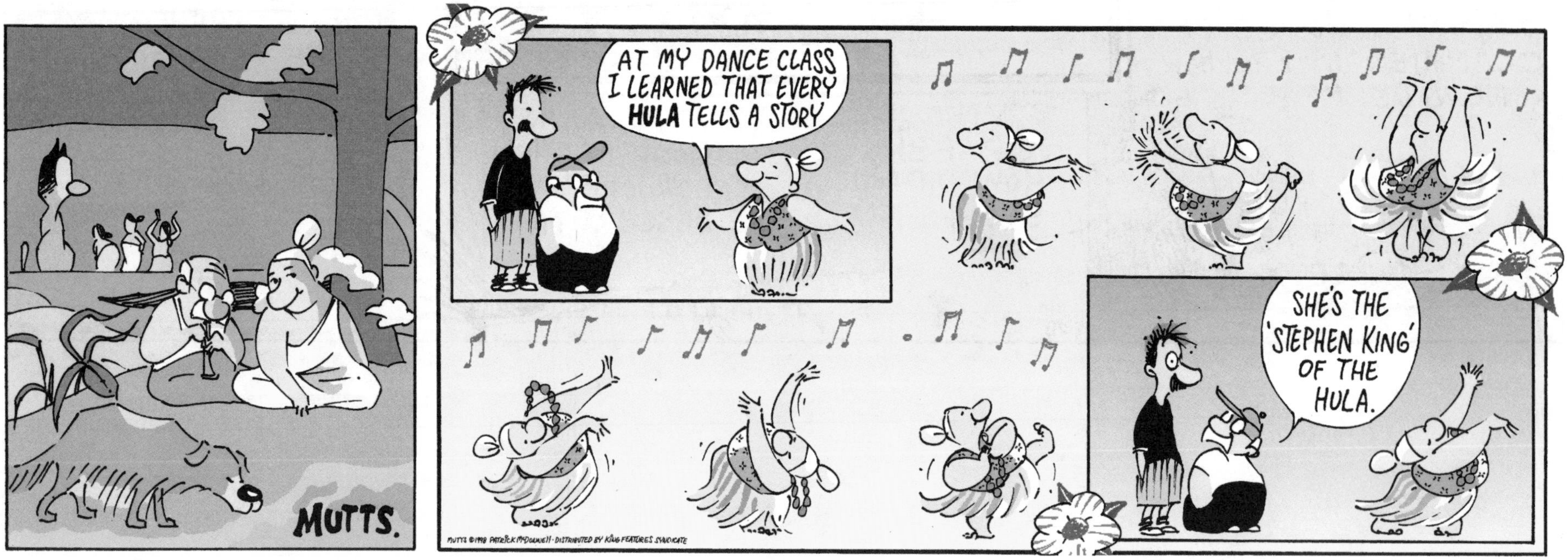
MUTTS.
AT MY DANCE CLASS I LEARNED THAT EVERY **HULA** TELLS A STORY
SHE'S THE 'STEPHEN KING' OF THE HULA.
MUTTS © 1998 PATRICK McDONNELL · DISTRIBUTED BY KING FEATURES SYNDICATE

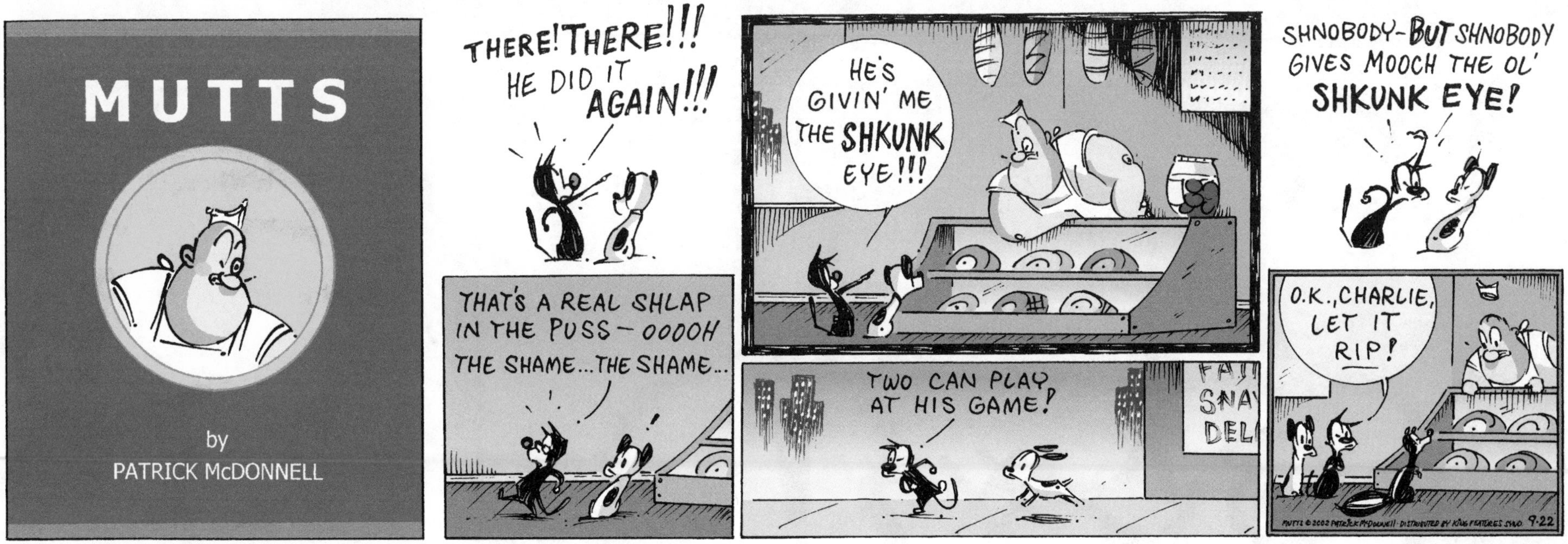
MUTTS
by
PATRICK McDONNELL
THERE! THERE!!! HE DID IT AGAIN!!!
HE'S GIVIN' ME THE SHKUNK EYE!!!
SHNOBODY–BUT SHNOBODY GIVES MOOCH THE OL' SHKUNK EYE!
THAT'S A REAL SHLAP IN THE PUSS–OOOOH THE SHAME...THE SHAME...
TWO CAN PLAY AT HIS GAME!
FA... SNA... DEL...
O.K., CHARLIE, LET IT RIP!
MUTTS © 2002 PATRICK McDONNELL · DISTRIBUTED BY KING FEATURES SYND 9·22

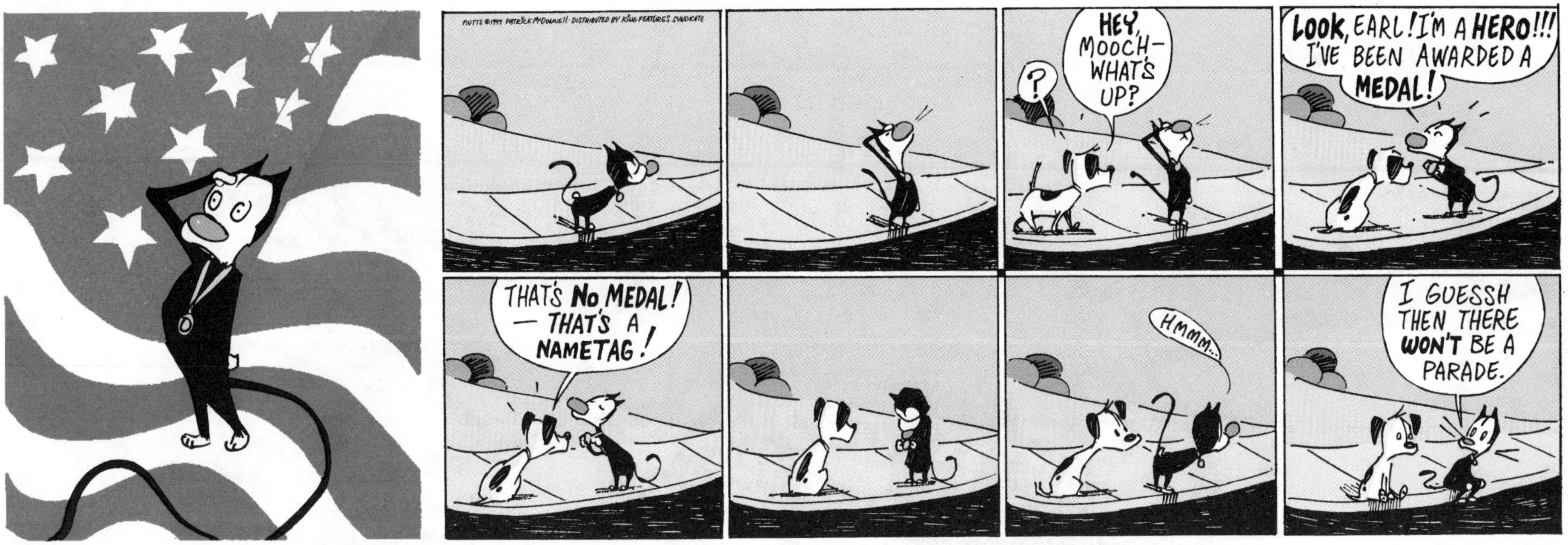
MUTTS ©1997 PATRICK McDONNELL · DISTRIBUTED BY KING FEATURES SYNDICATE
?
HEY, MOOCH– WHAT'S UP?
LOOK, EARL! I'M A HERO!!! I'VE BEEN AWARDED A MEDAL!
THAT'S NO MEDAL! –THAT'S A NAMETAG!
HMMM...
I GUESSH THEN THERE WON'T BE A PARADE.

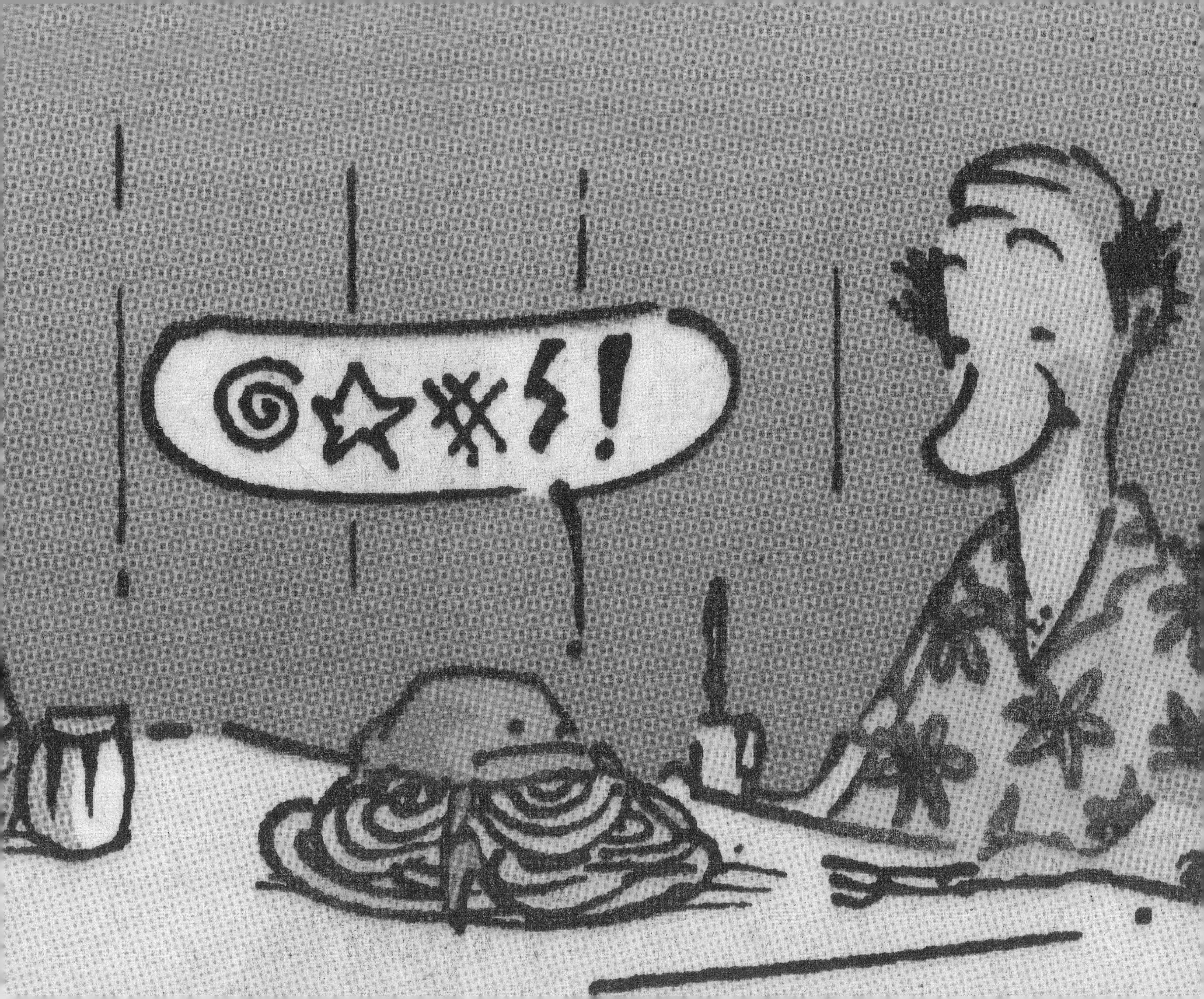

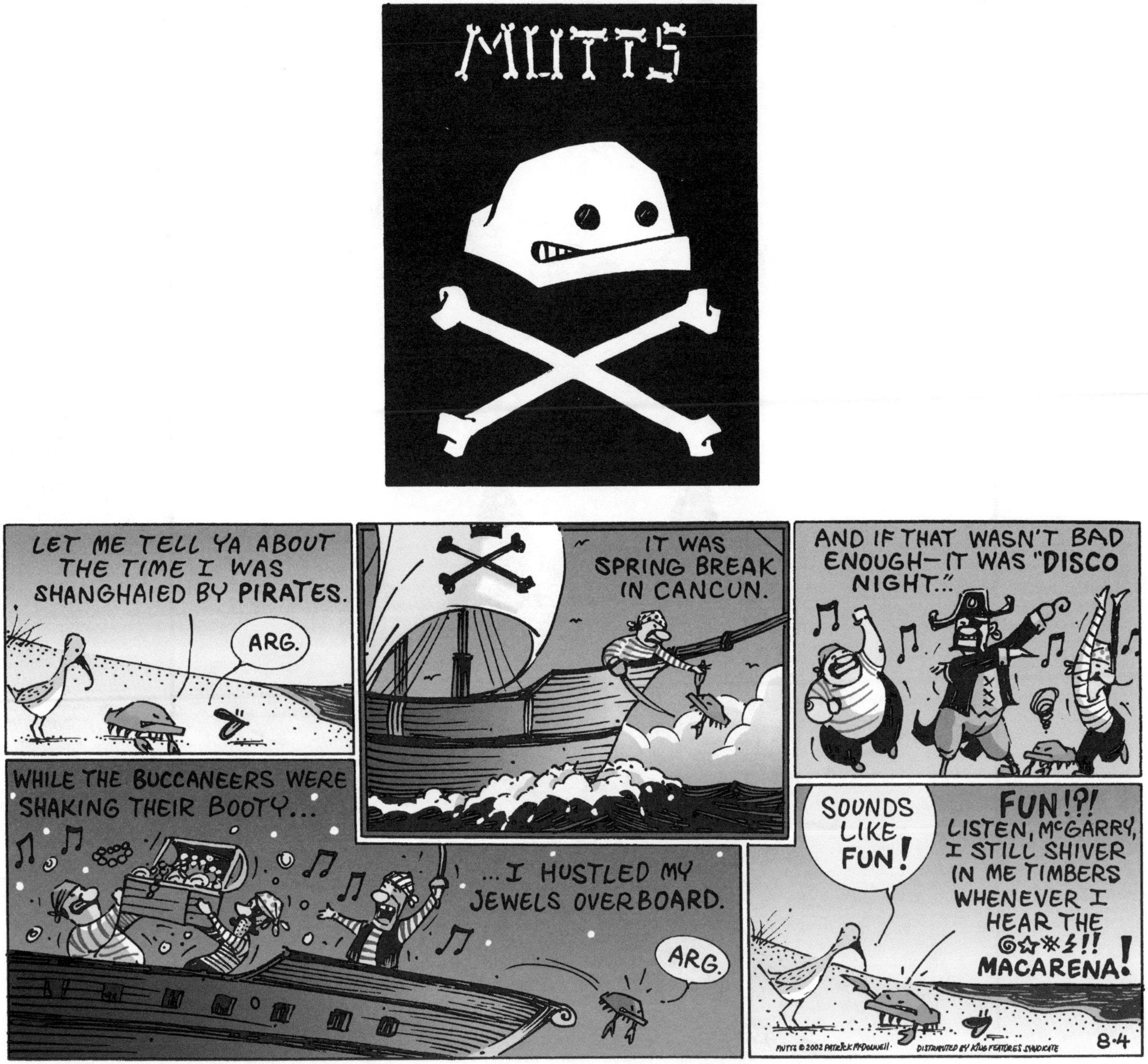
MUTTS
LET ME TELL YA ABOUT THE TIME I WAS SHANGHAIED BY PIRATES.
ARG.
IT WAS SPRING BREAK IN CANCUN.
AND IF THAT WASN'T BAD ENOUGH— IT WAS "DISCO NIGHT."
WHILE THE BUCCANEERS WERE SHAKING THEIR BOOTY...
...I HUSTLED MY JEWELS OVERBOARD.
ARG.
SOUNDS LIKE FUN!
FUN!?!
LISTEN, McGARRY, I STILL SHIVER IN ME TIMBERS WHENEVER I HEAR THE @☆*ϟ!! MACARENA!
MUTTS © 2002 PATRICK McDONNELL · DISTRIBUTED BY KING FEATURES SYNDICATE
8·4

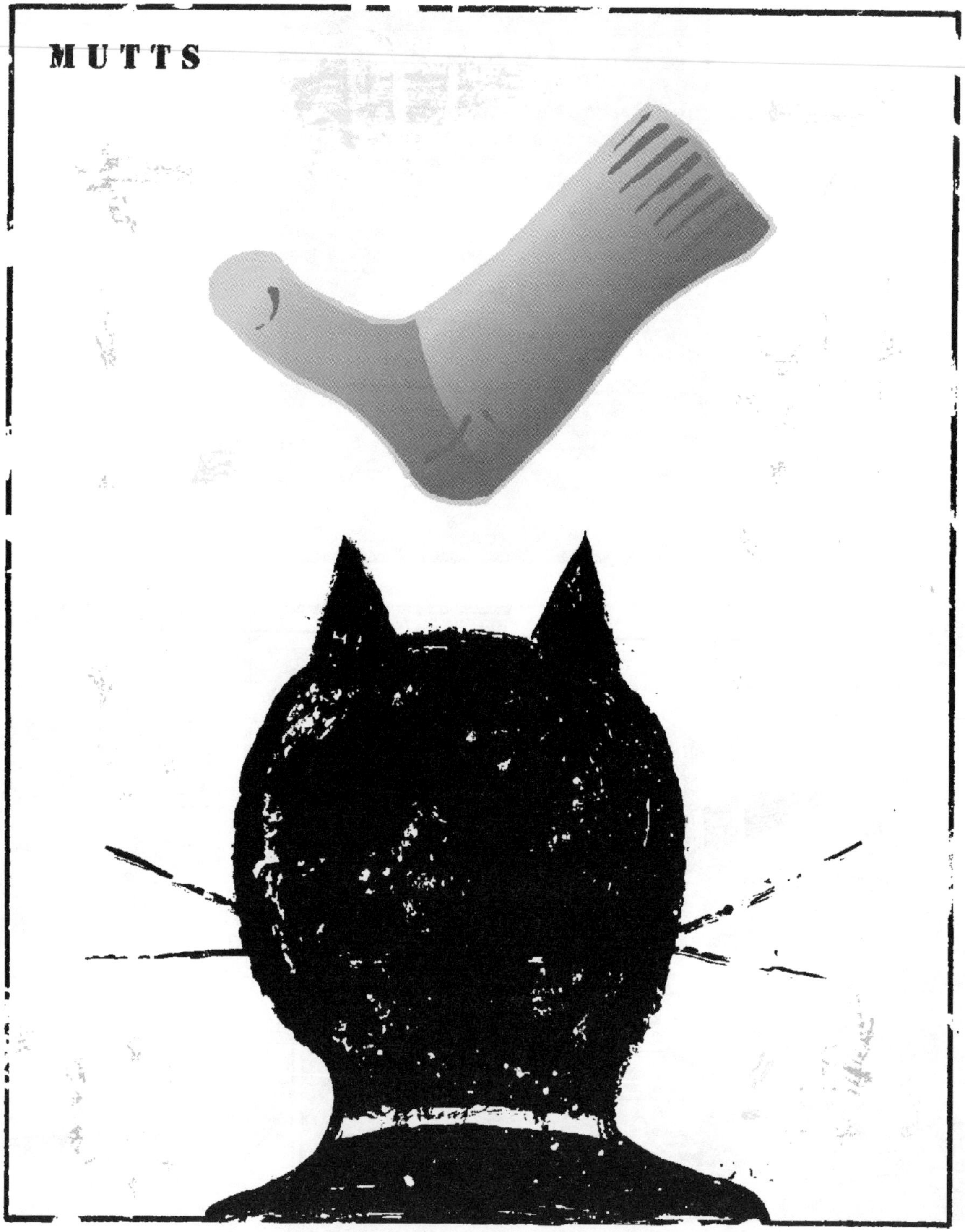
MUTTS

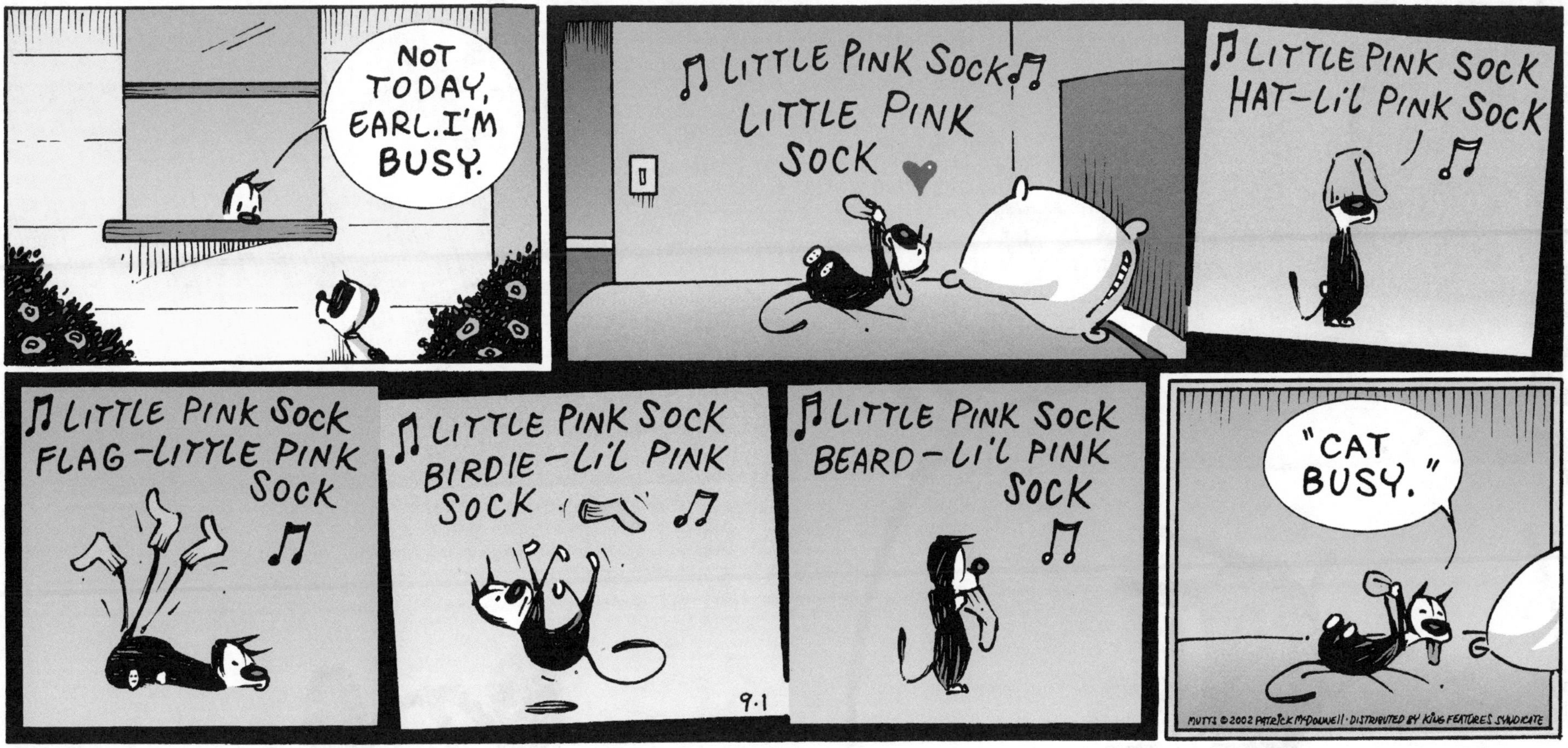
NOT TODAY, EARL. I'M BUSY.
♫ LITTLE PINK SOCK ♫ LITTLE PINK SOCK
♫ LITTLE PINK SOCK HAT—LI'L PINK SOCK ♫
♫ LITTLE PINK SOCK FLAG—LITTLE PINK SOCK ♫
♫ LITTLE PINK SOCK BIRDIE—LI'L PINK SOCK ♫
9·1
♫ LITTLE PINK SOCK BEARD—LI'L PINK SOCK ♫
"CAT BUSY."
MUTTS © 2002 PATRICK McDONNELL · DISTRIBUTED BY KING FEATURES SYNDICATE

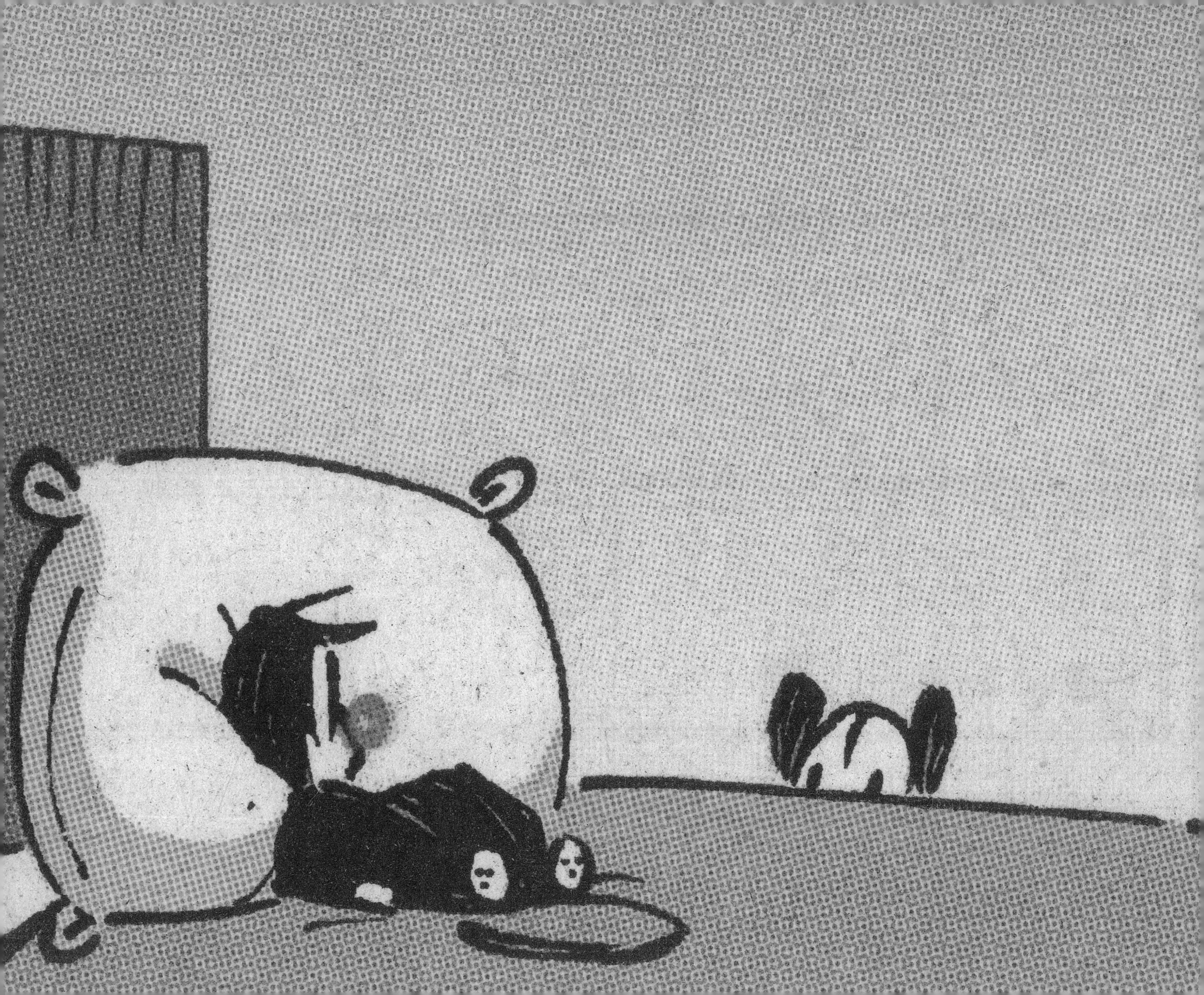

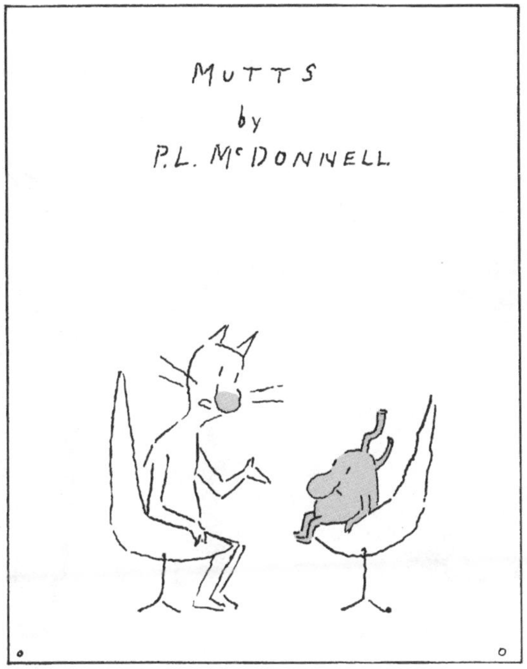
MUTTS
by
P.L. McDONNELL

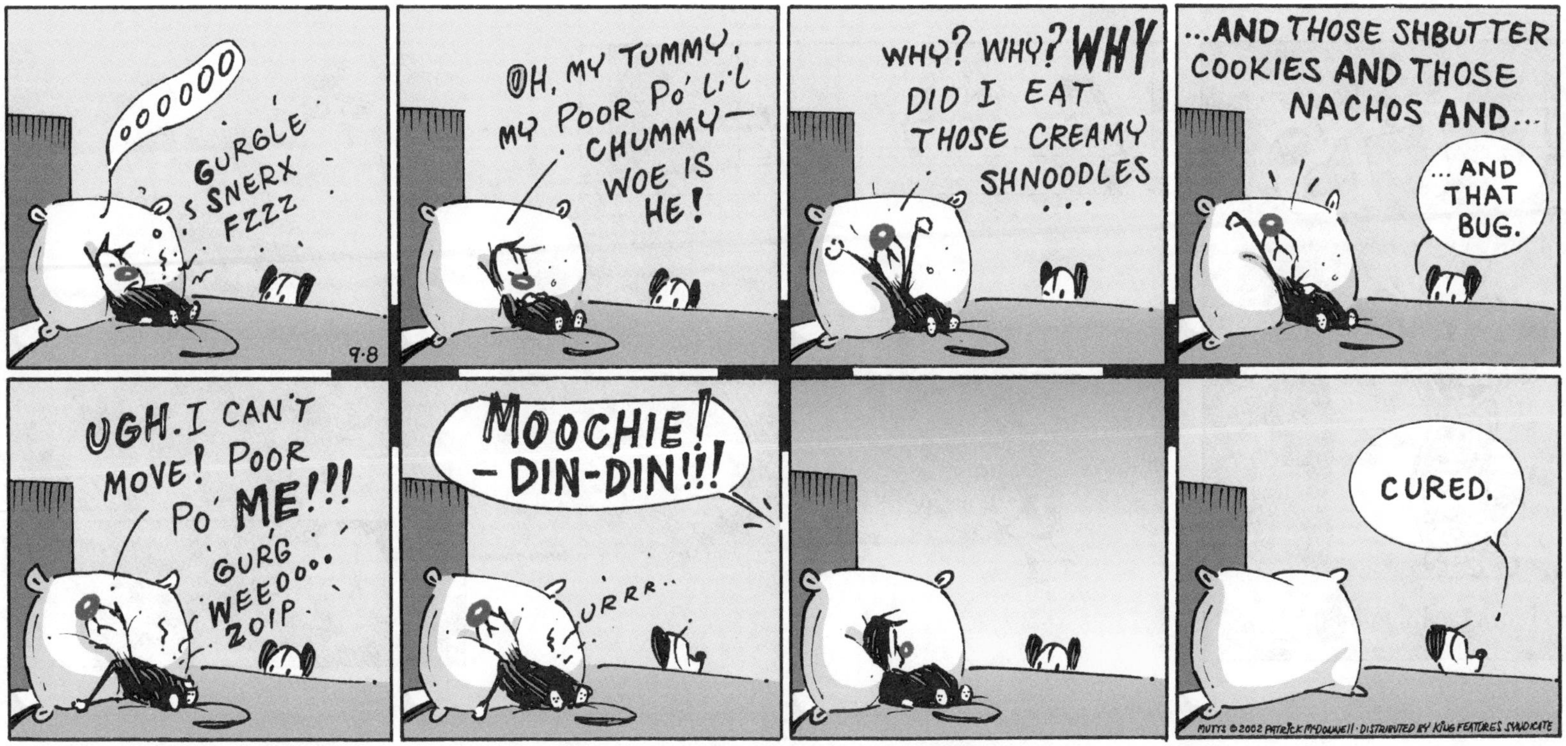
OOOOOO
GURGLE
SNERX
FZZZ
9·8
OH, MY TUMMY, MY POOR PO' LI'L CHUMMY—
WOE IS HE!
WHY? WHY? WHY DID I EAT THOSE CREAMY SHNOODLES . . .
...AND THOSE SHBUTTER COOKIES AND THOSE NACHOS AND...
...AND THAT BUG.
UGH. I CAN'T MOVE! POOR PO' ME!!!
GURG
WEEOOOO
ZOIP
MOOCHIE! —DIN-DIN!!!
URRR..
CURED.
MUTTS © 2002 PATRICK McDONNELL · DISTRIBUTED BY KING FEATURES SYNDICATE

PATRICK McDONNELL

MUTTS

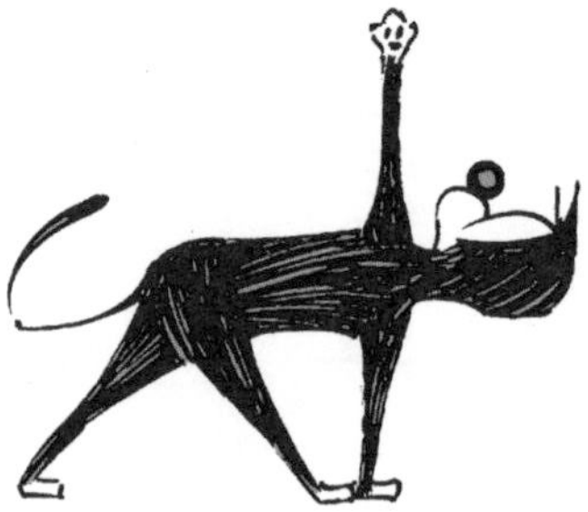

*with **earl** and **mooch***

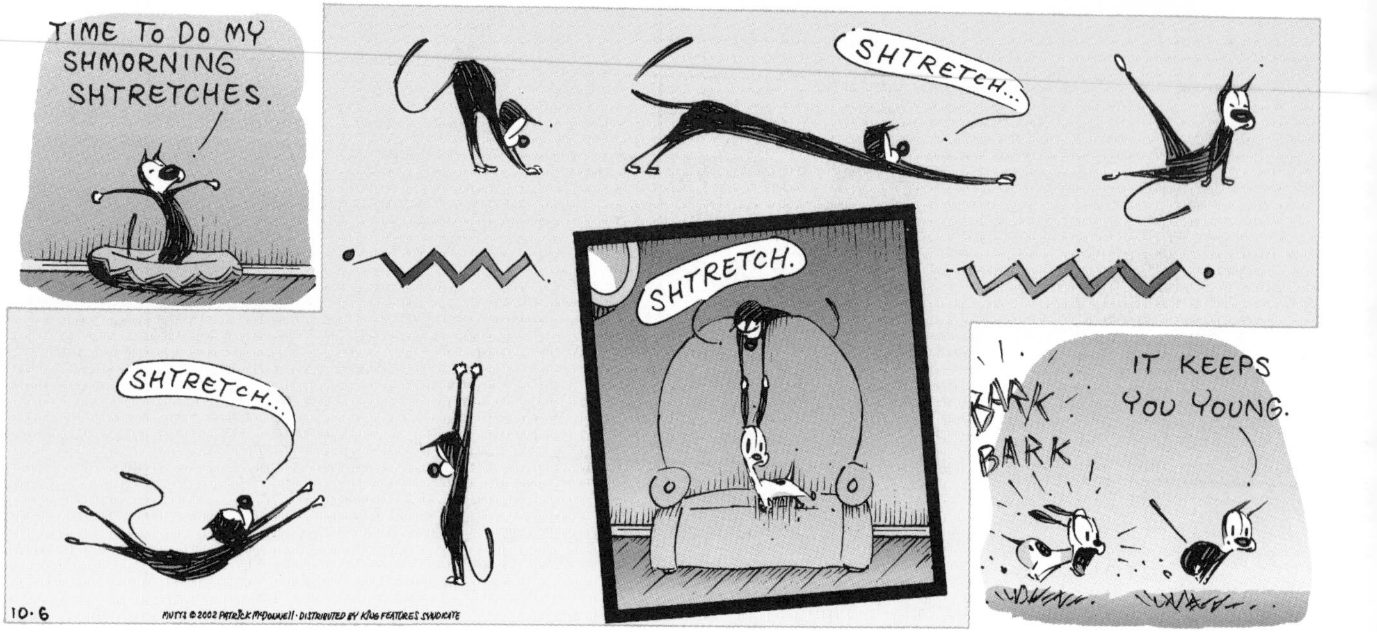

TIME TO DO MY SHMORNING SHTRETCHES.
SHTRETCH...
SHTRETCH...
SHTRETCH.
BARK BARK
IT KEEPS YOU YOUNG.
10·6
MUTTS © 2002 PATRICK McDONNELL · DISTRIBUTED BY KING FEATURES SYNDICATE

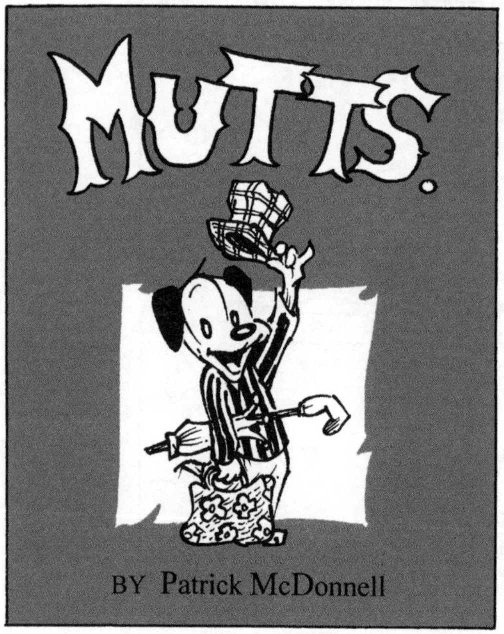

MUTTS.
BY Patrick McDonnell

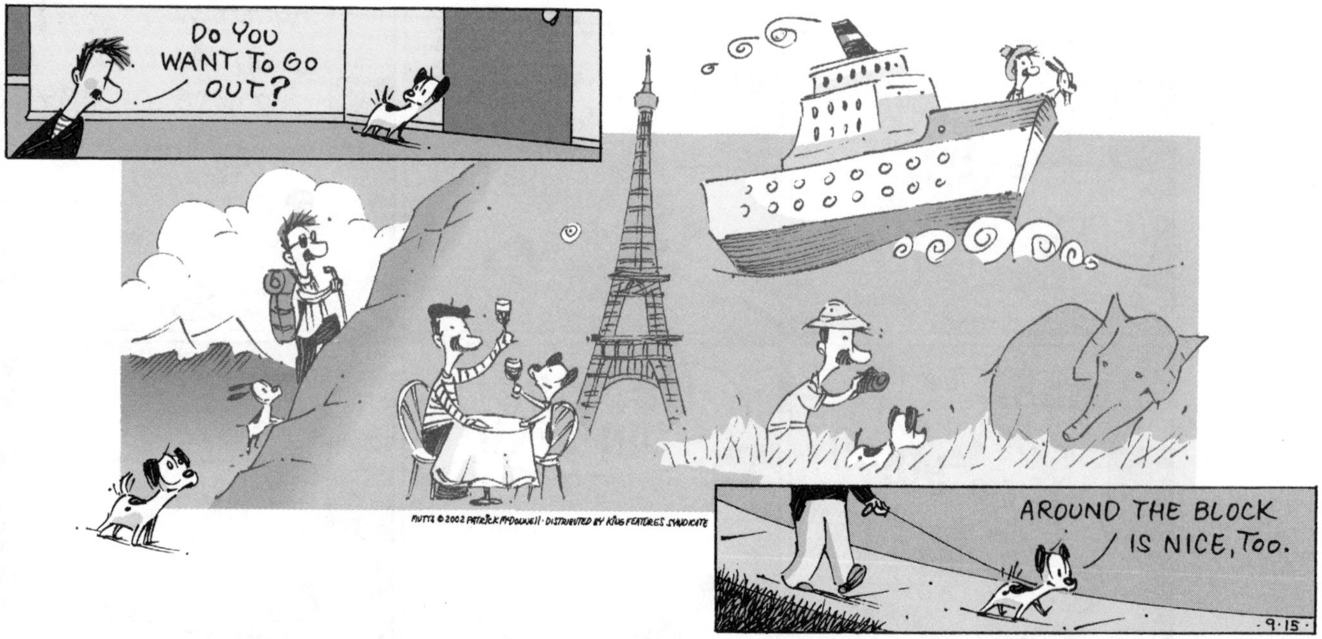

DO YOU WANT TO GO OUT?
MUTTS © 2002 PATRICK McDONNELL · DISTRIBUTED BY KING FEATURES SYNDICATE
AROUND THE BLOCK IS NICE, TOO.
·9·15·

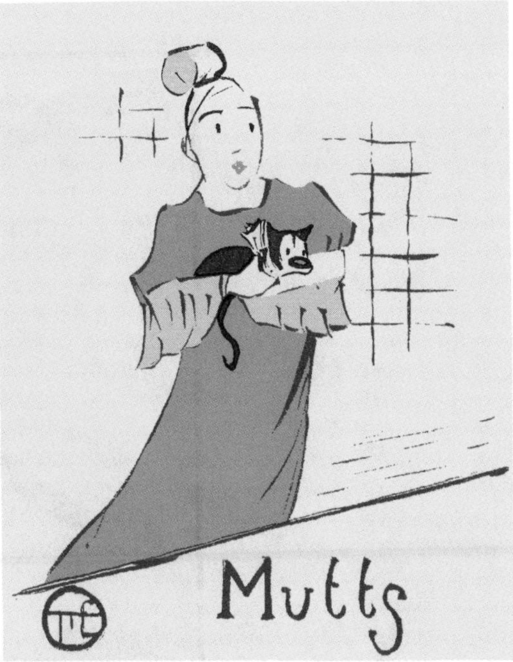
Mutts

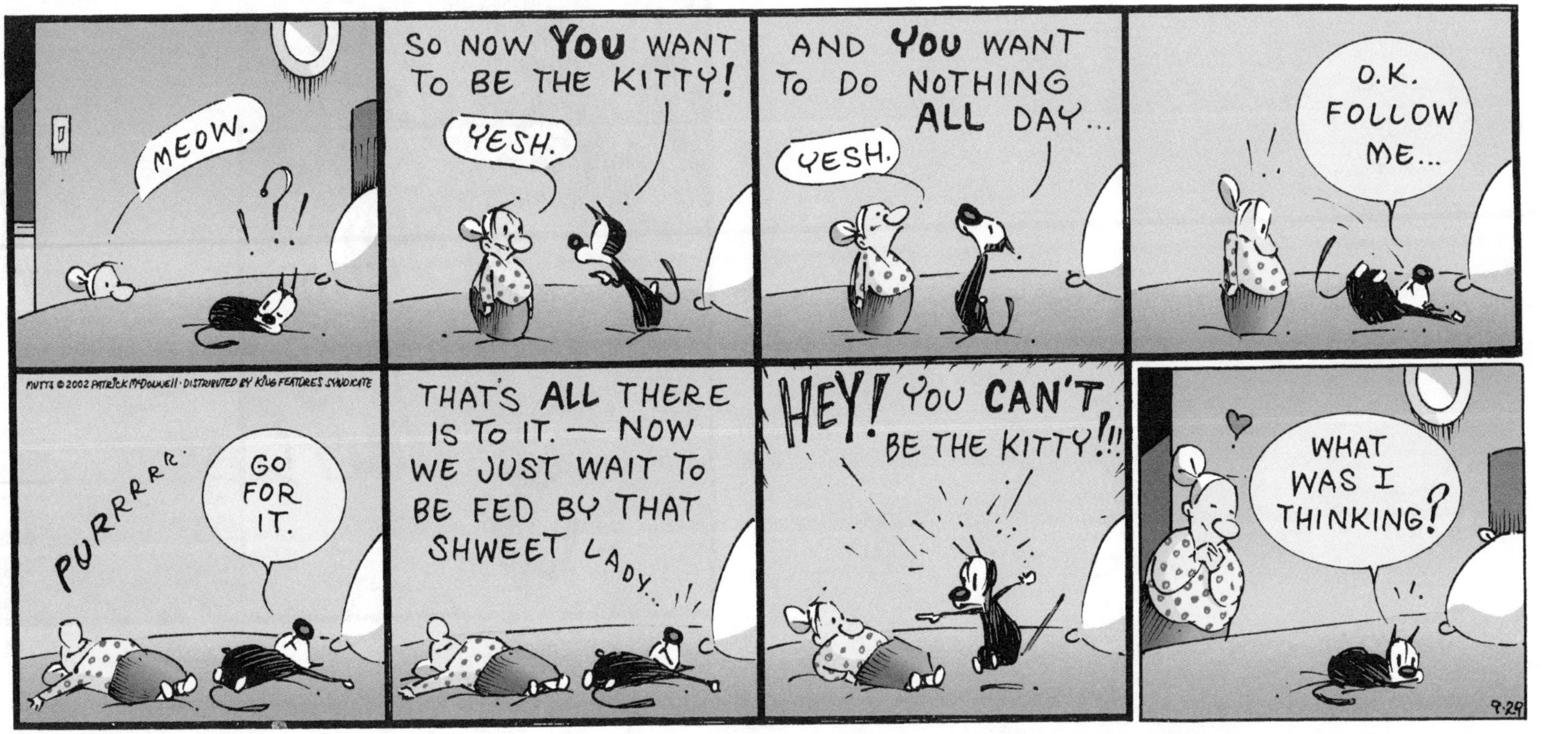
MEOW.
SO NOW YOU WANT TO BE THE KITTY!
YESH.
AND YOU WANT TO DO NOTHING ALL DAY...
YESH.
O.K. FOLLOW ME...
MUTTS © 2002 PATRICK McDONNELL · DISTRIBUTED BY KING FEATURES SYNDICATE
PURRRRR.
GO FOR IT.
THAT'S ALL THERE IS TO IT. — NOW WE JUST WAIT TO BE FED BY THAT SHWEET LADY...
HEY! YOU CAN'T BE THE KITTY!!!
WHAT WAS I THINKING?
9·29

MUTTS

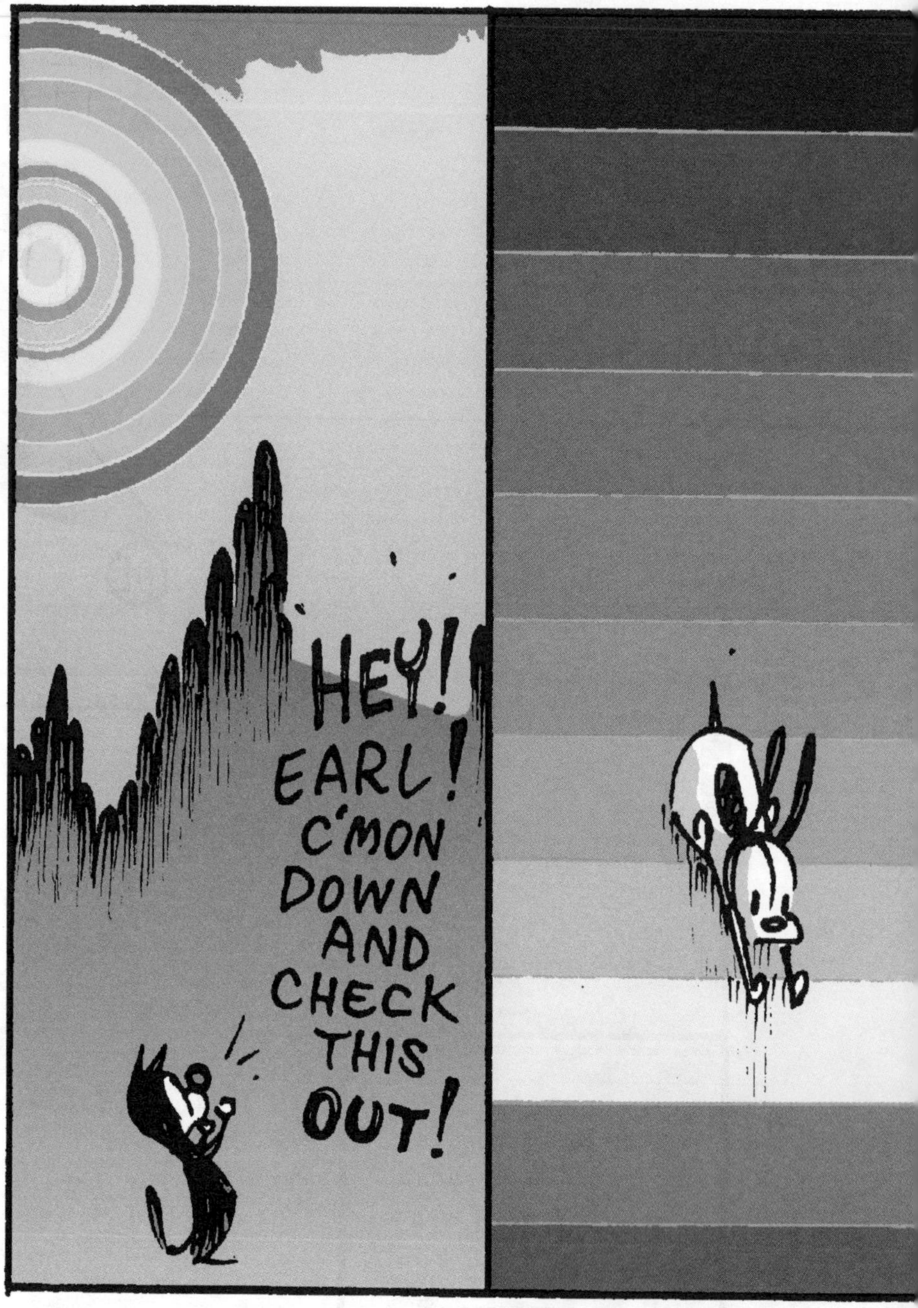
HEY! EARL! C'MON DOWN AND CHECK THIS OUT!

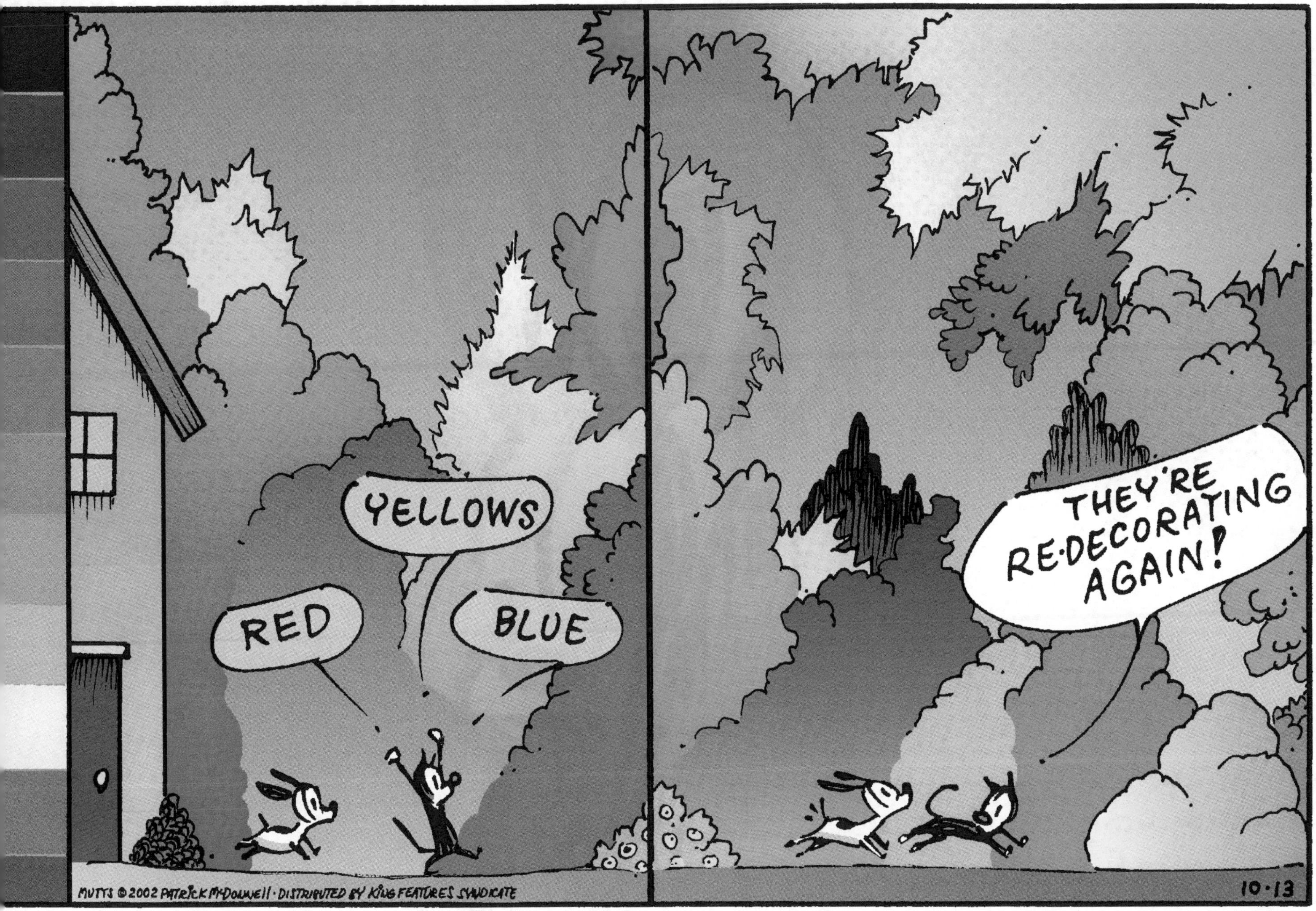
YELLOWS
RED
BLUE
THEY'RE RE·DECORATING AGAIN!
MUTTS © 2002 PATRICK McDONNELL · DISTRIBUTED BY KING FEATURES SYNDICATE
10·13

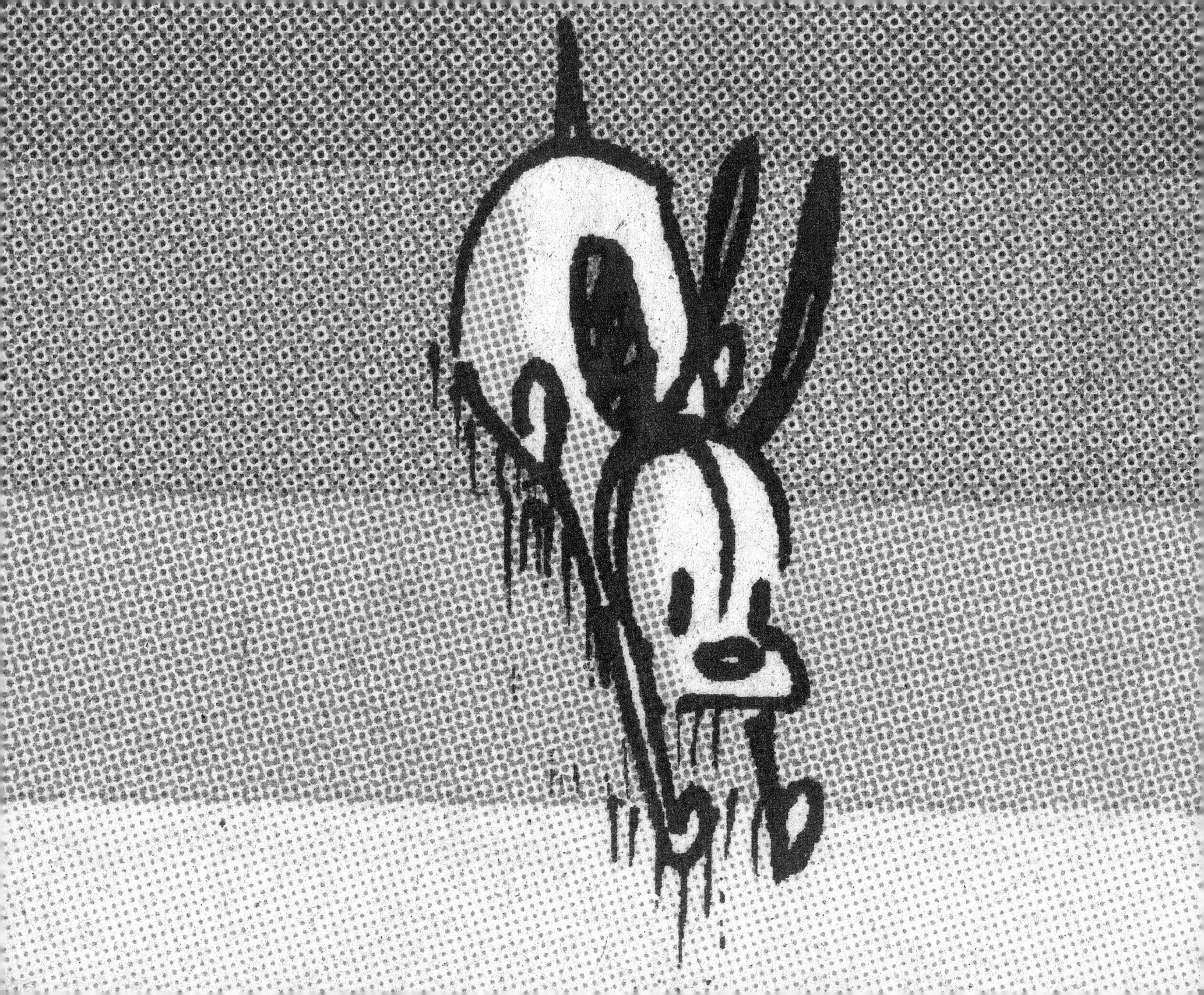

M U T T S

MUTTS
OOPS.
BONK
OOPS.
BONK
OOPS.
BONK
OOPS.
BONK
OOPS.
BONK
BONK
JUST CALL ME
"BUTTERFINGERS."
MUTTS © 2002 PATRICK McDONNELL · DISTRIBUTED BY KING FEATURES SYNDICATE
10·20

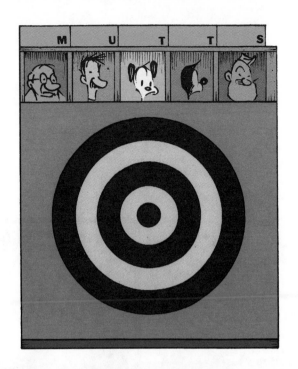

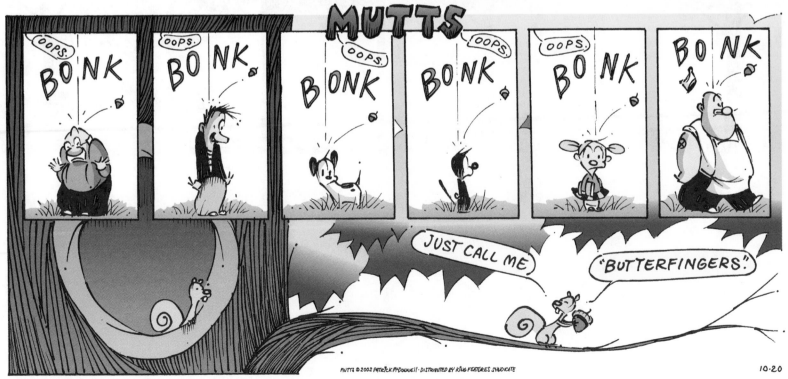

MUTTS
AAAHCHOO
BLESSH YOU.
MUTTS © 2002 PATRICK McDONNELL · DISTRIBUTED BY KING FEATURES SYNDICATE
11-10

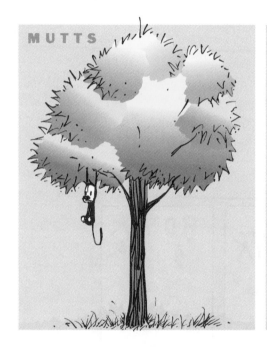

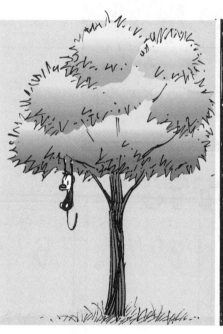

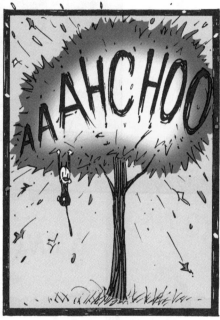

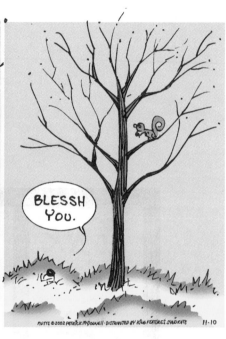

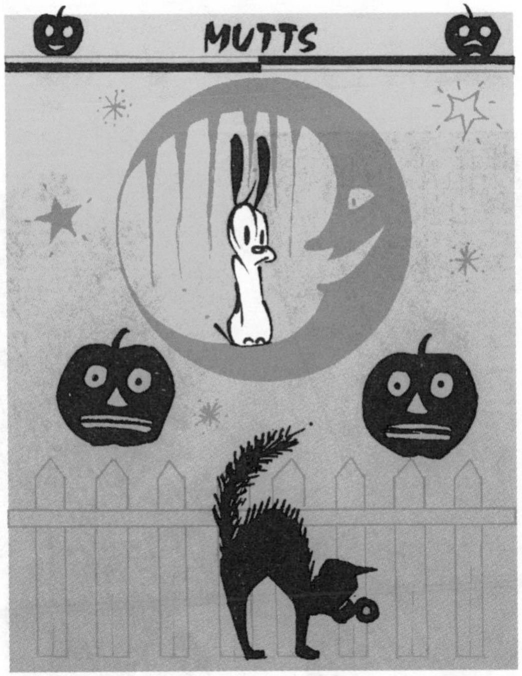
MUTTS

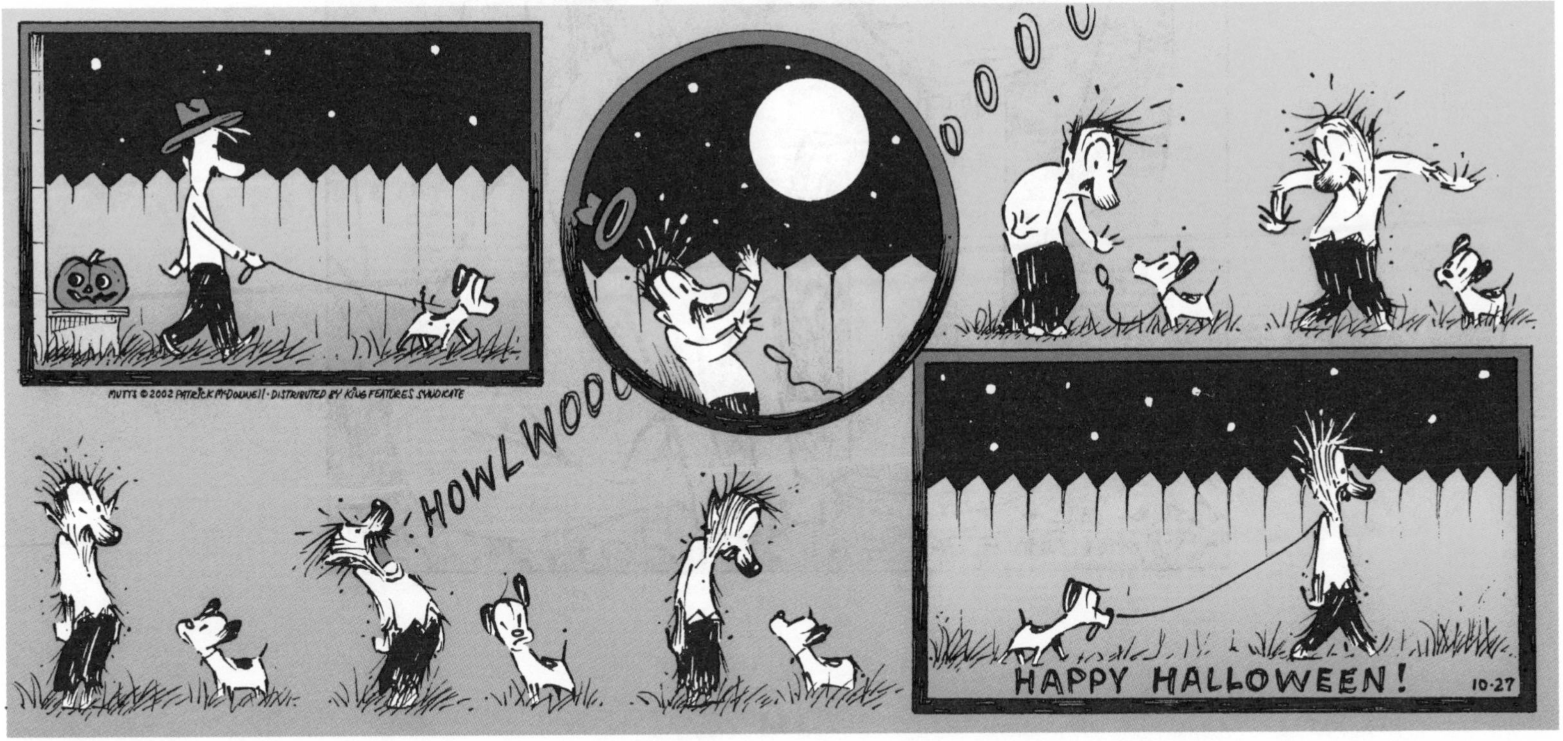
MUTTS © 2002 PATRICK McDONNELL · DISTRIBUTED BY KING FEATURES SYNDICATE
HOWLWOOO
HAPPY HALLOWEEN!
10-27

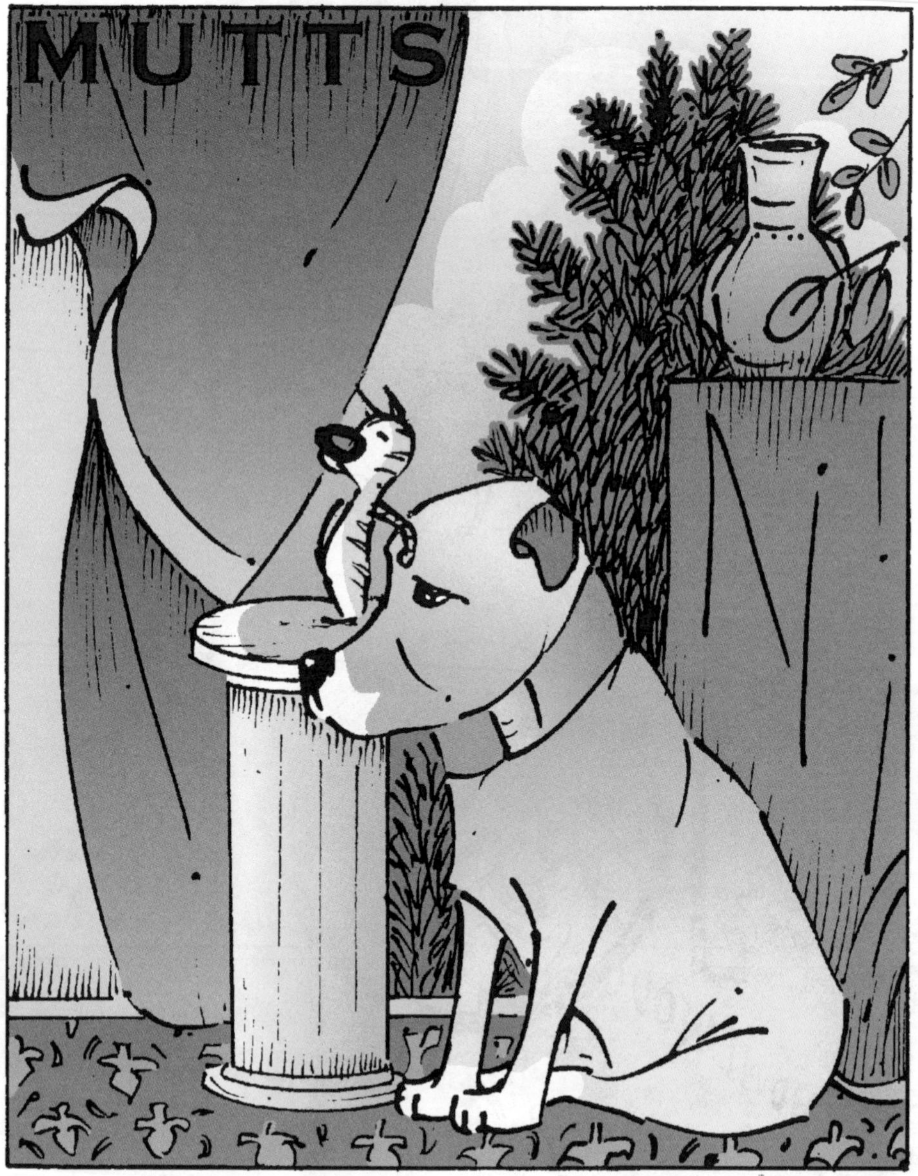
MUTTS

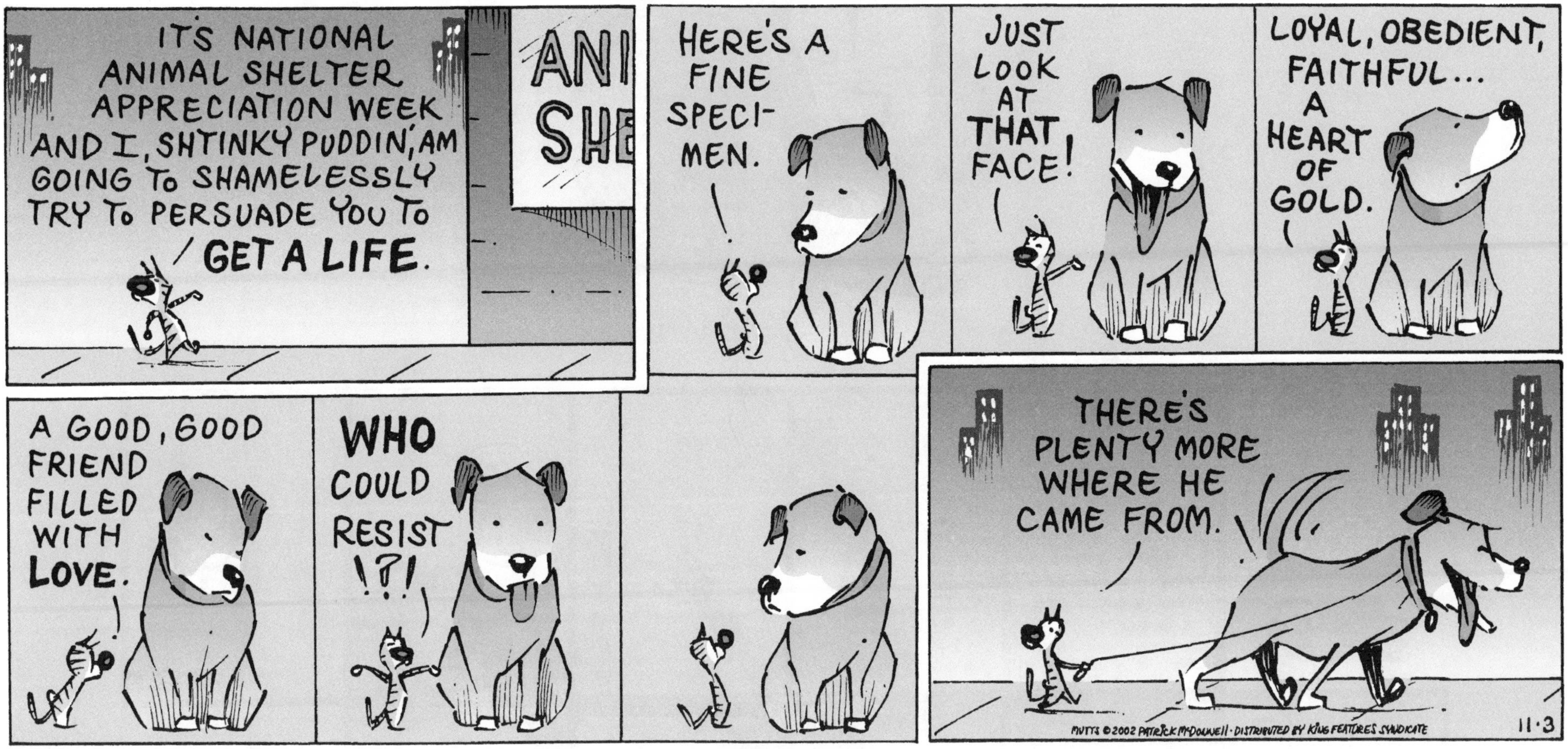
ANI
SHE
IT'S NATIONAL ANIMAL SHELTER APPRECIATION WEEK AND I, SHTINKY PUDDIN', AM GOING TO SHAMELESSLY TRY TO PERSUADE YOU TO **GET A LIFE**.
HERE'S A FINE SPECI-MEN.
JUST LOOK AT **THAT** FACE!
LOYAL, OBEDIENT, FAITHFUL... A HEART OF GOLD.
A GOOD, GOOD FRIEND FILLED WITH **LOVE**.
WHO COULD RESIST !?!
THERE'S PLENTY MORE WHERE HE CAME FROM.
MUTTS © 2002 PATRICK McDONNELL · DISTRIBUTED BY KING FEATURES SYNDICATE
11·3

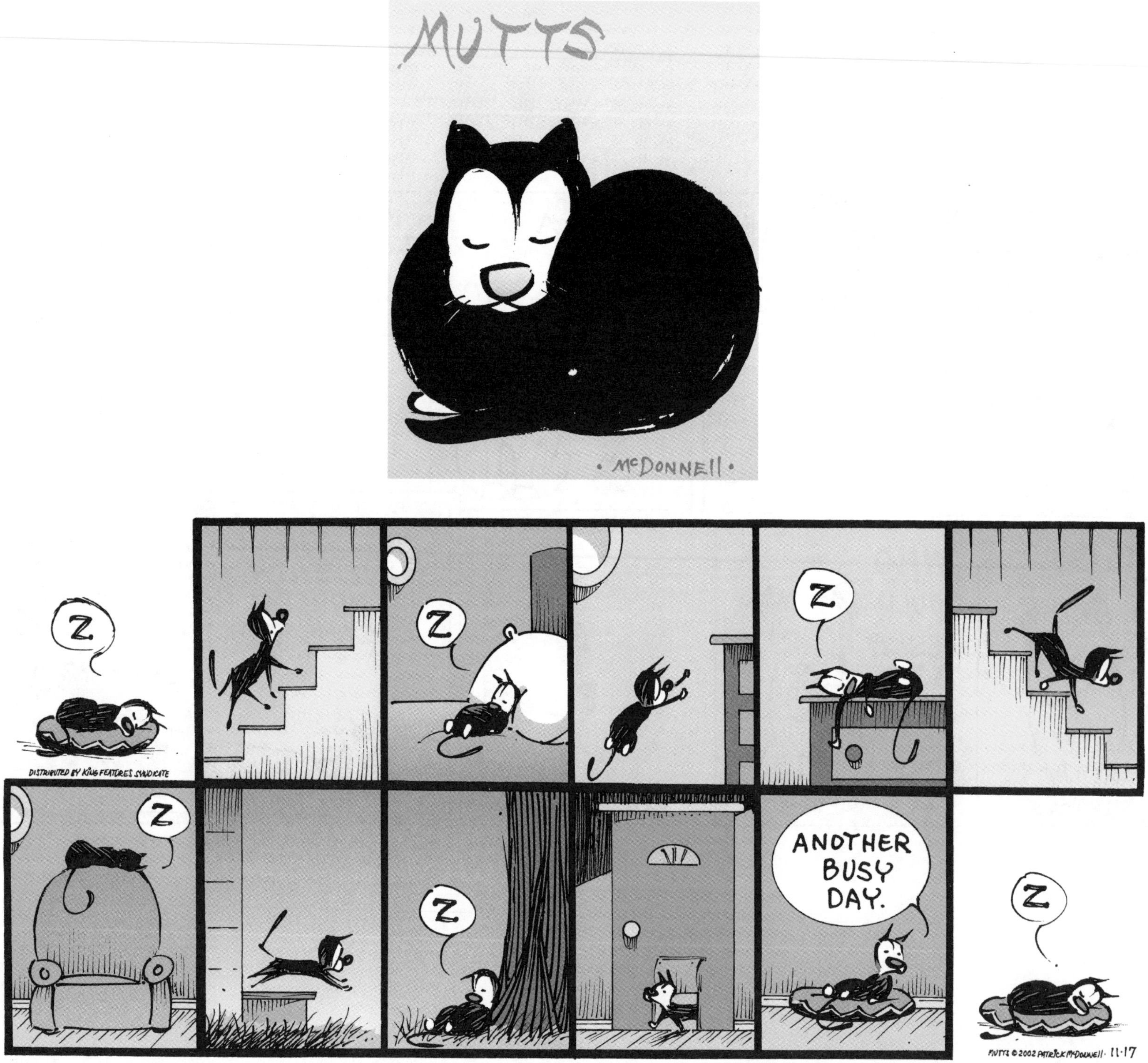
MUTTS
• McDONNELL •
Z
DISTRIBUTED BY KING FEATURES SYNDICATE
Z
Z
Z
Z
ANOTHER BUSY DAY.
Z
MUTTS © 2002 PATRICK McDONNELL 11·17

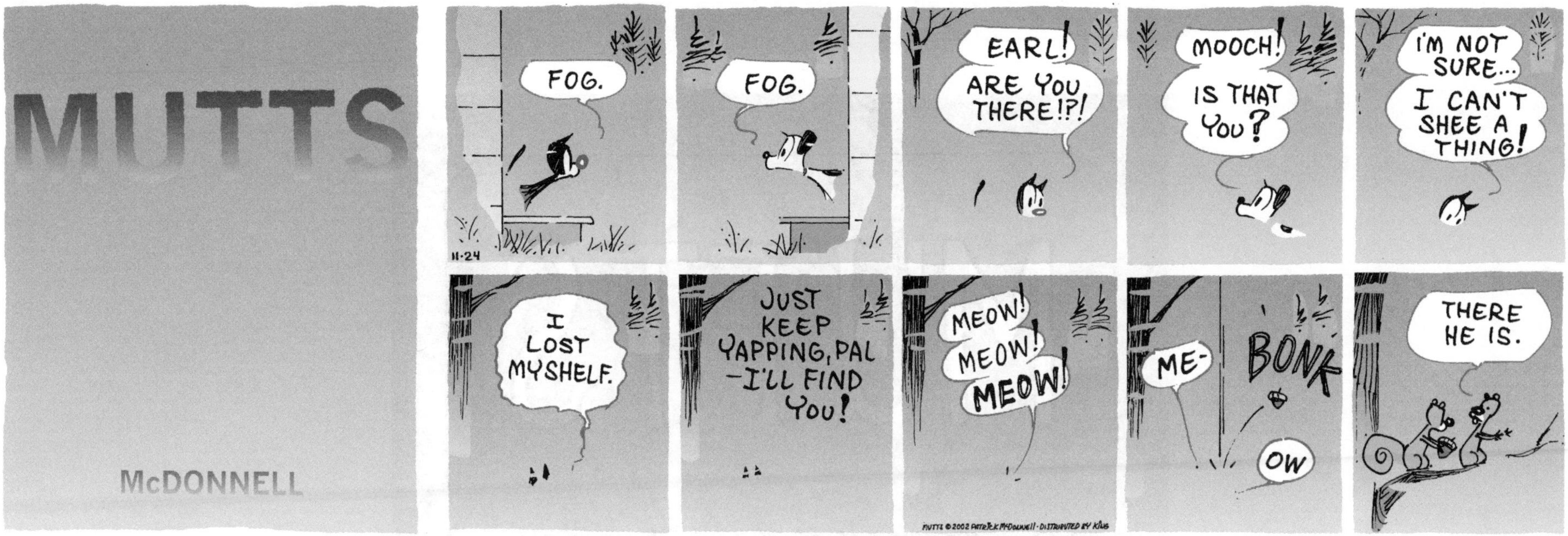
MUTTS
McDONNELL
FOG.
11-24
FOG.
EARL! ARE YOU THERE!?!
MOOCH! IS THAT YOU?
I'M NOT SURE... I CAN'T SHEE A THING!
I LOST MYSHELF.
JUST KEEP YAPPING, PAL — I'LL FIND YOU!
MEOW! MEOW! MEOW!
ME-
BONK
OW
THERE HE IS.
MUTTS © 2002 PATRICK McDONNELL · DISTRIBUTED BY KING

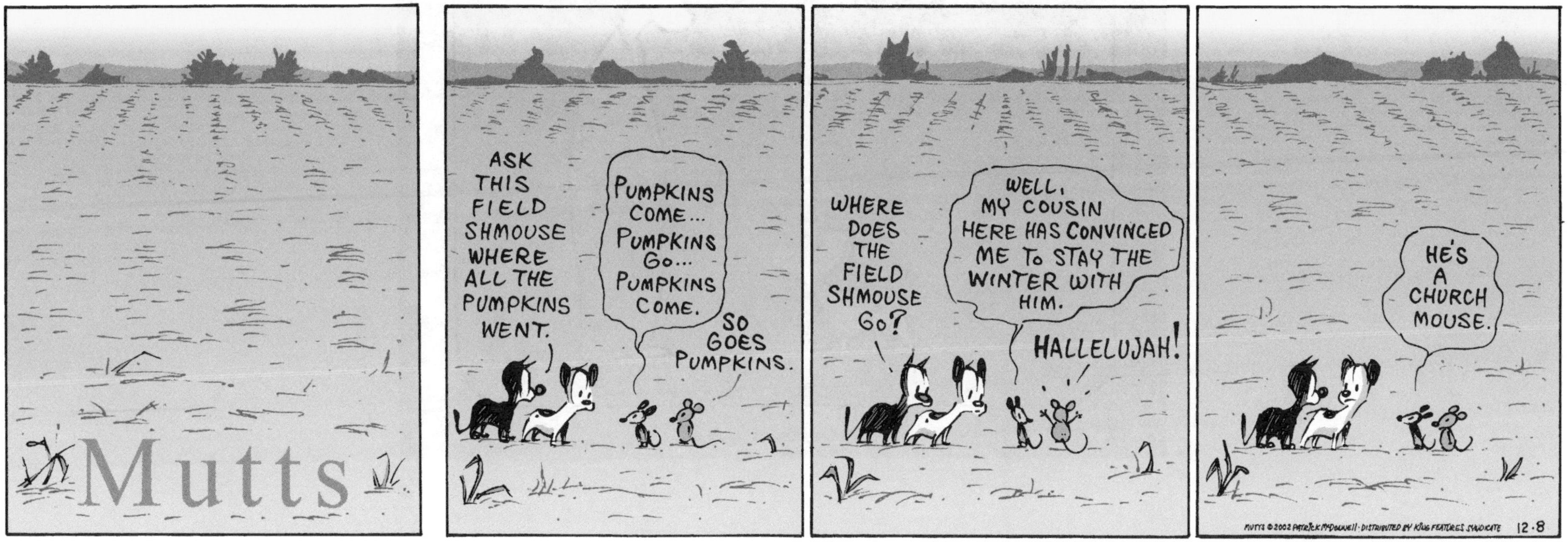
Mutts
ASK THIS FIELD SHMOUSE WHERE ALL THE PUMPKINS WENT.
PUMPKINS COME... PUMPKINS GO... PUMPKINS COME.
SO GOES PUMPKINS.
WHERE DOES THE FIELD SHMOUSE GO?
WELL, MY COUSIN HERE HAS CONVINCED ME TO STAY THE WINTER WITH HIM.
HALLELUJAH!
HE'S A CHURCH MOUSE.
MUTTS © 2002 PATRICK McDONNELL · DISTRIBUTED BY KING FEATURES SYNDICATE 12-8

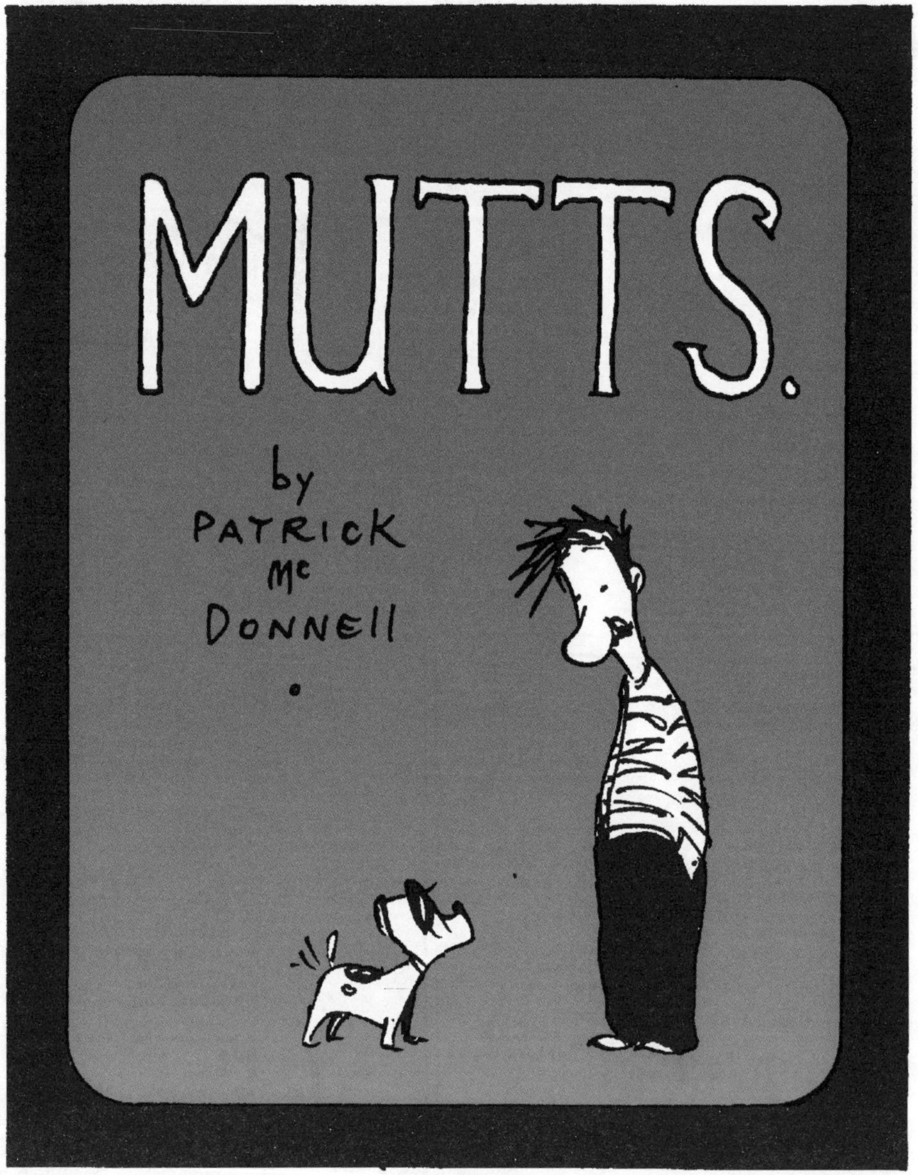
MUTTS.
by
PATRICK
Mc
DONNEll

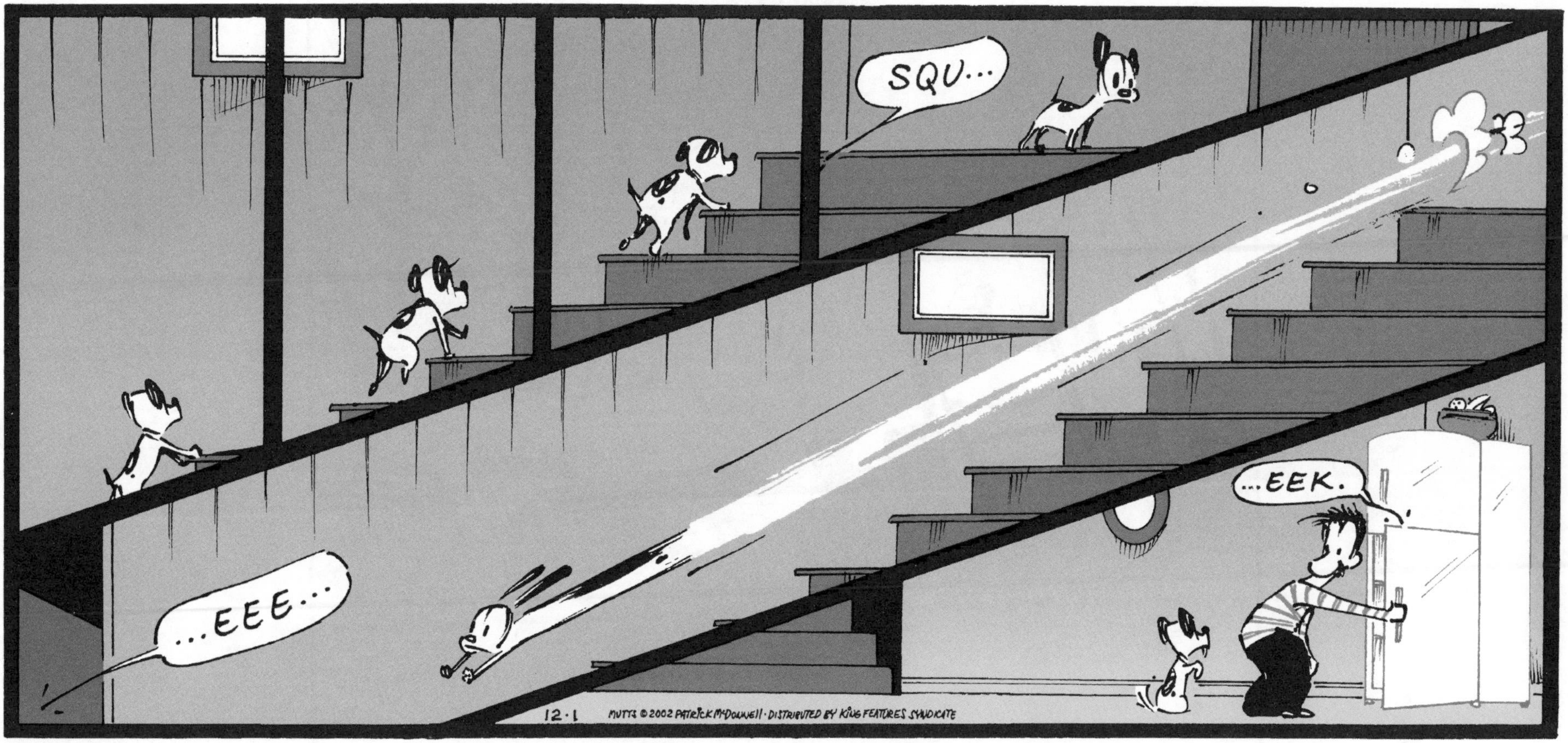
SQU...
...EEE...
...EEK.
12·1
MUTTS © 2002 PATRICK McDONNELL · DISTRIBUTED BY KING FEATURES SYNDICATE

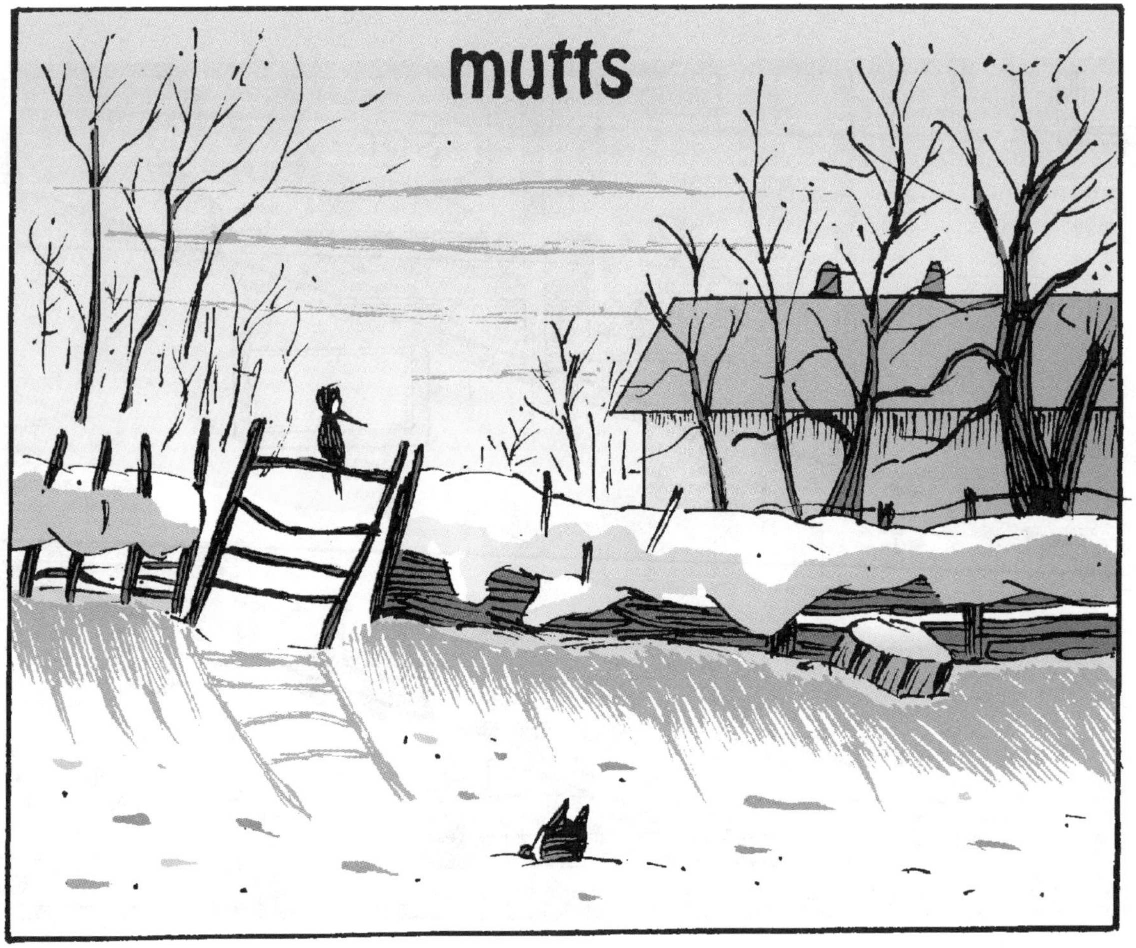
mutts

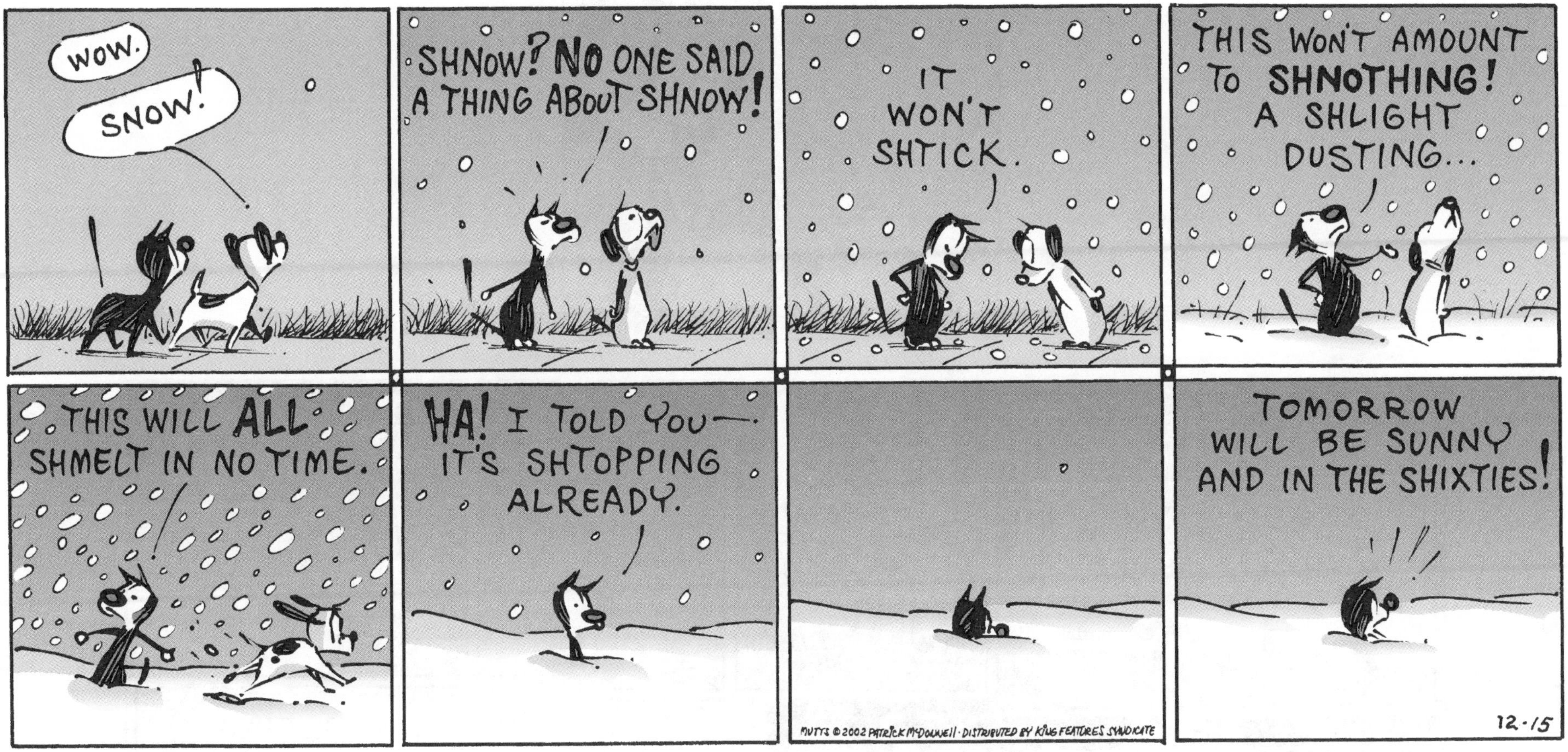
WOW.
SNOW!
SHNOW? NO ONE SAID A THING ABOUT SHNOW!
IT WON'T SHTICK.
THIS WON'T AMOUNT TO SHNOTHING! A SHLIGHT DUSTING...
THIS WILL ALL SHMELT IN NO TIME.
HA! I TOLD YOU— IT'S SHTOPPING ALREADY.
TOMORROW WILL BE SUNNY AND IN THE SHIXTIES!
MUTTS © 2002 PATRICK McDONNELL · DISTRIBUTED BY KING FEATURES SYNDICATE
12·15

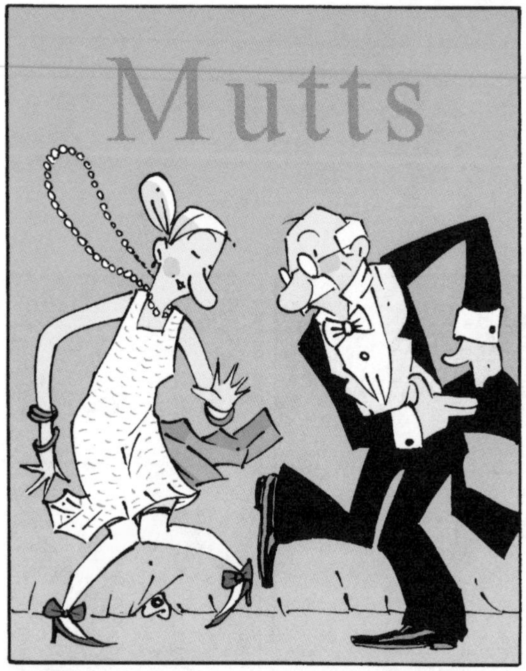
Mutts

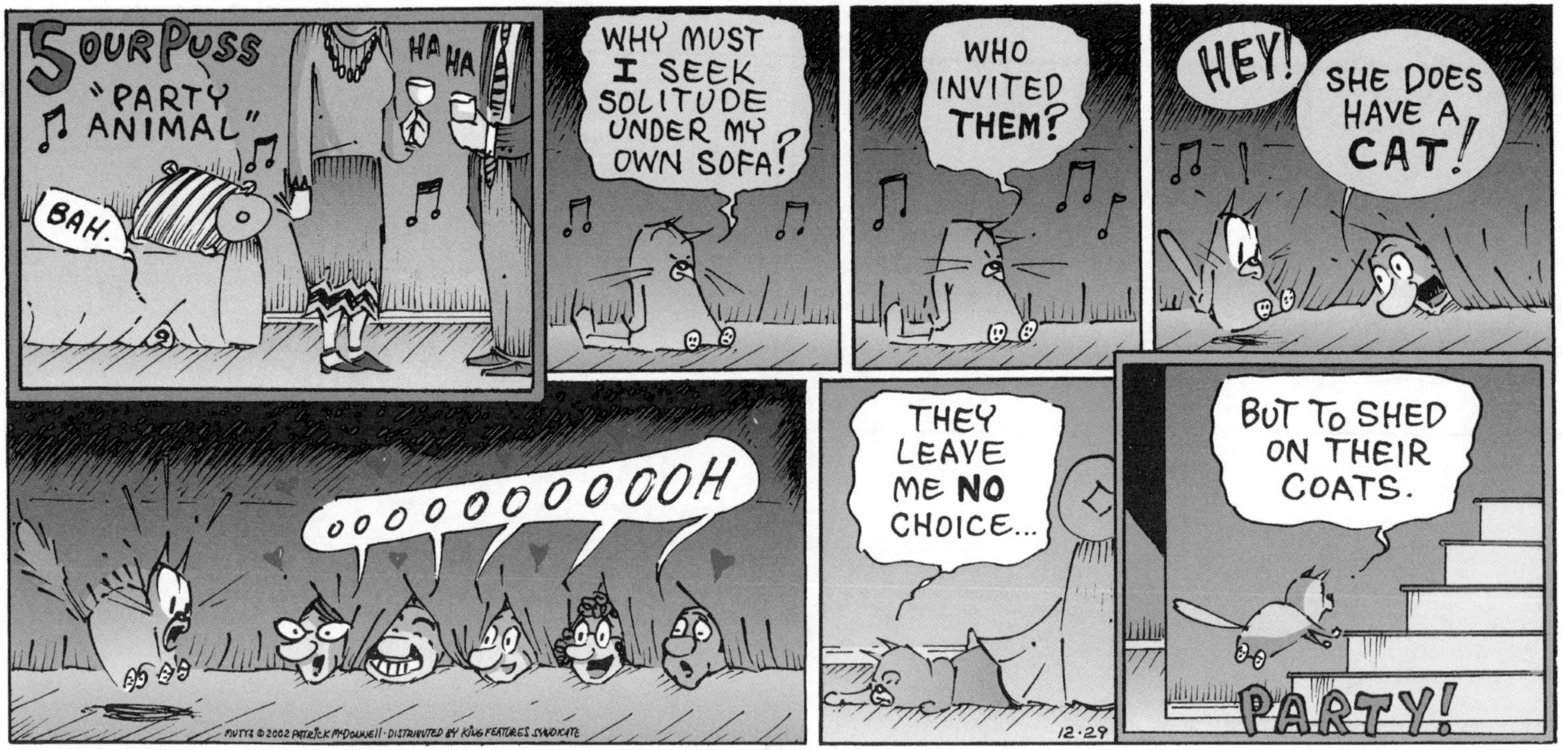
SOUR PUSS
"PARTY ANIMAL"
HA HA
BAH.
WHY MUST I SEEK SOLITUDE UNDER MY OWN SOFA?
WHO INVITED THEM?
HEY!
SHE DOES HAVE A CAT!
OOOOOOOOOOOH
THEY LEAVE ME NO CHOICE...
BUT TO SHED ON THEIR COATS.
PARTY!
MUTTS © 2002 PATRICK McDONNELL · DISTRIBUTED BY KING FEATURES SYNDICATE
12·29

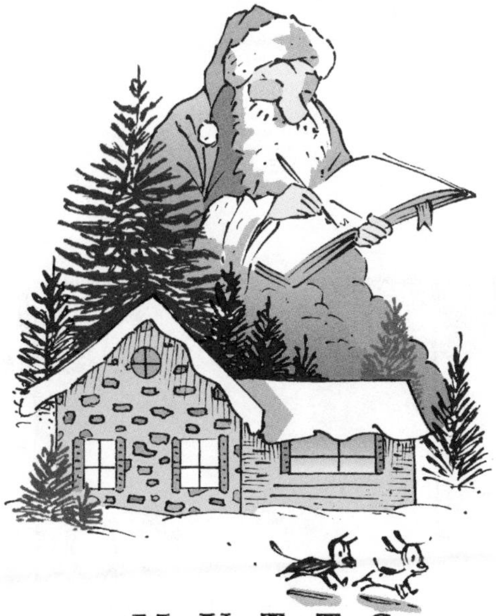

M U T T S

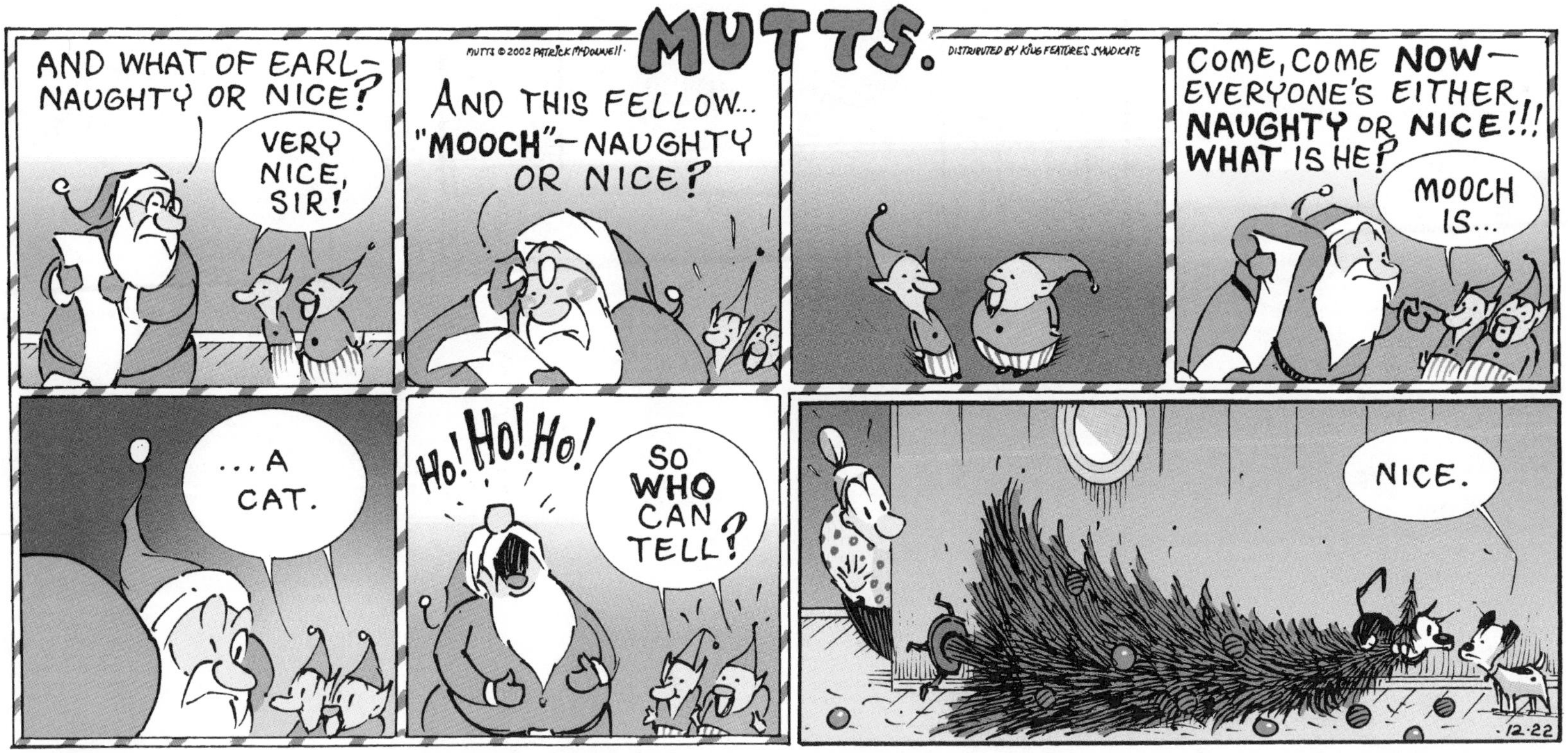

MUTTS
MUTTS © 2002 PATRICK McDONNELL
DISTRIBUTED BY KING FEATURES SYNDICATE
AND WHAT OF EARL– NAUGHTY OR NICE?
VERY NICE, SIR!
AND THIS FELLOW... "MOOCH"– NAUGHTY OR NICE?
COME, COME NOW– EVERYONE'S EITHER NAUGHTY OR NICE!!! WHAT IS HE?
MOOCH IS...
...A CAT.
HO! HO! HO!
SO WHO CAN TELL?
NICE.
12-22